FOOTBALL GROUNDS
A FANS' GUIDE

Written by Duncan Adams

First published in the UK in 2017
© G2 Rights Ltd

www.g2ent.co.uk

Printed and bound in Europe. Designed by Simon Pagett.
Publisher Jules Gammond

ISBN 978-1-78281-4191

INTRODUCTION

Welcome to the 2017/18 edition of Football Grounds - A Fans' Guide. This book covers every ground in the English Premier League and SkyBet Football Leagues, plus the cup finals and play offs venue; Wembley Stadium. Inside you will find a host of information useful to the travelling supporter. I have personally visited each of the venues, so that you get a real feel of what it is like to visit each stadium.

This upcoming season will see Tottenham Hotspur play all their home matches at Wembley Stadium, whilst their new stadium is being built on the White Hart Lane site. This promises to be yet another memorable season for the Club and for the fans who will pay visits to the largest stadium in the country. Last season Spurs proved the worth of the stadium when they had 85,512 in attendance for a Champions League game against Bayer Leverkusen. This became the highest ever attendance recorded by an English Club for a home match, beating the previous record of 84,569 set by Manchester City at Maine Road, way back in 1934.

The Football League this season welcomes the return of Lincoln City, after an absence of six years. I like many others have enjoyed visiting Sincil Bank in the past and will do so once again.

The other promoted team to the Football League is Forest Green Rovers. This Gloucestershire Club take their place in the Football League for the first time. With their home town of Nailsworth having a population of 5,800 they become the smallest town ever to have a Football League Club.

Although I have strived to make sure that every detail is as up-to-date as it can be, things can change over the course of a season; for example, a pub may close or another open, so please bear this in mind. I hope you find this guide useful and informative. But remember this is only a guide and should be treated as such. If you find that things have changed, or you feel that you can provide other useful information then please feel free to e-mail me at duncan@footballgroundguide.com. To see the latest updates to the Guide remember to visit the Football Ground Guide website: www.footballgroundguide.com.

As a member of the Campaign For Real Ale (CAMRA), I like nothing more than enjoying a good pint of real ale or traditional cider before a game. CAMRA produce a 'Good Beer Guide' each year. If there is a pub near to a particular football ground that is listed within the CAMRA Guide, that I have visited, then I have endeavoured to mention it, in the 'Pubs for away fans' sections.

I personally love sports stadiums and I have visited all of the 92 current league grounds (66 of those grounds with my team Birmingham City) and I am a member of the Ninety-Two Club. I have also visited many of the Scottish, Welsh Irish and National League Grounds and I have now been to over 300 venues. I hope you enjoy the book and that it will improve your away trips, as well as perhaps wetting the appetite to visit a ground that you hadn't thought about visiting before. So enjoy your footballing travels around the grounds and good luck to your team, except when they are playing Birmingham City of course!

The Ninety-Two Club

The Ninety-Two Club was formed in 1978 with just thirty-nine founder members, to commemorate their achievement of seeing a first team, competitive match at each of the Ninety-Two grounds of the then Football League; (now the Premiership, Championship, League 1 and League 2.)

The Club currently has over 1,200 registered members with around 800 still active. Secretary Mike Kimberley says: "Having followed Crystal Palace since 1968, my first away game was at Brighton in 1976 and I completed my last ground at Brunton Park, Carlisle in 1996. I have currently seen first team competitive matches at over 140 different League grounds.

I find the Football Ground Guide website an invaluable tool in planning each trip. The guide is very useful in detailing parking facilities, which railway station is best to use along with relevant bus services and a host of other useful information. Users also regularly add their own thoughts on their visits which can also be an important insight. This book version is a "must" for all fans embarking on all or part of this long journey. I am certain they will find it both a gruelling but ultimately fulfilling experience."

I am once more very pleased to see Duncan Adams' superb guide as a book which will grace any ground-hopper's book shelf.

I travelled around 25,000 miles to complete my original visits to the Ninety-Two grounds. I once suggested a long weekend in the Lake District to my ever-supportive wife Marie and after she accepted I casually mentioned, a visit to Deepdale at Preston on the way!"

You may find further details on the internet at www.ninetytwoclub.org.uk Or write to: The Ninety-Two Club, 153 Hayes Lane, Kenley, Surrey, CR8 5HP

Record Attendances & Ground Capacities

Please note that record attendances listed within the book are for the current stadium that a team plays at, rather an 'all-time record' including a previous venue.

The records are also for the Club that plays there, rather than being the stadium record. Also in some cases you may notice that the record attendance quoted is larger than the current capacity. This is due normally to when the grounds had larger terraced capacities, rather than current all seated capacities.

Special Thanks

To Owen Pavey, Graeme Rolf, Mike Cleave and Chris Hartford for helping me out by providing some of the photos for this book. Also a special thanks to all the fans who have contributed to the Guide, far too many to mention here, but Paul Willott, Barry Buttieg, Brian Scott, Darryl Marsh and James Walker deserve a special mention.

I am also indebted to Simon Inglis and his book 'The Football Grounds Of Great Britain' for some of the historical information contained within this Guide. Thanks also to my wife Amanda & daughter Sian who have both had to put up with me on many occasions disappearing to watch a game somewhere around the country.

Wham Stadium

Livingstone Road, Accrington, BB5 5BX

What is the ground like?

Although the Wham Stadium is on the smallish side, it is set in a picturesque area, with views over fields and hills behind the Coppice Terrace at one end. On one side of the ground is the Main Stand, which in fact is comprised of two small stands; the Main and Thwaites Stands. They sit on either side of the half way line, with an open gap between the two. Both are all seated covered stands and have an unusual array of tubular steelwork, running across the top of them.

Opposite is a very small covered seated area, called the Whinney Hill side. This former terrace had seating installed before the start of the 2009/10 season. Both ends are fairly new looking affairs, of which the home end, the William Dyer Electrical Stand covered, whilst the Coppice Terrace opposite is open to the elements. The William Dyer Electrical Stand looks a little odd, with a terracing at the rear, but with seating at the front, especially when you consider that the stand is quite a small structure. Another unusual aspect of the ground is that it has a total of eight floodlight pylons, with three on either side of the ground and another being located at one end.

What is it like for visiting supporters?

Away fans are mostly housed in the Coppice Terrace at one end of the ground, where up to 1,800 fans can be accommodated. If demand requires it then part of the Whinney Hill side can also be allocated. This small stand has a mixture of seating and terrace and has the benefit of some cover, unlike the Coppice Terrace which is open to the elements.

Adam Hodson a visiting Stockport County fan adds; "As it was raining I decided to head for one of the 200 or so seats in the Whinney Hill stand. I found that there is very little leg room between the rows of seats, of which there are only four. I was though located very close to the playing action as I sat in the front row."

Whilst Shirley Lawrence a visiting Swindon Town supporter tells me; "We had a pleasant day at the Crown Ground. Before the game we went to the Crown Pub which was crowded, but as they had six staff serving, we were able to get our drinks relatively quickly. Inside the ground there was not much atmosphere due to the away end being uncovered. Although we had over 800 supporters who were in good voice, the noise just wasn't carried around the ground."

Club nickname:	Ground name:	Capacity:	Opened:
The Reds, Stanley	Wham Stadium	5,057	1968

Pitch size:	Undersoil heating:	Record attendance:	Home kit:
111 x 72 yards	No	4,386 v Stevenage League Two May 7th 2016	Red and White Stripes

Telephone:	Website:	Programme:	
01254 356 950	accringtonstanley. co.uk	£3	

Pubs for away fans

The nearest pub is the Crown, which is just behind the ground on the main Whalley Road and welcomes all supporters. A little further down Whalley Road (five minutes walk in the direction of the motorway), is the Greyhound pub, which is a Sam Smith's house.

John Schmidt a visiting Darlington fan adds; 'If you go from the ground to the main road and head towards the town centre, then five a minute walk away, down on the right is the Grey Horse pub, It is only a small pub but served decent real ale. This area also seemed to be good for street parking.'

If you arrive early and have a bit of time on your hands then you may consider visiting the "Peel Park Hotel" in Turkey Street. This pub serves food and is listed in the CAMRA Good Beer Guide. It also overlooks Peel Park, the site of Accrington Stanley's old ground. It is around a 25 minute walk away from the Wham Stadium.

Directions & Car Parking

Leave the M65 at Junction 7 and take the left hand exit at the roundabout onto the A6185 towards Clitheroe (this is in the opposite direction to Accrington). At the first set of traffic lights turn right onto the A678, towards Padiham, and then at the next traffic lights,

turn right onto the A680 towards Accrington. After about half a mile along the A680 you will pass the Crown pub on your left. Take the next left into Livingstone Road and then left again for the Club car park, which costs £5, otherwise street parking.

By train

Accrington Railway Station is about a mile away. Exit the station and walk down the slope towards the large viaduct roundabout. Take the Milnshaw Lane exit at the opposite side of the roundabout. After 100m this

road then joins Whalley Road. Follow this for about a mile, passing the hospital, traffic lights and then a mini roundabout. Take the next right after the mini roundabout junction into Livingstone Road for the ground.

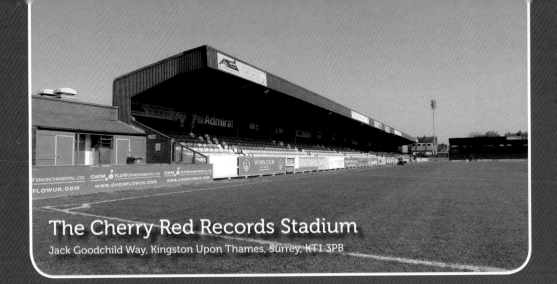

The Cherry Red Records Stadium

Jack Goodchild Way, Kingston Upon Thames, Surrey, KT1 3PB

What is the ground like?

The Cherry Red Records Stadium is a small but tidy ground, that is shared with Kingstonian FC. On one side is the Paul Strank Stand. This covered, all seated Main Stand looks fairly modern, having recently been extended. It accommodates 1,265 spectators and although only eight rows high, it is free of supporting pillars, resulting in uninterrupted views of the pitch. Surprisingly the team dugouts are not located in front of this Main Stand, but opposite in front of the Rygas Stand, which leads to a procession of players and club officials, at half and at full time. This terrace is partly covered to the rear and has open flanks to either side.

At one end is the Chemflow Terrace (aka the Athletics End, from the Athletics Stadium that sits behind), where the majority of the home supporters stand. This newish looking covered terrace is located quite close to the edge of the playing area, giving a reasonable view of the game. Opposite is the John Green Stand (Kingston Road End). This smart looking stand was opened in September 2012. It is covered having a raised roof and has an all seated capacity of 1,000.

What is it like for visiting supporters?

Away fans are housed in the Rygas Stand Terrace at one side of the pitch. If the away following is expected to be less than 600, then one side (towards the John Green Stand) is allocated and hence the terrace is shared with home supporters, although adequately separated. For larger followings then more of the terrace can be allocated, with the maximum allocation being 700.

This small shallow terrace is partly covered to the rear, with open standing areas on each side. In addition a number of seats are made available in the new John Green Stand, adjacent to the East Terrace.

Please note that the away terrace is not accessible by going through the main entrance into the stadium car park. Away fans should instead continue going along Kingston Road (keeping the main entrance on the right) and take the next right into Jack Goodchild Way.

Outside the stadium near the main entrance is a handy chip shop whilst a bit further along is the amusingly named 'Fat Boys Cafe'. I also noticed outside the Main Stand a vendor displaying and selling the largest array of different football badges, that I think I have ever seen.

Club nickname:	Ground name:	Capacity:	Opened:
The Dons or The Wombles	The Cherry Red Records Stadium	4,850	1989
Pitch size:	Undersoil heating:	Record attendance:	Home kit:
115 x 75 yards	No	4,870 v Accrington Stanley, League 2, May 14th 2016	Blue and Yellow
Telephone:	Website:	Programme:	
020 8547 3528	afcwimbledon.co.uk	£3	

Pubs for away fans

There are two large bars located inside the Paul Strank Stand. Away supporters are generally welcome to frequent the bars, however for the bigger games, and/or when it is all ticket, the bars are reserved for home fans only. On my visit I felt that the inside of the bar that I frequented, was a bit dim and drab looking, but with a real ale on offer from a local brewery and a barbecue selling burgers and hot dogs outside, its plus points outweighed the negative ones!

Otherwise, there is not much near to the ground, with a number of pubs closing in recent years. You could drink in Kingston or New Malden town centres and then get a bus to the ground (or a long walk!). The 131 bus passes the ground and goes through both town centres. If in Kingston, catch a bus heading to Tooting Broadway; if in New Malden, catch a bus heading to Kingston.

On New Malden High Street there is a Wetherspoons outlet called the Watchman., which is located near to the Fountain roundabout on the 131 bus route.

Directions & Car Parking

Leave the M25 at Junction 10, take the A3 northbound into London. At the exit for New Malden/Worcester Park, turn off and take the left turn into Malden Road (A2043) towards Kingston. Follow this to the next roundabout. Take the first exit into Kingston Road (A2043 still) and Kingsmeadow is one mile on the left. There is limited free parking available at the ground and, for Saturday games, to be in with a chance of securing a space you need to arrive before 1.30 pm at the latest. Otherwise street parking.

By train

The nearest railway station to the ground is Norbiton, which is about a 15 minute walk away. The station is served by trains from London Waterloo via Clapham Junction and Wimbledon.

New Malden station is also walkable from the ground albeit around 25 minutes.

Emirates Stadium
Highbury House, London, N5 1BU

What is the ground like?

With a capacity of over 60,000 the Emirates Stadium is one of the largest football grounds in London. It is the only stadium that I know of in this country that is four-tiered. The lower tier is large and shallow, set well back from the playing surface as a cinder track surrounds the playing area. A small second tier, which is called the Club tier, has seating, but is only eight rows high. Inside it has a number of lounges/restaurants, earning it the nickname the "Prawn Circle". This Club tier slightly overhangs the bottom tier.

The third tier is even smaller, being entirely comprised of executive boxes, some 150 in total and fits entirely under the large fourth tier.

This upper tier has been designed in a semi circular fashion and is topped by an impressive looking roof, that includes a lot of visible white tubular steelwork and perspex panels to allow more light to get to the pitch. The roofs though do not follow the semi circular shape of the stands but in fact run across the top of them and even dip down towards them giving them a strange look. Two excellent looking large video screens are situated in the North West and South East corners.

What is it like for visiting supporters?

Away fans at the Emirates Stadium are housed in the lower tier of the South East corner. The normal allocation for away fans is just under 3,000 tickets, but this can be increased for cup games. Although fans have big padded seats and plenty of leg room, the lower tier of the stadium is quite shallow (unlike the upper tiers which have plenty of height between rows), meaning that the view might not be as good as you would expect from a modern stadium.

Entrance to the stadium is by a 'smart ticket', whereby rather than giving your ticket to a turnstile operator, you enter it into a bar code reader to gain entry.

The concourse inside is not that spacious, but just about adequate. There is quite a choice of food on offer, although some of it is rather pricey. However the crowd of fans that had formed into a scrum around the kiosk put me off even trying to buy anything. It would have been nice if a proper queuing system had been put in place. There are plenty of flat screen televisions on the concourse to keep you entertained, plus there is a betting outlet.

Although some have questioned the amount of atmosphere at the Emirates, I personally found it okay. The away fans are also located very close to the home fans, which leads to a fair amount of banter between the two.

Club nickname: The Gunners	Ground name: Emirates Stadium	Capacity: 60,432 (all seated)	Opened: 2006
Pitch size: 105m x 68m	Undersoil heating: Yes	Record attendance: 60,161 v Man United Premier League November 3rd 2007	Home kit: Red and White
Telephone: 020 7619 5003	Ticket Office: 020 7619 5000	Website: www.arsenal.co.uk	Programme: £3.50

Pubs for away fans

The traditional pub for away supporters is the Drayton Park, which is located near to Arsenal tube station and Drayton Park Railway Station. This Courage pub overlooks the Emirates Stadium and is only a few minutes walk away. However as you would expect it can get extremely busy on matchdays, with drinkers spilling outside onto the pavements.

Just outside the entrance to the away turnstiles at the Emirates Stadium itself, there are some food and drink kiosks, one of which sells alcohol.

Mark Long recommends the Twelve Pins (formerly the Finsbury Park Tavern) near Finsbury Park Tube Station. 'Normally a good mix of home and away fans and about a ten minute walk from the ground.' Whilst Guy McIntyre adds; 'The Blackstock opposite The Twelve Pins, also welcomes away fans, plus it has a big screen showing Sky Sports.' Otherwise alcohol is available inside the stadium (Fosters, John Smith's and Strongbow), costing around £4.60 a pint.

Directions & Car Parking

Leave the M1 at Junction 2 and take the A1, following the signs for City (Central London). Keep going on the A1 for around six miles, until you see Holloway Road Tube Station on your right. Take the next left at the traffic lights into Hornsey Road and the stadium is

about a quarter of a mile further down this road. There is little parking at the stadium itself. It is probably better to park further out of London at a tube station such as Cockfosters and then take the tube to the Emirates.

By London Underground

Most fans head to Arsenal tube station which is on the Piccadilly line. It is only a few minutes walk from there to the stadium. On exiting the station turn right and follow Drayton Park Road around to the left. Then

take one of the large bridges over the railway line to the stadium. Other tube stations in walking distance of the stadium are Finsbury Park on the Piccadilly Line and Highbury & Islington on the Victoria Line.

Villa Park
Trinity Road Birmingham B6 6HE

What is the ground like?

Although the stadium has been completely rebuilt since the late 1970's, it has some individuality, as the four stands each have their own design, making it one of the more interesting in the League. At one end is the Holte End. This is a large two tiered structure which replaced one of the largest covered terraces in the country. Opened in the 1994/95 season it has a capacity of 13,500 seated supporters. At the other end is the North Stand, which is older (being built in the late 1970's), but still modern looking. This is two tiered, with a double row of executive boxes running across the middle. On one side of the pitch is the Doug Ellis Stand, which again is two-tiered and is roughly the same height as the other two stands. This stand was opened prior to the 1996 European Championships, for which Villa Park was a host venue. Opposite is the latest edition, the impressive looking Trinity Road Stand. Opened in 2001 it is three tiered, with a small tier at the front and then two larger tiers above, which are separated by a row of executive boxes. There are also two large video screens installed in opposite corners of the ground.

What is it like for visiting supporters?

Away supporters are located on one side of the Doug Ellis Stand, towards the North end of the stadium. Up to 2,972 fans can be accommodated in this area, split between both the upper and lower tiers of the stand. If only a small away following is expected then just the upper tier is allocated. The concourse at the back of the upper tier is particularly tight and easily becomes crowded, whereas there is more space behind the lower section. There is a fair selection of food available in the lower tier, but due to restricted space a limited offering is available in the upper tier; There are a selection of Pukka Pies and Pasties (all £3.30), Rollover Hot Dogs (£2.60) and then additionally in the lower tier; Cheeseburgers (£3.50), Fish & Chips (£6.50) and Chips (£2.80). There are wide screen televisions on the concourse, showing past encounters between the teams before kick off. There is also betting facilities available in the lower tier. Entrance to the stand is gained by entering your match ticket into an electronic reader.

A visit to Villa Park is normally an enjoyable experience, with the stewards normally taking a relaxed and friendly attitude. Atmosphere is normally good too. Although I support the other team in Birmingham (and no it isn't Solihull Moors), I have been to the ground on a number of occasions and I have to say that it is a very good one, with plenty of character.

Club nickname:	Ground name:	Capacity:	Opened:
The Villans	Villa Park	42,785 (all seated)	1897

Pitch size:	Undersoil heating:	Record attendance:	Home kit:
115 x 72 yards	Yes	76,588 v Derby FA Cup 6th Rd March 2nd, 1946	Claret and Blue

Telephone:	Ticket Office:	Website:	Programme:
0121 327 2299	0800 0149346	www.avfc.co.uk	£3

Pubs for away fans

The main pub for away fans is the Witton Arms, which is located near Witton Station and is only a few minutes walk away from the visitor's turnstiles. The pub has separate areas for home and away fans, but charges a £2 per person entry fee.

Alex Alexander a visiting Norwich City fan adds; 'We found a pub approximately 15 minutes walk from the ground where away fans were made welcome. It is called the Yew Tree. Although they don't serve real ale, they had a good range of beers and Magner's on draught. It is on the same road as the Witton Arms, but with this pub on your left carry straight on up the road, passing Witton Railway Station on your right. After about half a mile you will see the pub on the right hand side.'

Otherwise iit may be an idea to drink in Birmingham City Centre before the game, especially if arriving at New Street Station. where just outside on Lower Temple Street is the Shakespeare pub which is popular with away fans. Also nearby on Bennetts Hill is a real ale pub called The Wellington, & the "Sun On The Hill" which shows televised sports.

Directions & Car Parking

Leave the M6 at Junction 6 and take the slip road sign posted Birmingham (NE). At the roundabout below the motorway, turn right (the fourth exit), towards the City Centre. Villa Park is well signposted from here. Take the next right along Lichfield Road then at the second set of traffic lights turn right on to Aston Hall Road. This road will take you down to the ground. Mostly street parking or there is free parking available, but around 1.5 miles away (or a 30 minute walk) at the Star City leisure complex, which is signposted.

By train

Take the short ten minute train journey from Birmingham New Street to Witton Station. Witton Station is closer to the away section, than Aston Station and is only a few minutes walk from the ground. Turn left out of the station exit and continue down to a roundabout. Turn left at the roundabout into Witton Lane and the entrance to the away turnstiles is down this road on the right.

Hive Stadium
Camrose Avenue, Edgware, HA8 6AG

What is the ground like?

The Hive Stadium has seen some investment recently with the building of a new stand at the North End of the ground. Replacing a small terrace, the stand was constructed in only four months during the Summer of 2016. The stand is covered, all seated and is of a good size, having a capacity of 1,900. Pleasingly it is of the same height as the Main Stand and has a very similar design. The Main Stand on the West side of the stadium, is like the North Stand, single tiered and covered. It does though have a larger all seated capacity of just under 2,700 fans. On the opposite side is the East Stand. This is currently a rather plain looking affair, as essentially it is an office building that has had its roof extended outwards towards the pitch, and then had six rows of 750 seats installed in front of it, leaving a large back wall exposed of the office building. Oddly the roof doesn't extend the whole length of the stand, meaning that some of these seats are uncovered. Both sides of the stadium have small electronic scoreboards mounted at the back. At the South End of the ground is a small covered terrace which is only a few rows high and has a capacity of just under 900.

What is it like for visiting supporters?

Visiting supporters are housed in the new North Stand at one end, where just under 1,900 fans can be seated. The stand does not have any supporting pillars to impede your view and the facilities within the stand are excellent. The stand is also quite tall and steep. In fact from some of the top rows you can see the Wembley Stadium Arch in the distance.

The stewarding at the ground is vigilant, although generally relaxed and friendly. I did notice that the most of the singing Barnet fans tended to be in the Main Stand, rather than in a more traditional 'home end', although a drummer was sporadically trying to get things going in the home terrace.

The atmosphere created in the away end can be good especially if your team has a sizeable following.

Food on offer inside the stadium includes the standard fayre of Cheeseburgers (£4.50), Burgers or Hot Dogs (£4) and a selection of Baguettes (£3.50 whole, £2.50 half), but alas no pies.

I have enjoyed my trips so far to the Hive. Set in a nice part of town, it is a relaxed day out and one of the better in the League.

Club nickname:	Ground name:	Capacity:	Opened:
Bees	Hive Stadium	6,205	2013

Pitch size:	Undersoil heating:	Record attendance:	Home kit:
102m x 65.5m	No	5,233 v Gateshead Conference League April 25th, 2015	Black and Amber

Telephone:	Ticket Office:	Website:	Programme:
020 8381 3800	020 8381 3800 (ext. 1700)	www.barnetfc.com	£3

Pubs for away fans

Away supporters are treated to their own bar within the stadium, which is located behind the North Stand. This spacious bar has a large screen showing Sky Sports. It serves beers such as Fosters and Johns Smiths (£3.80) and Heineken (£4). The bar is open throughout the game and for a short time after the final whistle. The only downside is that the beer is served in plastic glasses.

There is also the Hive Bar at the stadium but this is for home fans only. The nearest pub is Moranos on Station Road, only a short walk from Canons Park Underground Station (come out of the station, turn right and it is in the row of shops further down on the right). This Irish themed wine bar is quite comfortable and has a number of large screens showing the early kick off on BT Sport. It is then only around a 10 minute walk to the away turnstiles, cutting through the playing fields (see by tube section below).

Quite close to Kingsbury Tube Station there is a Wetherspoons pub called JJ Moons If travelling on the Jubilee Line from Central London, then Kingsbury is only two stops before Canons Park.

Directions & Car Parking

Leave the M1 at Junction 4 and take the A41 towards Edgware. At the first roundabout take the 3rd exit onto the A410 towards Harrow & Stanmore. At the next small roundabout turn left at the Esso Garage towards Edgware. After passing through a set of traffic lights with the Masons Arms on one corner then at the next set of traffic lights turn right into Camrose Avenue. The entrance to the stadium is down this road on the right. There is a large car park at the stadium, with costs £5 or street parking.

By tube

The nearest tube station is Canons Park which is on the Jubilee Line. It is around a 10-15 minute walk away from the stadium. As you come out of the station turn left and at a convenient point crossover to the other side of the road. You will come to some metal railings where there is an entrance to some playing fields which you can walk through to the ground. This also brings you out at the North (Away) End of the stadium.

Oakwell
Grove Street, Barnsley, S71 1ET

What is the ground like?

Three sides of the Oakwell ground were redeveloped in the 1990's. On one side is the particularly attractive two-tiered covered East Stand running along one side of the pitch. Opened in March 1993, this stand has a capacity of 7,100. Opposite is the classic looking West Stand, part of which dates back to 1904. It was made all seated in the mid 1990's, but is only covered at the rear. At one end is the C K Beckett Stand which is an all seated, covered stand for home supporters, which has a capacity of 4,500. This stand was opened in 1995. The opposite end, the North Stand, is a relatively new single tier, covered stand, housing around 6,000 fans. This is the most recent addition to the ground being opened in 1999. Away supporters are housed in this stand.

An unusual feature of the stadium is a purpose built stand for disabled supporters. This is a three floor structure that sits at the corner between the East and C K Bennett Stands. There is also an electric scoreboard at one corner of the North Stand, on top of a security control room. The teams enter the playing area from one corner of the ground between the North and West Stands.

What is it like for visiting supporters?

Away fans are housed in the modern North Stand, where the facilities and view of the playing action are generally good. The concourse is of a fair size and has access to an open air area if fans need to smoke.

The normal allocation for away supporters is 2,000 tickets and fans are normally housed on one side of this stand on the East side. If demand requires it, then the whole of this stand can be allocated, increasing the number of tickets available to over 6,000. The acoustics of the stand are not bad meaning that visiting fans can really make some noise.

I found this club to be particularly friendly from the car park attendant to the programme seller. Even the P.A. announcer had a sense of humour (although a little optimistic), when he announced that perhaps the visiting fans would like to come up again to see the next Barnsley home game, so that we could see a decent game of football!

However, I have reports of fans getting hassle in the town centre. Although I've never personally had any problems at Oakwell, it may be advisable to keep colours covered especially around the town centre.

Club nickname:	Ground name:	Capacity:	Opened:
The Tykes or Reds	Oakwell	23,009 (all seated)	1888

Pitch size:	Undersoil heating:	Record attendance:	Home kit:
110 x 75 yards	Yes	40,255 v Stoke City FA Cup 5th Round February 15th, 1936	Red and White

Telephone:	Ticket Office:	Website:	Programme:
01226 211 211	01226 211 183	barnsleyfc.co.uk	£3

Pubs for away fans

Popular with away fans and in easy walking distance of Oakwell is the Metrodome Leisure Complex, which has a bar inside and also offers food.

Neil Tubby a visiting Norwich City fan, recommends the Dove Inn on Doncaster Road. This pub which is listed in the CAMRA Good Beer Guide, is an outlet for the Old Mill Brewery. It is only a five minute walk away from the ground down Oakwell Lane and is happily frequented by both home and away fans. Further along Doncaster Road (on the right after the Primary School on the left) is

the Barnsley East Dene Working Mens Club, which is happy to admit visiting supporters (including accompanied children) for a small donation. You can also leave your car there at a cost of £2. Kevin Downsworth a visiting Hull City fan adds; 'The Barnsley East Dene Club was very welcoming to us as away fans for a pre-game pint. Handy parking too and only about a ten minute walk away from Oakwell.' There is also the Harbour Hills Working Mens Club on Vernon Street, which also normally admits visiting supporters. Alcohol is also on sale inside the Oakwell Stadium.

Directions & Car Parking

Leave the M1 at Junction 37 and take the A628 towards Barnsley. Stay on this road (the ground is well signposted) and you will eventually see Oakwell on your right. There are a couple of car parks located at the ground, but they are mainly for permit

holders only. In between the ground and the MetroDome is a car park for visiting supporters called Queens Ground (post code S71 1AN)., which costs Cars (£4), Mini Buses (£8) and Coaches (£15).

By train

Barnsley Railway Station is about a ten minute walk away from Oakwell. On exiting the station turn left along Midland Street and at the bottom of this road turn left again into Kendray Street. Proceed down underneath

the road bridge and take the next left into Bala Street. After going up the one way street turn left into Windermere Road and then the next right onto Queens Road. You will soon see Oakwell on your right.

St Andrews

Birmingham B9 4RL

What is the ground like?

Approximately three quarters of the ground have been rebuilt since the mid 1990's. One large two-tiered tiered stand, incorporating the Tilton Road End and Spion Kop, completely surrounds half the pitch and replaced a former huge terrace. The new Tilton Road End was opened for the start of the 1994-95 season, with the new Spion Kop following in 1995. At the back of the Spion Kop Stand, which runs along one side of the pitch, are a row of executive boxes; as well as a central seated executive area which also incorporates the Directors 'box'. The other newish stand, the Gil Merrick Stand

(previously known as the Railway End) was opened in February 1999. It is a large two tiered stand and unusual in having quite a small top tier, which overhangs the lower area. Again there is a row of executive boxes in this stand, housed at the back of the lower section.

Only one older stand, the former Main Stand, which was opened in 1952, now remains of the former St Andrews. This is a two tier stand running along one side of the pitch and has a row of executive boxes running across its middle.

What is it like for visiting supporters?

Away supporters are housed on one side of the Gil Merrick Stand, which is located at one end of the stadium in the lower tier. The normal allocation is 3,000 tickets, but this can be increased to around 4,500 for cup games (when the whole of the lower tier is allocated). This stand is normally shared with home fans housed on the other side, who are separated by a sizeable gap which is covered in plastic netting. Although for most of the 2016/17 season the upper tier of the Gil Merrick Stand has been closed, when it has been opened then this results in home fans being housed above the away support.

The facilities and the view from the Gil Merrick Stand are pretty good. Food on offer

inside the ground includes the legendary Chicken Balti Pie (£2.90) and away fans can also purchase alcohol. However if your team has a large following then in the absence of a queuing system then this can result in somewhat of a scrum outside the food and drink kiosks.

Directly outside the away turnstiles is a large separated compound, where the away coaches are parked. Fans are normally searched on entry. The atmosphere inside St Andrews can be a bit 'hit and miss'. But on its day and with the home fans singing the club anthem "Keep Right On To The End Road" then a visit to St Andrews can be a memorable one.

Club nickname:	Ground name:	Capacity:	Opened:
The Blues	St Andrews	30,016 (all seated)	1906

Pitch size:	Undersoil heating:	Record attendance:	Home kit:
115 x 75 yards	Yes	66,844 v Everton FA Cup 5th Round February 11th, 1939	Royal Blue & White

Telephone:	Ticket Office:	Website:	Programme:
0121 772 0101	0121 772 0101 (Option 2)	www.bcfc.com	£3

Pubs for away fans

There are not a great deal of pubs located near to St Andrews and what ones there are can be quite intimidating for away supporters and are not recommended. However there is the Cricketers Arms on Little Green Lane which does tolerate away fans in small numbers. This pub is located behind the nearby Retail Park and is only a 5-10 minute walk away from the ground.

It arriving by train into Birmingham City Centre, then there are plenty of pubs to be found. Just outside New Street Station on Lower Temple Street is the Shakespeare pub which is popular with away fans. Also nearby on Bennetts Hill is a specialist real ale pub called The Wellington as well as a handy Wetherspoons outlet called the Briar Rose, as well as the "Sun On The Hill" pub, which also shows televised sports. You can then get a taxi up to the ground (about £9).

If you are walking to the ground from the city centre, then there is the Anchor Pub on Bradford Street. Renowned for its range of real ales on offer, it normally has a friendly mix of beer loving supporters. Oherwise alcohol is served within St Andrews.

Directions & Car Parking

Leave the M6 at Junction 6 and take the A38(M) to Birmingham. Leave the A38(M) at the Inner Ring Road exit, turning left at the top of the slip road onto the Ring Road East (the ground is signposted). Continue along the ring road for two miles, crossing straight across three roundabouts. At the fourth roundabout take the first exit onto Coventry Road going towards Small Heath. St Andrews is about a quarter of a mile up this road. There is a private car park located on the left just before the ground (£5) or street parking.

By train

The nearest station is Bordesley, but very few trains call there on Saturdays. You are more likely to end up at Birmingham New Street Station in the City Centre. New Street is located one and a half miles away from St Andrews and is around a 30 minute walk away, some of which is uphill. Otherwise you can take the following buses from the city centre; No: 58, 60, 97 & 97A from stops ME & MF located near Moor Street Railway Station.

Ewood Park
Blackburn, Lancashire, BB2 4JF

What is the ground like?

Ewood Park is quite impressive, having had three new large stands built during the 1990's. These stands are at both ends and at one side of the ground. They are of the same height and of roughly similar design, being two tiered, having a row of executive boxes and similar roofs. The ends are particularly good, both having large lower tiers. The only downside is the open corners, although there is a huge screen at one corner by the away end. There is also an electric scoreboard at the Bryan Douglas Darwen End of the ground. The Riverside is the only undeveloped stand, running down one side

of the pitch. This is a smaller single tiered stand and is not as pleasing to the eye as its more modern counterparts. In fact it looks older than what it is having been opened in 1988. It contains a fair number of supporting pillars and is partly covered to the rear. Just to highlight how much the ground has changed, this was at one time the 'best' stand at Ewood Park.

One other interesting feature of the ground, is the fact that the pitch is raised. This means that players have to run up a small incline, whilst taking throw-ins and corners.

What is it like for visiting supporters?

Away fans are housed in the Bryan Douglas Darwen End, where the facilities provided are good. However, the spacing between the rows of seats leaves a lot to be desired, being quite tight. The Darwen End is shared with home supporters, but if demand requires it the whole of the stand can be made available. Normally the away allocation is for three quarters of the stand, at just under 4,000 tickets, which are split between the whole of the upper tier and part of the lower tier (with the lower tier being allocated first). If you have not bought a ticket in advance, then you need to buy one from the away supporters ticket office at the ground as you can't pay on the turnstiles. The ticket office is located on one corner of the Darwen End.

On the concourse the food available includes; Pies (Chicken Balti, Peppered Steak, Potato and Meat, Cheese and Onion all £2.70), Sausage Rolls (£2.30) and Hot Dogs (£3.20). The refreshment areas are opened 90 minutes before kick off and close 15 minutes into the second half. If you are looking to eat something prior to entering the ground, then there is a baker in Bolton Road selling hot pies from one of its windows. Across the Bolton Road by the home end is a McDonalds, which I noticed had a walk through service for fans!

I found the Blackburn fans both friendly and helpful, plus coupled with the relaxed stewarding, has made it so far for me, four pleasant visits so far to Ewood Park.

Club nickname:	Ground name:	Capacity:	Opened:
Rovers	Ewood Park	31,367 (all seated)	1890
Pitch size:	Undersoil heating:	Record attendance:	Home kit:
115 x 76 yards	Yes	62,522 FA Cup 3rd Rd v Bolton Wanderers March 2nd 1929	Blue and White
Telephone:	Ticket Office:	Website:	Programme:
01254 372 001	01254 372 000	www.rovers.co.uk	£3

Pubs for away fans

Behind the Bryan Douglas Darwen End, the Club have created a fanzone area, into which away fans are admitted. It has some large screens showing previous meetings between the two sides and more importantly food and drink outlets, where you can buy a 'Pie and a Pint' for £4.90. The closest pub to Ewood Park that away fans can use is the Fernhurst pub on Bolton Road, which is only a five minute walk away. Part of the Hungry Horse chain, it quickly fills up on matchdays and once full no further fans are allowed entry, until people leave. However please note that in keeping with the 'family atmosphere' of the pub, fans are asked to refrain from singing.

There is also the Golden Cup pub which is further on past the Fernhurst (going away from Ewood Park) on Bolton Road and is tucked in by the motorway bridge. However this Thwaites pub is quite small, gets rather crowded and it is a good 20 minute walk (and mostly uphill) from the football ground. It is friendly though and also offers a range of pies. You can also park at the pub for a cost of £5. Alcohol is also served within the ground itself. The Club offer two pints of lager or bitter served in a two pint pot!

Directions & Car Parking

Ewood Park is well signposted from the M65. Leave the M65 at Junction 4 and take the A666 towards Blackburn/Darwen. Turn right at the first set of traffic lights and Ewood Park is about one mile down the road on the right hand side. Various private car parks are available in the area around Ewood Park costing in the region of £5. There are a number situated along Branch Road, which you can access from the A666, turning right into Branch Road at the traffic lights after passing a BP Garage on your left.

By train

The closest railway station is Mill Hill which is around a 15 minute walk away from Ewood Park. Mill Hill is served by trains from Blackburn and the rail journey only takes a few minutes. Blackburn Railway Station itself is at least a couple of miles from the ground and is a good 25-30 minute walk away. Blackburn Railway Station is served by trains from Manchester and Leeds.

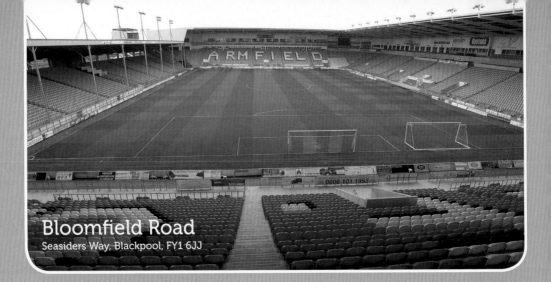

Bloomfield Road
Seasiders Way, Blackpool, FY1 6JJ

What is the ground like?

Bloomfield Road has been almost completely re-developed over the last 15 years, with three permanent stands being built, along with a temporary stand on the East side. The three permanent sides are of similar design, being single-tiered, all of the same height, seated and covered. The Stanley Matthews (West) Stand on one side of the stadium and the Mortensen Kop (North Stand) at one end, were both opened in 2002. The North West corner between these stands has also been filled with seating, enclosing this area of the ground. Behind the main seating in the West Stand and the North West corner, is a hospitality balcony with executive boxes at the rear from the south end to the Directors' Box at the halfway line, from which point to the North West corner is the Sir Stanley Matthews Hospitality Suite.

In 2010 the long awaited South Stand was finally opened, now called the Armfield Stand which is a mirror image of the North Stand. It has a capacity of 3,600 seats. On the East side of the ground the Club have erected a covered temporary stand. Although temporary it is of a good size housing some 5,000 fans in a single tier of seating.

What is it like for visiting supporters?

Away fans are housed in the Stan Mortensen Kop (North) Stand, at one end of the ground. Up to 2,500 supporters can be accommodated in this area. For visiting supporters this is an improvement on the East Stand that has been used in previous seasons, as the facilities are generally better and there are no supporting pillars to contend with, meaning that you get a fine view of the action.

Food on offer inside the ground includes a range of Pies; Potato & Meat, Steak, Cheese & Onion (all £3), Sausage Rolls (£2), Cheese Pasties (£2) and Hot Dogs (£3).

Please note that in recent seasons a number of Blackpool Fans have sadly felt the need to boycott watching games at Bloomfield Road, which has resulted in a big drop in matchday attendances. So if you are wondering why the stadium looks quite empty and the atmosphere pretty flat, then this is the reason. Hopefully the Club will find the good times again soon and the missing fans will return.

A trip to Blackpool is normally a highlight of the season for most visiting fans. With good night life, reasonably priced accommodation and plenty of visitor attractions then many make a weekend of it in this traditional seaside resort.

Club nickname:	Ground name:	Capacity:	Opened:
The Seasiders or Tangerines	Bloomfield Road	16,750 (all seated)	1899

Pitch size:	Undersoil heating:	Record attendance:	Home kit:
112 x 74 yards	No	38,098 v Wolves Division One Sept 19th 1955	Tangerine and White

Telephone:	Ticket Office:	Website:	Programme:
01253 685 000	0844 847 1953	blackpoolfc.co.uk	£3

Pubs for away fans

Popular with away fans is the Old Bridge House pub on Lytham Road. It is only short walk away from Bloomfield Road (head towards the sea front and then turn right into Lytham Road and the pub is down on the right). This pub has screens showing BT and Sky Sports.

Further along Lytham Road on the corner with the seafront is the Manchester Bar. This pub has large screens showing televised sport and normally has a DJ playing loud music, who tries his best to entertain the visiting fans. Also on Lytham Road (but this

going in the direction of the Pleasure Beach) is the Albert Pub which normally has a good mix of home and away fans in attendance. This pub also shows BT and Sky Sports.

If you are a fan of Wetherspoons pubs than on the seafront near to the Pleasure Beach is the Velvet Coaster. Opened in 2015 it is the largest Wetherspoons outlet in the country. It is though a good twenty minute walk from Bloomfield Road. Whilst nearer is another Wetherspoons called 'The Auctioneer' on Lytham Road. Otherwise beer is on sale inside the ground.

Directions & Car Parking

Leave the M6 at Junction 32 and take the M55 to Blackpool. Then at the end of the M55 continue straight onto the A5230 and then Yeadon Way towards the town centre. The ground which is signposted from here, you will reach on the right hand side. A huge pay

and display car park is located on the left just before you reach the ground on Seasiders Way. It costs £3.50 for three hours and £6 for up to 6 hours (some of the pay machines also accept credit/debit cards). Charges also apply to evening games.

By train

The closest railway station is Blackpool South which is around a ten minute walk away. However fewer trains stop at this station with most calling at Blackpool North. Blackpool North Station is around two miles away and

therefore you may wish to jump in a taxi to the ground. Or take the number 11 bus to Lytham from the nearby Bus Station. This bus passes the end of Bloomfield Road every 15 minutes.

Macron Stadium

Burnden Way, Horwich, Bolton, BL6 6JW

What is the ground like?

The Macron Stadium as it i snow called was opened in 1997. From the outside the stadium looks simply stunning and can be seen for miles around. I still think the view of it driving down the slip road from the M61 motorway, is one of the greatest sights to be seen in English football, especially when it is lit up at night. It has a great eye catching design and is unlike anything else in the country.

The inside is functional and tidy, but not unsurprisingly lacks the wow factor of the stadium's external appearance. It is totally enclosed and each stand has a conventional rectangular lower tier, with a semi circular upper tier above. Situated between the two tiers is a row of executive boxes. Above the stands there is a gap between the back of the stands and the roof to allow additional light to reach the pitch. The roofs are then topped with some diamond shaped floodlights that sit above a striking supporting tubular steel supporting structure. There is large video screen in one corner. One unusual feature of the ground is that the teams emerge from separate tunnels on either side of the halfway line. Outside the stadium is a statue of former player and legend Nat Lofthouse.

What is it like for visiting supporters?

Away fans are housed in the two tiered South Stand at one end of the ground, where up to 5,000 supporters can be accommodated, although the normal allocation is nearer 3,000. The lower tier is sometimes shared with home supporters, but the upper tier is given entirely to away fans.

The leg room and facilities within this stand are good and the atmosphere is boosted in the home end by the presence of a drummer. Although I did not experience any problems at the ground myself, I have received some reports of stewards being rather strict with fans, so it is advisable to be on your best

Alex Smith adds; 'away fans should note that the bottom rows of the lower tier are not covered by the roof and therefore you may get wet if it rains'.

Normally a visit to the Macron Stadium is one of the better in the League. It is easy to get to, looks spectacular and has plenty of eating and drinking facilities around.

It is the only ground where I have ever seen a squirrel running across the pitch. The visiting Birmingham fans soon adopted it by chanting "The squirrel is a bluenose...." which made me chuckle at the time.

Club nickname:	Ground name:	Capacity:	Opened:
The Trotters	Macron Stadium	28,723 (all seated)	1997

Pitch size:	Undersoil heating:	Record attendance:	Home kit:
105 x 68 metres	Yes	28,353 v Leicester City, Premier League December 28th 2003	White and Navy Blue

Telephone:	Ticket Office:	Website:	Programme:
01204 673 673	0844 871 2932	www.bwfc.co.uk	£3

Pubs for away fans

The most popular pub for away fans is the Beehive, which is about a 10-15 minute walk away from the visitors turnstiles. It is a good sized pub that also serves food. You can also park your car there (see below).

Also there is the Barnstormers pub on Lostock Lane (from the M61, go past the stadium on your left, move into the right hand filter lane and turn right at the traffic lights into Lostock Lane, the pub is down on the right) which also admit away fans. There is normally a mixture of home and away supporters in this pub.

Otherwise alcohol is served within the ground, although for some games such as local derbies, the Club opt not to sell any.

In another good move then the Club allow your to pre-order and pay for your half time drinks, before the game has kicked off, through the purchase of tokens. Thus making it quicker to get your hands on your.interval liquid refreshments.

There are a number of bars on the nearby Middlebrook Retail Park however most do not admit away fans.

Directions & Car Parking

The stadium is located adjacent to Junction 6 of the M61, from where it is clearly visible. There is a car park at the ground itself which costs £7 for cars. Alternatively there are a number of units in the industrial estate around Lostock Lane that cost around the

£4-£5 mark. Also there is the Beehive pub which costs £5 to park (but you can get this £5 back off your drinks and food bill bought inside). From the M61 continue past the stadium on your left and the Beehive pub is situated at the next roundabout.

By train

Just a few minutes walk away from the Macron Stadium is Horwich Parkway Railway Station. This station is served by trains from Bolton and Manchester Victoria.

As you come out of the station you will see the stadium in front of you. The away turnstiles are located around to the right hand side of the stadium.

Vitality Stadium

Kings Park, Bournemouth, BH7 7AF

What is the ground like?

The Vitality Stadium has been greatly improved with the addition of the Ted MacDougall Stand at the South End of the ground. Although temporary in nature, the stand which is named after a former centre forward, fills what was an open end, making the ground four sided. The stand itself was erected in the Summer of 2013 and looks quite impressive. Having a capacity of 2,400 seats it is of a decent size and is all seated. The only drawback is that it has a couple of supporting pillars at its front.

The rest of the stadium was literally built in 2001 in a matter of months. All three stands are of roughly the same design and height and are quite smart looking, with the Main Stand having a row of executive boxes to its rear. Each is a covered single tiered stand, with good views of the playing action with perspex windshields at each side. One nice touch is that the windshields to either sides of the stands have been brightened up with the addition of some huge player photos. There is also a small video screen installed beneath the roof of the Main Stand towards the South End.

What is it like for visiting supporters?

Away fans are located on one side of the East Stand, which is situated at one side of the pitch. The normal allocation for this area is 1,500 seats, but this can be increased to 2,000 if required. The stand is shared with home supporters and offers a good view of the playing action. The facilities are okay and normally there is a good atmosphere.

Please bear in mind though that if you have tickets for the lower rows in this stand, then at the beginning and towards the end of each season, the sun can shine quite brightly into this area, so make sure you bring your shades and a cap!

For the bigger FA Cup games then visiting supporters are housed in the Ted MacDougall Stand at one end of the ground, which has a capacity of 2,150. I had a fairly relaxing visit to the stadium with no problems experienced.

Food on offer inside the ground includes a range of Pies; Steak and Ale, Chicken & Mushroom Chicken Balti (all £3.50), Burger/Cheeseburgers (£4), and Hot Dogs (£4).

For night games in the build up to kick off, the stadium puts on a short lights show. Which although entertaining, doesn't really resemble a stadium light show as such, but to me more of being in a very large disco!

Club nickname:	Ground name:	Capacity:	Opened:
The Cherries	Vitality Stadium	11,464 (all seated)	1910

Pitch size:	Undersoil heating:	Record attendance:	Home kit:
115 x 71 yards	Yes	28,799 v Man United FA Cup 6th Round March 2nd 1957	Red & Black Stripes

Telephone:	Ticket Office:	Website:	Programme:
0344 576 1910	0344 576 1910 (Option 1)	www.afcb.co.uk	£3.50

Pubs for away fans

There is the 1910 Supporters Bar at the ground, but this is for home fans only. Similarly the closest pub to the stadium, the Queens Park Hotel on Holdenhurst Road (alongside the A338 Wessex Way) also does not allow in away supporters.

Around a 10-15 minute walk away in nearby Boscombe is the Mello Mello Bar located on Christchurch Street. Away fans are welcome at this pub as well as Baxters which is a little further down on the opposite side of the road. Baxters also has the added benefit of showing televised sport.

Otherwise it may be the case of drinking in Bournemouth Town Centre before the game, although it is around three miles away from the Vitality Stadium.

Alcohol is made available to visiting supporters inside the stadium, in the form of cans of John Smith's Bitter or Fosters Lager.

Directions & Car Parking

Follow the A338 towards Bournemouth. The ground is situated on the left of the A338 in the outskirts of town. You should be able to spot the tops of the ground floodlights on the left. Otherwise leave the A338 via the slip road which is signposted Kings Park and

Football traffic. You will then reach a small roundabout at which you take the second exit into Kings Park Drive. The entrance to the stadium is down this road on the left. There is a pay & display car park at the ground which costs 50p per hour.

By train

Pokesdown station is located one mile away or around a 15 minute walk from the Vitality Stadium. Pokesdown Station is served by trains from Bournemouth and London Waterloo. On leaving the station

(there is only one exit) turn right down the main Christchurch Road (A35). Proceed for about 400 metres and then turn right into Gloucester Road. The ground is located down the bottom of this road.

Northern Commercials Stadium

Bradford, West Yorkshire, BD8 7DY

What is the ground like?

The term; "a game of two halves" is often applied to a football game; but in the case of the Northern Commercials Stadium "a ground of 'two halves" comes to mind. The stadium has been completely re-built since the mid-1980's, but the initial impression is that one side is twice as big as the other. The Kop End, is a relatively new two tiered stand, that is simply huge and looks quite superb. It once towered over the rest of the ground, but the addition of another tier to the Co-operative Main Stand during 2001 has led to it meeting its once larger neighbour. With the corner between these stands also being filled, one

has a truly impressive spectacle.

The rest of the ground now looks somehow rather out of place. The Northern Commercials (Midland Road) Stand is a covered single tiered stand. At some other grounds this would look impressive, as it is of a fair size and is free of supporting pillars. However it almost is lost in the shadow of its larger newer neighbours. At the remaining end is the TL Dallas Stand which is an odd looking small 'double decker' type stand, with the upper tier largely overhanging the lower tier, giving this 'double decker' effect.

What is it like for visiting supporters?

After an absence of a few seasons, away fans now find themselves back in the TL Dallas Stand at one end of the ground, where 1,840 fans can be accommodated. If possible try to get tickets for the upper tier, as the view of the action is far better. On the downside there are a number of supporting pillars that could impede your view.

Roger Mulrooney a visiting Barnsley fan informs me; 'On my last visit I found the home crowd friendly and non-threatening. The stewards were particularly good natured and helpful. It is still a very good away day for a visiting fan.'

Fred Benson a visiting Scunthorpe United fan adds; 'On our recent visit, the lower tier of the TL Dallas was closed to away fans, apart from disabled spectators. With the upper tier being sold out other Scunthorpe fans were accommodated in the Midland Road Stand, which seemed strange.'

Pleasingly I have found Bradford to have become rather more friendly towards away supporters in recent years. It is quite an enjoyable day out especially if you enjoy what the city has to offer. Make sure that you wrap up well unless the weather forecast is 80 degrees. This is because Bradford is situated at a bottom of a valley, down which a rather cold wind normally prevails.

Club nickname:	Ground name:	Capacity:	Opened:
The Bantams	Northern Commercials Stadium	25,136 (all seated)	1903

Pitch size:	Undersoil heating:	Record attendance:	Home kit:
113 x 70 yards	No	39,146 v Burnley FA Cup 4th Round March 11th, 1911	Claret & Amber with Black Trim

Telephone:	Ticket Office:	Website:	Programme:
0871 978 1911	0871 978 8000	bradfordcityfc.co.uk	£3

Pubs for away fans

Chris O'Sullivan a visiting Bury fan recommends the Bradford Arms on Manningham Lane; 'It is only about two minutes from the ground and was welcoming to away fans.'

About a ten minute walk away from the stadium along Manningham Road (going away from the City Centre) is the Cartwright Hotel, which has a sizeable bar. Also about a ten minute walk away (this time towards the City Centre) is the "Corn Dolly" on Bolton Road, which is listed in the CAMRA Good Beer Guide.

Near to Bradford Forster Square Station is the Sparrow Bier Bar. Neil Le Milliere a visiting Exeter City fan adds; 'The Sparrow was superb. Although on the small side (it is probably only good for 50 or so supporters), it is still an excellent place to visit with a superb choice of ales and special drinks. Plus the pork pies were to die for!'

Alcohol is not available to away fans in the TL Dallas Stand. If there is a large following and the Club allocate a portion of the Midland Road Stand to visiting supporters, then beer is on sale in that stand.

Directions & Car Parking

Leave M62 at J26 and take the M606 to Bradford. At the end of the M606 take the Ring Road East (A6177 City Centre). At the next roundabout turn left along the Ring Road East. At the next roundabout turn left onto the A650 (signposted City Keighley).

After crossing a further 2 roundabouts, keep to the right (signposted Skipton). Continue towards Skipton, at Kia Cars, turn left into Station Road, then left along Queens Road, then the second left into Midland Road for the away entrance. Street parking.

By train

If arriving at Bradford Interchange Station, then although it is not a particularly long walk to the ground (about 20 minutes), it is not a straightforward route through the city centre. Either take a taxi (£6) or alternatively the bus station is located next to the train station (Bus No's 622, 623, 626 or 662). Alternatively Bradford Forster Square Station is only ten minutes walk from the ground and is served by trains from Leeds.

Griffin Park
Braemar Road, Brentford, TW8 0NT

What is the ground like?

The ground is rather compact and certainly has an individual feel. On one side is the Bill Axbey Stand, which is named after a long time supporter who watched the Bees for an incredible 89 years before passing away in 2007. This stand is a single tiered, covered all seated stand, which has a number of supporting pillars running across the front of it. The roof of the stand is painted with a large advert, designed to catch the eye of passengers flying into Heathrow Airport. Opposite is the Braemar Road Stand. Again this stand is single tiered, all seated and has a number of supporting pillars. It has a very low roof, which makes you wonder what the view would be like from the very back row of the stand.

At one end is the Ealing Road Terrace, which is a small covered stand. Opposite is the Brook Road Stand. This stand which was opened in 1986, is a strange affair; a small double decker stand that has seating on the first tier and terracing below. It is known affectionately by the Brentford fans as the 'Wendy House'. The ground is complete with a set of four imposing floodlights.

What is it like for visiting supporters?

Away fans are housed in the Brook Road Stand at one end of the ground. This covered two tiered stand has 600 seats in its upper tier and room for around 1,000 fans below in the terrace. The upper tier has good unhindered views of the playing area, whilst below in the lower terraced area there are a couple of prominent supporting pillars, which may affect your view.

There are a good selection of refreshments on offer including a selection of Pies (£3.30), Pasties (£3), Hot Dogs (£3.50), Burgers (£3.50), Cheeseburgers (£3.60) and Sausage Rolls (£2). I also have been informed that an enterprising home owner has set up a hot dog and cake stall in their front garden on Brook Road South, just along from the away supporters entrance, which is proving popular.

Tim Porter a visiting Torquay United supporter adds; 'The home fans were the most friendly I've come across for a long time - before kick-off, the stadium announcer asked all the home fans to put their hands together for the Torquay fans who had made such a long journey. I expected indifferent silence or abuse, but there was almost universal clapping!' I also had an enjoyable visit to Griffin Park and didn't experience any problems.

Club nickname: The Bees	Ground name: Griffin Park	Capacity: 12,763	Opened: 1904
Pitch size: 110 x 73 yards	Undersoil heating: No	Record attendance: 39,626 v Preston FA Cup 6th Round March 5th, 1938	Home kit: Red, White & Black
Telephone: 0208 847 2511	Ticket Office: 0208 847 2511 (Option 1)	Website: brentfordfc.com	Programme: £3.50

Pubs for away fans

Brentford is famous for being the only ground in England that has a pub at every corner of the ground. The surrounding land was formerly owned by the Griffin Brewery, hence the name Griffin Park. However one of these pubs the Royal Oak is currently closed.

The other three are; The Griffin (which serves Fullers real ale), The Princess Royal and The New Inn. The New Inn is the favoured pub for away supporters. Derek Hall a visiting Hartlepool United fan adds; 'Probably the best pub out of the four is the Griffin, with the New Inn a fairly close second, although this was packed on our visit'.

Roger Stamp informs me; 'Probably the best real ale pub in Brentford is the 'Magpie & Crown' which is only ten minutes walk away from the ground, on Brentford High Street. The pub has four real ales on tap and welcomes both home and away supporters.'

Please note that alcohol is NOT available for away fans to purchase inside the stadium.

Directions & Car Parking

Leave the M4 at J2 and take the A4, going around the Chiswick Roundabout so that you end up coming back on yourself. Continue along the A4 and at the first roundabout take a left onto the B455 (Ealing Road). The ground is located about half a mile down this road on your right. There is no parking at the ground. There is a small pay & display car park in Layton Road (first right off Ealing Road) which costs £5 for three hours (but is free after 6.30pm). Otherwise street parking, but check signs for any restrictions.

By train

Brentford Railway Station is around a five minute walk away from Griffin Park. This station is on the London Waterloo to Reading line, which normally has services running every 15 minutes on Saturday afternoons. To get from the station to the ground, exit onto Station Road. Take the first right into Orchard Road, right again into Windmill Road and then first left into Hamilton Road which leads into New Road and the ground.

American Express Community Stadium

Village Way, Falmer, East Sussex, BN1 9BL

What is the ground like?

The Amex Stadium is a spectacular sight when viewed from a far, set against the pleasant backdrop of the Sussex Downs.

On one side is the impressive looking West Stand. This three tiered stand, has a large lower tier, a small middle tier and a medium sized upper tier. The seating in the upper tier follows the semi-circular design of the stand, giving it an interesting effect. The team dugouts are located on this side. Opposite is the smaller East Stand. This two-tiered stand had its upper tier added in the Summer of 2012. The gap in-between the two tiers is occupied by the Clubs' administrative offices.

Both ends are also small single tiers of seating, and have an electric scoreboard to the rear. One of these ends, the South Stand, has a hospitality area containing a number of executive boxes, which is situated above the seated area. The roofs over both ends slope down from the larger West Stand on one side to the East Stand opposite, giving the ground a different look. The stadium is totally enclosed with all the corners filled with seating. The stadium has an eye catching roof made up of transparent panels.

What is it like for visiting supporters?

Away fans are housed in the South East corner of the stadium. This area not only includes the corner section but also part of the East and South Stands lower tiers. Around 3,300 fans can be accommodated in this area. It is worth noting that the Club charge away fans more for sitting in the East Stand rather than the South Stand or South East corner. As you would expect from a new stadium, the view of the playing action and leg room are both good. Plus the added bonus of padded seats is a rare 'luxury'.

Food on offer inside the stadium include locally handmade Pies from Piglets Pantry in Shoreham-on-sea, which are baked on-site. You can choose from Steak & Harveys Ale with mushrooms, Chicken & Ham with leek and Vegetarian butternut squash with spicy tomato. However, it will cost you £4.20 for the privilege. Also on offer are Cheeseburgers (£4.70), Burgers (£4.60) and Hot Dogs (£4.20).

Peter Llewellyn adds; 'The Amex Stadium is an excellent venue, very nicely set in the countryside. The concourse is extraordinarily wide and spacious for such a small stadium. Comfy cushioned seats, excellent views, plenty of leg room, great pitch and the best acoustics of any stadium I've been to. The home fans singing, was deafening, all down to the acoustic effect of the stadium design.'

Club nickname:	Ground name:	Capacity:	Opened:
The Seagulls	Amex Stadium	30,750 (all seated)	2011
Pitch size:	Undersoil heating:	Record attendance:	Home kit:
115 x 75 yards	Yes	30,338 v Bristol City, Championship League, 29/4/17	Blue and White Stripes
Telephone:	Ticket Office:	Website:	Programme:
0344 324 6282	0844 327 1901	www.seagulls.co.uk	£3.50

Pubs for away fans

There is not much in the immediate vicinity around the stadium. There is one pub called the Swan Inn located on Middle Street in Falmer, which is about 15 minute walk away, but for most fixtures this is for home fans only.

Alcohol is served within the ground in the form of; Harveys real ale (£4.30) which is brewed in nearby Lewes, Fosters (£4.20), White or Red Wine (£4.20). Harveys have also produced a special Albion bottled beer which is only available at the stadium or from the Harveys shop in Lewes. 5p from every bottle sold will be donated to the Macmillan Cancer Support charity.

It may be an idea if travelling by train to drink beforehand in Brighton. Outside Brighton Mainline Station there are a number of excellent pubs. Phil Kramer's pick is the Evening Star on Surrey Street. 'It is away fan friendly and only two a minute walk away from the station. It is in the CAMRA good beer guide and serves real Sussex ale and cider.'

Directions & Car Parking

At the end of the M23, continue onto the A23, heading into Brighton. At the roundabout which is the junction with the A27, take the A27 towards Lewes. After around 4 miles you will see the stadium on your right hand side. Leave at the A27 and take the slip road sign posted Falmer (B2123). At the top of the slip road turn right crossing back over the A27 and the entrance to the stadium is down on the right. Parking at Bridge Car Park (off the A27, near Stanmer Park £15) or use official free Park & Ride at Mill Road (BN1 8ZF).

By train

The nearest railway station is Falmer, which is situated right by the stadium. Kevin Bartholomew informs me; 'Falmer station is three stops from Brighton Central Station on the line to Lewes and Seaford. Alternatively, you can avoid Brighton completely by getting a train to Lewes and changing there for Falmer. There are four trains an hour in either direction and both reach the ground in less than ten minutes.'

Ashton Gate
Ashton Road, Bristol, BS3 2EJ

What is the ground like?

Ashton Gate has undergone some major transformation recently with the building of two new stands and the refurbishment of a third. The most recent and largest edition is the new Lansdown Stand on the West side of the ground. Opened in August 2016 this huge stand has a capacity of around 11,000, spread over two tiers. It has a large lower tier, with a smaller one above, whilst in-between the tiers there is row of corporate boxes stretching across its middle. At one end is another new stand. The South Stand was opened in August 2015 and is a good sized single tiered stand, having a capacity of just

over 6,000 seats. It extends around both corners of this end of the stadium.

Of the remaining parts of the ground, then the Atyeo Stand at one end of Ashton Gate is a handsome, covered all seated single tiered stand. It was opened in 1994 and is named after former playing legend John Atyeo. On the remaining side is the Dolman Stand which was opened in 1970. It is a two-tiered all seated stand that has a large upper tier and a smaller lower tier. There are two large video screens located in opposite corners. The ground is shared with Bristol Rugby Club.

What is it like for visiting supporters?

Away fans are housed at one end of the stadium in the Atyeo Stand, where around 4,200 fans can be accommodated. The stand is free of supporting pillars and offers good views of the playing action. The stand is also located quite close to the pitch and with good stand acoustics a good atmosphere can be created.

Entrance to the ground is gained through the use of electronic turnstiles, whereby your ticket needs to be inserted into a bar code reader. Normally fans are searched on entry.

Unless there is a large following then the seats are unreserved, so if you want a

particular view then make sure you get into the ground early.

Inside the stand the facilities are adequate. Although don't make the mistake that some fans do and queue at the first refreshment kiosk located inside the turnstiles. If you proceed up the stairs and through the double doors, then this leads to a larger area that has a number of refreshment outlets.

Refreshments available include; Steak & Ale Pies (£3.70), Cheese & Onion Pasties (£3.70), Steak Pasties (£3.70) and Sausage Rolls (£3).

Club nickname:	Ground name:	Capacity:	Opened:
The Robins	Ashton Gate	27,000 (all seated)	1904

Pitch size:	Undersoil heating:	Record attendance:	Home kit:
115 x 75 yards	Yes	43,335 v Preston FA Cup 5th Round February 16th 1935	Red and White

Telephone:	Ticket Office:	Website:	Programme:
0117 963 0600	0117 963 0600 (Option 1)	www.bcfc.co.uk	£3

Pubs for away fans

Bedminster Cricket Club is located about a 10-15 minute walk away from Ashton Gate, on Clanage Road (A369). It has a bar which welcomes visiting fans, plus you can also park your car there (see Directions below).

Alternatively, alcohol is normally made available to away fans inside the ground. Brands available include; Fosters, Butcombe Bitter, Guinness and Thatchers Cider (all £4).

Domenic Brunetti a visiting Nottingham Forest fan informs me; 'Before kick off we were directed by a club steward to the "Tobacco Factory" cafe bar which is a five minute walk from the road behind the Atyeo stand next door to an Aldi store on Raleigh Road. On route we passed several pubs which clearly have signs saying Home Fans only. When we got in the Tobacco House we found the bar friendly and trouble free and the food was good too.'

Otherwise there is not much near to the ground in the way of pubs for away fans to drink in.

Directions & Car Parking

Leave the M5 at Junction 18 and travel along the Portway (A4) following signs for the Bristol Airport/Taunton (A38). As you go over the swing bridge (Brunel Way), branch left into Winterstoke Road, and you will see the ground on your left.

Alternatively leave the M5 at Junction 19 and take the A369 towards Easton-in-Gordano. Stay on the A369 towards Bristol for around ten miles. You will reach Bedminster Cricket Club on your left, which you can park at (cost £5). Otherwise street parking.

By train

The nearest railway station is Parson Street which about a mile away from Ashton Gate and is served by trains from Bristol Temple Meads. The journey time is only four minutes to Parson Street. Bristol Temple Meads Station itself is around two miles from the ground. There is a shuttle bus to the ground from outside the station which costs £2 return.

Memorial Stadium
Filton Avenue, Horfield, Bristol, BS7 0BF

What is the ground like?

On one side is the West Stand, which with its pavilion looks more like a cricket stand. It has a row of hospitality boxes across the top, with a few rows of seats in front. Below is an area of terrace. The stand runs for about half the length of the pitch and straddles the half way line. On one side of it, towards the Blackthorn end is a small covered terrace, used as a family area, whilst the other side has a small covered area of temporary seating, called the South West Stand. Opposite is the Uplands Stand, taller than the West Stand, but similar in length. This stand has covered seating to its rear and terracing at the front. It has open terracing to either side.

At one end is the unusual looking South Stand. Although it has been in place for a number of seasons now, it was originally erected as a temporary stand, to fill the previously empty end. The stand only runs for just over half the width of the pitch, has several supporting pillars running across the front of it and has been nicknamed 'the tent' by Rovers fans. Opposite is the Blackthorn End, which is a covered terrace for home supporters.

What is it like for visiting supporters?

Away supporters are mostly housed in an open terrace on one side of the East Stand. This area is open to the elements so you might get wet if it rains. The open terrace makes it difficult for away fans to really generate some noise. Up to 1,100 away supporters can be accommodated in this area.

If the weather is poor then it may be a better bet to head for one of the seats that are made available to away fans in the South Stand at one end of the ground. I must recommend the huge Cornish Pasties (£3.20) that are sold at the ground, big and tasty, plus they even do vegetarian ones which makes a change.

I did not experience any problems on my visits, however I noted that the Rovers fans seemed to tolerate away fans rather than being over friendly. They can still do a good rendition of their club anthem 'Goodnight Irene', when the occasion stirs.

I find it quite amusing that the Rovers fans are nicknamed 'gasheads'. Nick Wootten informs me that this term comes from where the Club's old Eastville stadium was sited. It was next to a (sometimes rather smelly) gas works. In fact it was rumoured that if Rovers were losing at half time, the gas would be turned up, to put off the opposition!

Club nickname:	Ground name:	Capacity:	Opened:
Pirates	Memorial Stadium	12,011	1921

Pitch size:	Undersoil heating:	Record attendance:	Home kit:
110 x 73 yards	No	12,011 v West Brom FA Cup 6th Round February 9th 2008	Blue and White Quarters

Telephone:	Ticket Office:	Website:	Programme:
0117 909 6648	0117 909 8848	bristolrovers.co.uk	£3

Pubs for away fans

There is a bar behind the clubhouse terrace at the ground that allows in away supporters. Not far from the Memorial Stadium on Gloucester Road is the Wellington. This pub which is owned by Bath Ales, serves food too and normally has a mix of home and away fans on matchdays. Also on Gloucester Road is a recently opened micropub called the Drapers Arms.

Rhys Gwynllyw a visiting Wrexham supporter recommends the Annexe Inn on Seymour Road. Located half mile a way from the stadium, this pub along with the Drapers Arms are listed in the CAMRA Good Beer Guide. It is close to the County Cricket Ground, going further along the A38 towards Bristol. After passing an Indian Restaurant called Guru, turn left into Nevil Road and then right at the Sportsman Pub into Seymour Road. Other pubs near to the stadium are best avoided by visiting supporters.

Please note that alcohol is NOT made available to away fans inside the stadium.

Directions & Car Parking

Exit M5 at junction 16 (Signposted Filton) and join the A38 (South) towards Bristol City Centre. The ground is about five miles down the A38. You will pass the large British Aerospace works and further on, you will pass the Wellington pub on your right and continuing along the A38 Gloucester Road, turn left into Filton Avenue. The entrance to the Club car park is the second right down this road. There is a fair amount of street parking around the sides and back of the Wellington pub.

By train

The nearest railway station is Filton Abbey Wood, which around one and a half miles away from the Memorial Ground, or a 20-25 minute walk away. More likely though you will end up at Bristol Parkway which is about two miles away from the ground and is really too far to walk from. So you are probably best to jump in a taxi (cost about £10) or buses 73/73A/73B run from the railway station past the stadium.

Turf Moor
Harry Potts Way, Burnley, BB10 4BX

What is the ground like?

Burnley have played continually at Turf Moor since 1883, which is one of the longest continual occupations of ground by any club in the League. Half the ground was re-developed in the mid 1990's with two smart looking new stands being opened. The first of these the James Hargreaves Stand was opened in early 1996. It has two large tiers, with a row of executive boxes, housed between them. This stand replaced the famous Longside Terrace, which was a big steep covered terrace. Later in 1996 the Jimmy McIlroy Stand was opened at one end of the ground. This two-tiered stand is similar in design to the James Hargreaves Stand, which gives half the ground a uniform look.

The other two sides of the ground are much older and look out of place next to their shiny new neighbours. The Bob Lord Stand at one side of the pitch was opened in 1974. It is a small all seated single tiered stand, with a row of supporting pillars running across its middle. The David Fishwick Stand at one end of the ground was opened in 1969. Again it is a simple looking single tiered stand that has some supporting pillars.

What is it like for visiting supporters?

Away fans are housed on one side of the David Fishwick Stand (towards the Bob Lord Stand) at one end of the ground. Up to 2.414 visiting fans can be seated in this area. This stand is shared with home supporters, who are separated by a single gangway, which is fenced off and lined with stewards. However the close proximity of the home fans coupled with the stand having good acoustics, normally makes for a good atmosphere.

The Club have recently spent some money on improving the facilities in this stand. This includes new turnstiles as well as a refurbishment of the undercroft and toilets. What was a dark dank concourse is now quite pleasant complete with television large

screens. However, these areas can get quite uncomfortably crowded, especially at half time.

The seats inside the stand are still the old wooden type (although they have been painted recently) and if you end up being seated behind a supporting pillar, then the view is not great.

On a brighter note, then in one open corner at the far end, you can see beyond the stadium, the Pennine hills rolling into in the distance.

Club nickname:	Ground name:	Capacity:	Opened:
The Clarets	Turf Moor	22,546 (all seated)	1883

Pitch size:	Undersoil heating:	Record attendance:	Home kit:
115 x 73 yards	Yes	54,775 v Huddersfield Town FA Cup 3rd Rd, 1924	Claret and Blue

Telephone:	Ticket Office:	Website:	Programme:
01282 446 800	0844 807 1882	burnleyfootballclub.com	£3

Pubs for away fans

The main bar for away fans is the Cricket Club, which is located right next to Turf Moor. It normally has a friendly mix of home and away supporters and you can also park there. Paul Hanson adds 'Another place I could recommend is the Queen Victoria Public House, which is a Brewers Fayre establishment, located on Queen Victoria Road. The ground is no more than 10 minutes walk away from this pub. Away fans visit regularly wearing their colours.' You can also park at the Queen Victoria at a cost of £5 (which you can get refunded back at the bar against the cost of food and drink).

Matthew Harrison informs me; 'The Bridge Bier Huise pub', which is around ten minutes walk away from the ground, serves good beer and food and is fine for away supporters'. This pub which is in the centre of Burnley is listed in the CAMRA Good Beer Guide.

Otherwise alcohol is normally available for away fans to purchase inside the ground.

Directions & Car Parking

Leave the M6 at Junction 29 and take the M65. Leave the M65 at Junction 10 and follow signs for Towneley Hall. This road eventually goes past the ground.

There is a car park at the adjacent cricket ground by Turf Moor which costs £6. There is also a private car park available on Doris Street, off Belverdere Road (BB11 3DL), which is around 400 yards from the stadium and costs £5. Otherwise, street parking.

By train

There are two railway stations that are in walking distance of Turf Moor; Burnley Central and Burnley Manchester Road. Central station is around a 20 minute walk away from the ground and is mostly served by local trains. Manchester Road is a 15 minute walk away and is served by the faster express service from Manchester Victoria.

Pirelli Stadium
Burton Upon Trent, Staffs, DE13 0AR

What is the ground like?

In 2005 the Club left their Eton Park ground, which had been their home since 1958 and moved to a new £6.5m purpose built stadium nearby (well almost across the road to be exact!). The Club in 2005 were a non-League outfit, but since then they have steadily progressed into and up the Football League.

On one side of the Pirelli Stadium is the attractive looking Main Stand, which is covered and all seated. The Club's administration offices and corporate facilities are located in this stand and so at the back of the seated area is a row of windows running across it. Above this glassed area is white panelling, which gives the stand an interesting look.

The other three sides are small, steep covered terraces. They are a little ugly looking as they each have a large visible back wall. Each of these terraced stands has solid windshields to either side, apart from one side of the South Stand where there is a Police Control Box present. The stadium is completed with a set of four tall looking floodlights.

What is it like for visiting supporters?

Away fans are predominantly housed in the East Stand Terrace at one end of the ground, where just over 1,400 fans can be accommodated. In addition 400 seats are also made available to visiting supporters in the Main Stand.

As you would expect from a modern stadium, the view of the playing action (there are no supporting pillars) and facilities are good. The atmosphere is not bad too (although there is a bit of a monotonous drummer in the home end), as well as the grub available including the legendary Faggots & Mushy peas (£3.20). Other food on offer includes; Double Cheeseburgers (£4.50), Double Burgers (£4), Cheeseburgers (£3.50), Burgers (£3.20), Pukka Pies (£3.50), Sausage Rolls (£1.80), Hot Dogs (£3.20), Chip Butties in crusty bread (£2.90) and Chips (£2.50).

There is also a bar for away fans in which you can sit inside. There are TV screens showing Sky Sports News and then live coverage of the match itself. The bar is open until 15 minutes after the second half has started.

On the whole Burton is one of the better days out in the league, with excellent pubs, a good stadium with good facilities, atmosphere and virtually hassle free.

Club nickname:	Ground name:	Capacity:	Opened:
The Brewers	Pirelli Stadium	6,912	2005

Pitch size:	Undersoil heating:	Record attendance:	Home kit:
110 x 72 yards	No	6,746 v Derby Championship League 26/8/2016	Yellow and Black Stripes

Telephone:	Ticket Office:	Website:	Programme:
01283 565 938	01283 565 938 (Option 1)	burtonalbionfc.co.uk	£3

Pubs for away fans

A ten minute walk away is the 'The Beech Inn' which is popular with away fans. It is located up the A5121 Derby Road (going in the opposite direction to Burton town centre) on the left.

Otherwise there is the Great Northern pub, which has a mixture of home and away fans. It serves Burton Bridge Beers. This pub is located on Wetmore Road, which leads off the roundabout near to the stadium entrance, go up and over the railway bridge and the pub is on the left. If you particularly like your real ale then just under a half a mile away from the stadium is the Burton Town Brewery. Situated in a small industrial unit in Falcon Close (off Hawkins Lane, which itself also runs off the main roundabout by the ground), it opens its doors before matches.

Near to the railway station are the Roebuck, Devonshire, the Last Heretic micropub and the Cooper's Tavern which are all recommended, If you walk from the station to the ground, you will pass the Albert Ale House on your left which also serves well kept Burton Bridge Beers. Alcohol is also served within the stadium to away fans.

Directions & Car Parking

Leave the A38 at the Burton North exit and follow the A5121 towards Burton. Go straight across a roundabout and you will then pass a McDonalds on your right. Just before the next roundabout you will see the stadium on your right. Turn right at the roundabout into Princess Way. A short distance along Princess Way on the right, is the entrance to the Club Car Park, which costs £5. Car parking is also available at the Ryknild Trading Estate (also costing £5), just off the roundabout right by the stadium. Otherwise street parking.

By train

Burton-on-Trent Railway Station is located around a mile and a half away from the Pirelli Stadium. As you come out of the station turn left and go down the hill. Turn right into Derby Road and from there it is a straight road up to the stadium. It should take about 25 minutes to walk. Otherwise there is a taxi rank at the station and the cost up to the ground is around £6.

Gigg Lane
Bury, BL9 9HR

What is the ground like?

The Gigg Lane football ground was completely re-built in the 1990's with the Cemetery End being the last stand to be completed in 1999. These modern stands which are all covered, have vastly improved the overall look of the ground, whilst at the same time making it an all seated one. The only real disappointment is three of the stands contain a number of supporting pillars. On one side is the Main Stand. This all seated stand has its spectators area raised up above pitch level meaning that supporters have to climb a small set of steps to enter it.

Part of the front has a small box like structure, with a number of windows running along the front. It particularly caught my eye, as with the windows being almost at pitch level, I wondered just how many broken windows they get each season?

Opposite is the Les Hart Stand, a single tiered affair which extends around to meet the Cemetery End, enclosing that corner of the stadium. The Les Hart Stand also has a small TV gantry, plus there are a number of supporting pillars running across the stand that may impede your view.

What is it like for visiting supporters?

Away fans are housed in the Ratio Law Stand (aka the Manchester Road Stand) at one end of the stadium, where just over 2,000 away supporters can be accommodated. There is a row of supporting pillars about a third of the way up the stand, which could cause problems if you are seated behind one of them. The stand is also situated quite well back from the pitch and is slightly below pitch level, meaning that those seated in the first few rows don't get a great view, especially if the action is going on down at the other end. However unless your team has a large following then for most games, fans can sit (or allowed to stand) in whichever area of

the away end they wish, so you can normally enjoy a good view of the game.
The catering is your standard football fayre of Cheeseburgers (£3.50), Hot Dogs (£3.80), Sausage Rolls (£2.80) and Pies including the Chicken Balti Pie (£3.20).

My only grumble was the archaic looking toilets in this relatively modern stand. On the whole, however, Gigg Lane still has the feel of a proper football ground about it.

A visit to Gigg Lane is normally a good and relaxed day out, although sometimes the ground lacka a little in atmosphere.

Club nickname: The Shakers	Ground name: Gigg Lane	Capacity: 11,640 (all seated)	Opened: 1885
Pitch size: 112 x 73 yards	Undersoil heating: No	Record attendance: 35,000 v Bolton FA Cup 3rd Round January 9th, 1960	Home kit: White and Royal Blue
Telephone: 0161 764 4881	Ticket Office: 0161 764 4881 (Option 1)	Website: www.buryfc.co.uk	Programme: £3

Pubs for away fans

There is a supporters club at the ground, which sometimes allows in small numbers of away fans, for a small fee (£1). Geoff Blanthorne a visiting Tranmere Rovers fan adds; 'The Bury set-up is a very friendly one, with a nice supporters club where I enjoyed a pre-match drink together with a reasonably priced lunch whilst watching the early match on a big screen.'

My pick of the pubs on nearby Manchester Road, is the Swan & Cemetery, around a ten minute walk from the ground. This Thwaites pub, is quite comfortable, serves good hand pulled beer and also serves food. Neil Le Milliere a visiting Exeter City supporter recommends the Rose & Crown on Manchester Old Road. "It's not the biggest pub but it was very friendly; served a variety of real ales and is only a ten minute walk away from Gigg Lane.' Otherwise Bury town centre is around a 15 minute walk away where there are plenty of pubs to be found including a Wetherspoons pub called the "Art Picture House" on Haymarket Street. Alcohol is available to away fans inside the ground albeit in plastic bottles or cans (£3.50).

Directions & Car Parking

Leave the M66 at Junction 3. Take the left hand exit at the junction and follow this road until you come to the junction with the A56 Manchester Road. At this T-junction which has traffic lights, turn right towards Bury. You will pass the Swan & Cemetery pub on your left and then some playing fields. At the end of the playing fields just before the traffic lights, turn right into Gigg Lane for the ground. Street parking, although beware of a residents only parking scheme in operation in the nearby streets.

By Metro/Train

There is no railway station in Bury itself, so most fans travelling by train are likely to end up at one of the Manchester railway stations.

You can travel to Bury from Manchester by Metro. Bury Metrolink Station is served by trams from Manchester Victoria & Piccadilly railway stations. Bury Metrolink Station is about a 10-15 minute walk from the ground.

Cambs Glass Stadium
Newmarket Road, Cambridge CB5 8LN

What is the ground like?

The Main Stand on one side is a covered two-tiered all seated stand, part of which is used as a Family enclosure. This stand has a number of supporting pillars. Opposite is the Habbin Stand, which is for home supporters and is mostly covered. Again there are a number of supporting pillars.

At one end of the ground is the Marstons Smooth South Stand, which was opened in 2002. This good sized covered single tiered, all seated stand, replaced a former open terrace. The seating area is raised in this stand, meaning that supporters enter the stand via a small flight of stairs. The North Terrace at the other end of the ground is covered. However, it only runs for about half the width of the pitch, with one side ending in line with the eighteen yard box. Thus there is a large open area at one corner of the ground that is unused for spectators but houses the supporters club.

In 2016 the Abbey Stadium was renamed the Cambs Glass Stadium, in a corporate sponsorship deal.

What is it like for visiting supporters?

Away fans are housed in the Marstons Smooth South Stand at one end of the ground, where up to 1,600 supporters can be seated. This relatively new covered, all seated stand has good facilities. For some larger games then the South part of the Habbin terrace can also be made available. This covered terrace can accommodate almost 1,000 supporters.

The entrance to the away section is reached by walking along a path through what appears to be a common field that is used from time to time to graze cows (well judging from the number of cow pats!). Not much fun at the best times and especially when it is a bit more difficult to see for those night games! Adam Hodson a visiting Stockport County fan informs me; 'The away end is a nice modern stand with good views of the playing action.

The refreshments on offer included the legendary bacon rolls (£2), which have apparently returned after an absence, due to demand from fans'. Other food on offer include Cheeseburgers (£3.50), Burgers (£3), Hot Dogs (£3.50), Steak Pies (£3), Chicken Balti Pies (£3) and Potato, Cheese & Onion Pasties (£3).

Normally a visit to the Abbey Stadium is an enjoyable and relaxed one.

Club nickname: The U's	Ground name: Cambs Glass Stadium	Capacity: 8,127	Opened: 1931
Pitch size: 110 x 74 yards	Undersoil heating: No	Record attendance: 14,000 v Chelsea Friendly Match May 1st 1970	Home kit: Amber and Black Stripes
Telephone: 01223 566 500	Ticket Office: 01223 566 500 (Option 1)	Website: cambridge-united. co.uk	Programme: £3

Pubs for away fans

There is a supporters club at the ground itself, that normally allows in away supporters except for high profile games. The club charges a £2 entrance fee and also serves food. However as you would expect on matchdays it gets rather busy and sometimes has to turn away fans because it is full. With a number of pubs in the local area having closed down, there is little choice for away fans in the way of a pre-match pint. Along Newmarket Road going to towards the city centre is the Wrestlers pub, which also offers Thai food. Otherwise it may be in an idea to drink in the centre of Cambridge before the game or on route.

Jeff Beastall a visiting Mansfield Town fan adds; 'We found an interesting pub called The Tram Depot. It is a character pub offering a broad selection of beers and lagers, with meals and snacks, It is just over a mile away from the ground. It is located on Dover Street just off East Road (A603). However the pub prefer that you keep team colours covered.'

Please note that alcohol is NOT made available to away fans inside the ground.

Directions & Car Parking

Take the A14 to Cambridge, heading towards Newmarket. Turn off onto the B1047 sign posted for Cambridge Airport. At the top of the slip road turn right towards Fen Ditton. Go through Fen Ditton until you reach a T-Junction, where at the traffic lights you turn right into Newmarket Road. Go straight across the roundabout (there is a McDonalds on one corner) and you will come to Abbey Stadium on your left hand side. There is no parking available at the ground so street parking.

By train

Cambridge Railway Station is over two miles away, so best to catch a taxi (about £9). Or you can catch the Citi 3 bus from outside the station, which runs past the ground in the direction of Fen Ditton. It costs £2.50 return and the bus journey takes 10-15 minutes. If you decide to walk to the ground, then it is a fair old stroll, and a mazey route, but should only take 30 minutes at a good pace.

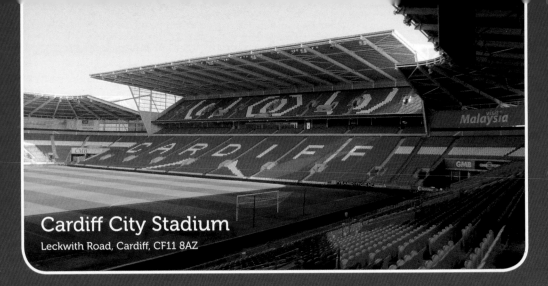

Cardiff City Stadium
Leckwith Road, Cardiff, CF11 8AZ

What is the ground like?

The Club moved to the new stadium in 2009, just a short distance from their old Ninian Park home. The capacity was further increased by 5,000 seats in 2014, chiefly by expanding the Ninian Park Stand on one side by adding a small second tier and then an overhanging third tier. Making it the tallest and largest stand at the stadium. However, it's most striking feature is its roof, which is simply huge, elevating and extending quite a distance forward to provide cover to those below.

Located opposite is the Grandstand. This stand is two-tiered, with a small second tier of seating that overlaps the back of the lower tier. In this area at the rear of the lower section there is a row of executive boxes. Whilst at the back of the second tier there is visible, a glassed frontage area used for corporate entertainment. The team dug outs are located at the front of this stand. Both ends are virtually identical, being single tiered, all seater affairs. The stadium is completely enclosed with all four corners having spectator seating. Above each end there is digital video screen.

What is it like for visiting supporters?

Away fans are located in one corner of the stadium, between the Ninian and Grange stands. Up to 1,800 fans can be accommodated in this area. The Club operate automatic turnstiles, where you have to put your ticket (which has a bar code on it) into a slot reader, which then allows the turnstiles to admit you.

As you would expect from a new stadium the view of the playing action and facilities are good. The acoustics are also good, with the stadium having a loud PA system. The concourses are spacious, have televisions to keep you entertained and serve the usual football fayre of food.

Inside the stadium away fans are kept separate from home fans, by an area of 'no mans land' to each side. Whilst outside there is a fenced in compound, which is also used to accommodate the away coaches, but again keeps fans separated after the game has finished which should avoid most problems.

Since moving to the new stadium, then a visit to Cardiff is now normally a more enjoyable one that it was at Ninian Park. Even so I would still advise to be cautious around the stadium and the city centre and to keep colours covered.

Club nickname:	Ground name:	Capacity:	Opened:
The Bluebirds	Cardiff City Stadium	33,300 (all seated)	2009

Pitch size:	Undersoil heating:	Record attendance:	Home kit:
110 x 75 yards	Yes	28,680 v Derby Championship League 2/4/16	Blue With White Trim

Telephone:	Ticket Office:	Website:	Programme:
0845 365 1115	0845 345 1400	cardiffcityfc.co.uk	£3

Pubs for away fans

There are no bars in the close vicinity to the stadium that I could see. As the stadium is close the old Ninian Park supporters will tend to use the pubs they did previously, most of which can be quite intimidating for away supporters and are not recommended.

One suggestion that I have received is the Gol Centre on Lawrenny Avenue (off Leckwith Road, See Google Map below) which has amongst other facilities a bar. Gwilym Boore informs me; 'We are a 5-a-side centre located about an eight minute walk from Cardiff City Stadium. We charge £5

to park at the centre but this is returned to customers in the form of a bar voucher which can be used against purchases of Hot Dogs, alcoholic and soft drinks, tea and coffee and confectionery. We also encourage FREE use of our pitches by visiting children.' Plus further along Lawrenny Avenue is the Canton Rugby Football Club, which has a bar, large screen television showing Sky Sports and also offers free parking.

Otherwise it is probably best to drink in the city centre and then go on up to the stadium. Alcohol is also available inside the ground.

Directions & Car Parking

Leave the M4 at junction 33 and take the A4232 towards Cardiff/Barry. Leave the dual carriageway at the B4267 exit. At the end of the slip road, turn left at the roundabout, signposted 'City Centre'. If you continue past the ground on your right and then turn right

at the next lights into Sloper Road. Then if you then turn right at HSS this leads you into a fenced off area adjacent to the away turnstiles. You can normally park here at a cost of £8, or if full then street parking.

By train

The nearest railway station is Ninian Park Halt, which is only a five minute walk from the stadium. This station is on a local line (City Line-direction Radyr) which is served by trains from Cardiff Central, which run every

30 minutes on Saturday afternoons (although occasionally extra services are put on). On leaving Ninian Park Halt Station proceed left along Leckwith Road and you will see the stadium over on your left.

Brunton Park
Warwick Road, Carlisle, CA1 1LL

What is the ground like?

The Pioneer (East) Stand on one side of the pitch, is a covered all seated stand, which looks quite smart. This stand was opened in 1996. The other side is an old partly covered (to the rear) Main Stand, which has seating at the back and a terraced paddock to the front. The central part of this stand was built in 1954 and the wings added at a later stage.

The Warwick Road End is a covered terrace that has a peculiar looking roof, which consists of three triangular sections. The other end, the Petterill End (aka The Waterworks End), is largely a small open terrace, which oddly contains a small section of seating on one side. This end is only used for the bigger games. On one side of this end is a Security Control Box, which also has a small electric scoreboard mounted below it. There is also a video screen situated at the back.

The ground also has some strange looking floodlights that don't have the normal bank of lighting on top of the pylon, but instead have the lights mounted up the side. Outside the ground entrance is a statue of former Carlisle favourite Hughie McIlmoyle.

What is it like for visiting supporters?

Away fans are housed on one side of the Pioneer (East) Stand (towards the Petterill End). This stand is of a decent size and around 2,000 fans can be accommodated.

The East Stand is all seated, covered and is located at one side of the pitch. It is fairly modern and the facilities within, plus the view of the playing area are good. Unless your team has a large following then normally fans can sit where they like, rather than be allocated a specific seat.

For larger games then the Petterill End terrace can also be allocated which houses around 1,700 supporters. Please note though that this end does not have a roof so is open to the elements, so hope it doesn't rain.

Most fans enjoy their trip to Brunton Park. The ground has a mixture of old and modern stands and has plenty of character.

I personally found the Carlisle fans to be friendly and helpful. The atmosphere was also particularly lively and I had an enjoyable afternoon there.

Club nickname:	Ground name:	Capacity:	Opened:
The Cumbrians	Brunton Park	17,949	1909

Pitch size:	Undersoil heating:	Record attendance:	Home kit:
112 x 74 yards	No	27,500 v Middlesbrough FA Cup 5th Rd 7/2/70	Blue and White

Telephone:	Ticket Office:	Website:	Programme:
01228 526 237	0844 371 1921	carlisleunited.co.uk	£2

Pubs for away fans

The Carlisle Rugby Club next to Brunton Park on the Warwick Road, has a club bar which allows in away supporters and is family friendly. Simon Tunstall informs me; "At the back of the main football club car park there is the Stoneyholme Golf Club, which has a bar, serves food and welcomes away fans on matchdays".

Paul Sawyers adds; 'I would recommend the Lakeland Gate for a drink on match days, which is a family friendly pub that also serves food.' Also if you leave the M6 at Junction 43 and take the A69 towards Carlisle, then you will pass a recently opened Toby pub/carvery, which is not that far from the ground. There is also the Beehive on Warwick Road and the Howard Arms on Lowther Street. Although these two pubs that serve real ale, may be for home fans only for high profile games.

Steve Ellis a visiting Exeter City fan adds; 'You can get a beer inside the ground. Also a bit like a theatre you can also pay and pre-order half time drinks before the game starts. At half time the drinks are already poured and there is no need to queue. Just go to end of bar and hand over your receipt.'

Directions & Car Parking

Brunton Park is very easy to find. Simply leave the M6 at junction 43 and take the A69 towards Carlisle. After a mile you will reach the ground on your right.

The club car park which costs £2.50, can be found by turning right immediately before Brunton Park (it is well advertised). Otherwise street parking.

By train

Brunton Park is situated about a mile from Carlisle Citadel Railway Station and takes around 20 minutes to walk. Upon exiting the station's main entrance, walk the short distance around the Crescent until reaching Warwick Road. You will be able to see the Brunton Park stands in the distance. Continue straight along Warwick Road and you will reach the ground on your left. Thanks to James Prentice for these walking directions.

The Valley
Floyd Road, Charlton, SE7 8BL

What is the ground like?

The opening of the North Stand in 2002, completely transformed the look of the ground. What was a single tiered separate stand, is now a large two tiered affair, extending and completely enclosing the North East & North West corners. In total it houses 9,000 fans. Both sides were also redeveloped in the mid 1990's. The West Stand on one side is a good sized two tiered stand, whilst opposite is the smaller single tiered East Stand, where the vast open terrace, reputedly the country's biggest, was located until demolished in the 1990's. There is a row of executive boxes that run across

the back of this stand and it has a television gantry suspended beneath its roof. The older South Stand, behind the goal, is given to away supporters and now looks out of place in its smart surroundings. On one side of this is a police control box.

The stadium doesn't have any floodlight pylons as such, but has rows of small floodlights running across the tops of the stands. In one corner of the stadium between the South & East Stands is a large video screen. Outside the ground there is a statue of Charlton's former goalkeeper Sam Bartram.

What is it like for visiting supporters?

Away fans are housed in the Jimmy Seed (South) Stand at one end of the ground, which is slightly raised above pitch level, making for a generally good view. Up to 3,000 away fans can be accommodated in this end. Peter Inwood a visiting Leeds fan adds; "There is one solitary supporting column in the entire ground and guess where it is? Right in the middle, behind the goal in the away supporters end. Very annoying it is as well. However, I would commend the stewards, who took a relaxed attitude to the away supporters who stood throughout the match, although expect to be searched on the way in". Otherwise the height between rows is good and the stand quite steep, keeping you fairly close to the playing action. It is worth

noting that there are refreshment areas on either side of the stand. As to be expected those located by the entrance turnstiles, tend to be busiest, whilst those on the other side of the stand are normally less congested.

Food on offer includes a range of Pies; Peppered Steak (£4), Chicken Balti (£4) and Cheese & Onion Pies (£4). These outlets are supplemented by separate Hot Dog stalls (£4). There is also a betting kiosk inside the ground. Adam Hodson a visiting Stockport County fan adds; "There is a decent fish and chip shop at the top of Floyd Road, which you pass on the way to the away fans entrance."

Club nickname:	Ground name:	Capacity:	Opened:
The Addicks	The Valley	27,111 (all seated)	1919

Pitch size:	Undersoil heating:	Record attendance:	Home kit:
112 x 73 yards	No	75,031 v Aston Villa FA Cup 5th Round February 12th 1938	Red and White

Telephone:	Ticket Office:	Website:	Programme:
020 8333 4000	03330 144 444	www.cafc.co.uk	£3

Pubs for away fans

The main pub for away fans is the 'The Antigallican' which is situated close to Charlton Railway Station. However as you would expect it can get very busy and this is not helped by the local Police not allowing fans to drink outside. It is a rather basic pub but has real ale available (albeit a lone handpump) and also offers a selection of filled rolls and pork pies.

Whilst Colin Gilham recommends the 'Rose of Denmark' on Woolwich Road. 'The pub not only allows in away supporters but absolutely welcomes them. They have a photo display

on the wall of fans from visiting clubs that have frequented the pub this season and it also has SKY television.' They also serve Fullers London Pride. Please note that this is a home supporters only pub after the game. To find these pubs come out of Charlton station and turn left into Charlton Church Lane and the Antigallican pub is down on the right hand corner. If you continue down to the T-junction with the Woolwich Road and turn left you will reach the Rose of Denmark further down on the left. Alternatively alcohol is available in the away end.

Directions & Car Parking

Leave the M25 at Junction 2 and take the A2 towards London. After around 12 miles keep right leading onto the A102 towards the Blackwall Tunnel. Leave the A102 at the next slip road (sign posted Woolwich & Ferry A206). At the bottom of the slip road turn

right at the traffic lights towards Woolwich. Proceed along the A206 and on reaching the Antigallican pub, you can see the ground diagonally behind this pub. Parking at the ground is by permit only. Street parking but check signs for parking restrictions.

By train or tube

The ground is a short walk from Charlton Railway Station, which is served by trains from Charing Cross, London Bridge and Waterloo East stations. On Saturdays there are also services from Cannon Street.

Alternatively you can take the London Underground, using the Jubilee Line to get to North Greenwich station. Then take a short ride on buses 161, 472 or 486 to get to the Valley.

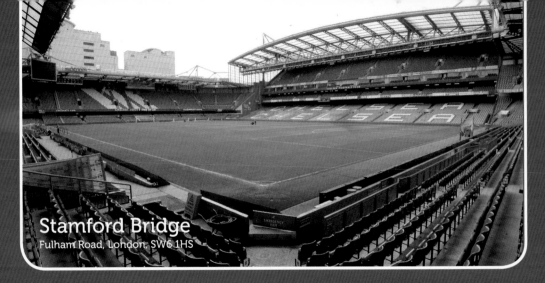

Stamford Bridge
Fulham Road, London, SW6 1HS

What is the ground like?

Stamford Bridge is quite impressive looking, having had three new stands built since the mid-1990's. The developers have taken advantage of the fact that the 'old' Stamford Bridge was oval shaped and have stretched the new stands right around the ground 'filling in' the corners, so that the stadium is totally enclosed. The latest addition to the stadium is the attractive looking West Stand, which was opened in 2001. Located on one side of the pitch, it is a superb three tiered affair having a row of executive boxes running across its middle. Its roof is virtually transparent, allowing more light to reach the pitch and gives it a unique look. Opposite is the older East Stand. Opened in 1973 this towering stand is also three tiered and has the team dugouts situated at its front.

Both ends are smaller being two-tiered. One of these is the Matthew Harding Stand, named in memory of the man who did so much to transform the club. Opposite is the Shed End which has a Police Control Box suspended below its roof. There are two large video screens located in opposite corners of the stadium. Outside the ground is a statue of former playing legend, Peter Osgood.

What is it like for visiting supporters?

Away fans are located on one side of the Shed End lower tier (towards the East Stand side), where the normal allocation for league games is 3,000 tickets. For cup games the whole of the Shed End can be allocated. The view from this area of the ground is pretty good and the refreshment areas are modern looking. There are televisions on the concourses, showing amongst other things at half time, highlights from the first half. There is a range of food and drink on offer, but like a number of London Premier League Clubs it is quite pricey; CheeseBurgers (£4.90), Hot Dogs (£4.50), Pasties (£4.50), Tandoori Chicken Wraps (£5) and Vegetarian Pasties (£5).

On the whole I found Stamford Bridge a pleasurable day out. There was a good atmosphere within the ground and even though there wasn't a lot of space between the home and away fan sections, in didn't feel intimidating. The stewards were also pretty laid back. I was seated in the Shed End and I did find a little difficult to go up and down the steps of the stand, due to the stand itself being quite steep and the steps between rows quite small. The only 'real hassle' I had was trying to get through the lines of stewards situated outside the stadium at the entrance to the away section. They seemed to assume that I was a Chelsea fan and kept ushering me towards the home end. Only after showing my ticket for the visiting section for a third time did I finally make it inside!

Club nickname:	Ground name:	Capacity:	Opened:
The Blues	Stamford Bridge	41,623 (all seated)	1905
Pitch size:	Undersoil heating:	Record attendance:	Home kit:
113 x 74 yards	Yes	82,905 v Arsenal Division One October 12th, 1935	Royal Blue With White Trim
Telephone:	Ticket Office:	Website:	Programme:
0371 811 1955	0371 811 1905	www.chelseafc.com	£3

Pubs for away fans

The pubs near the Stamford Bridge ground can be quite partisan, so I would recommend getting a drink somewhere on the journey there. A number of away fans drink in the pubs around the Earl's Court area, which is only a couple of tube stops away from Fulham Broadway station. The Courtfield Tavern, which is almost opposite the main entrance to Earls Court Tube Station, is a particular favourite with away supporters.

John Ellis a visiting Leicester City fan adds; 'We found that away fans were allowed into the Goose pub on North End Road, which is located about a mile away from Stamford Bridge. The beer was reasonably priced by London standards and it showed Sky Sports.'

Alcohol is available inside the stadium to away fans in the form of Singha Beer (Pint £4.60), London Pride (500ml Bottle) £4.90 or Red or White Wine (187ml miniature bottle). However for certain fixtures the Club opt not to sell any to away supporters, so don't bank on it!

Directions & Car Parking

Leave the M25 at Junction 15 and take the M4 towards London, which then becomes the A4. Carry on over the Hammersmith flyover and after a further one and half miles, take the Earls Court turning (A3220). Continue past Earls Court station and down the one way system until you reach the junction with Fulham Road (A304). At this junction, turn right at the traffic lights and after about half a mile, you will see the ground on your right. Parking is at a premium in the local area and so rather pricey.

By train or tube

The nearest tube station is Fulham Broadway which is on the District Line. Take a tube to Earls Court and if necessary, change for a Wimbledon bound tube. The nearest over ground train station is West Brompton, which is served by trains from Clapham Junction (which is in turn served by trains from London Waterloo and Victoria stations). It is around a 15 minute walk to the ground from West Brompton station.

LCI Rail Stadium
Whaddon Road, Cheltenham, GL52 5NA

What is the ground like?

At one end of the ground is the newest addition to the stadium. The Hazlewoods Stand was opened in December 2005 and has a capacity of 1,100 fans. It is particularly steep in its design, has a perspex windshield to one side and perspex panels incorporated into its roof, to allow more light to reach the pitch. The stand is unusual in the respect that it has a couple of more rows of seats on one side of it. There is also a small electric scoreboard on its roof. On one side of the ground is another relatively new stand. The Wymans Road Stand was opened in November 2001. This stand sits proudly at one side of the pitch and houses 2,034 supporters. It is a covered, all seated, single tiered stand, part of which is given to away supporters. The ground is now enclosed in one corner where the two new stands meet, although it is not used for spectators. On the other side of the pitch is the Main Stand, which was opened in 1963. It has seating to the rear and terracing at the front. Straddling the half way line, it does not extend the full length of the pitch, having open spaces to either side. At one end is the small covered terrace, called the Prestbury Road Stand, which is the home end of the ground.

What is it like for visiting supporters?

Away supporters are housed in the Hazlewoods Stand at one end of the ground. Just over 1,100 supporters can be accommodated in this area. The view of the playing area from the Hazlewoods Stand and the facilities inside are good, plus it has good leg room.

If demand requires it, then part of the Wymans Road Stand can also be allocated to away fans.

The food on offer within the ground is not bad; you can choose from Burgers (£2.80, including for those with a bigger appetite a half pounder with cheese £4), Hot Dogs (£3), Homemade 'Gourmet' Pies (£3.20),

Bacon Rolls (£3), Cornish Pasties (£3) and Sausage Rolls (£2.50).

I found Cheltenham itself to be quite pleasant and the supporters friendly. The picturesque Cotswold Hills around Cheltenham can easily be seen from inside the ground. The atmosphere is also pretty good and there is a drummer in the home end. I did find the p.a. to be a bit deafening though.

Club nickname:	Ground name:	Capacity:	Opened:
The Robins	LCI Rail Stadium	7,066	1932

Pitch size:	Undersoil heating:	Record attendance:	Home kit:
111 x 72 yards	No	8,326 v Reading FA Cup 1st Round November 17th 1956	Red and White

Telephone:	Ticket Office:	Website:	Programme:
01242 573 558	01242 573 558 (Option 1)	www.ctfc.com	£3

Pubs for away fans

There is a club bar at the ground called the Robins Nest which allows in small numbers of away fans for a £1 admittance fee. Also close to the ground is the Parklands Social Club, where you can also park your car (£4). Simply go down Whaddon Road, passing the ground and the bowling club on your left. Take the first left hand turn and the entrance to the social club car park

Around a ten minute walk away are the "Sudeley Arms" and 'The Conservatory" on Prestbury Road on the outskirts of the town centre. There is even a decent fish and chip shop situated in-between the two.

To find these pubs, turn right out of the club car park, and then turn left at the end of the road. Go straight over the roundabout, and The Sudeley Arms is on your left and the Conservatory is further up on your right. It is no more than a ten minute walk from the ground.

Neil Le Milliere a visiting Exeter City fans recommends the Kemble Brewery Inn on Fairview Street. This pub which is listed in the CAMRA Good Beer Guide, serves up to six real ales.

Directions & Car Parking

Leave the M5 at J10 and take the A4019 to Cheltenham. On reaching a large roundabout with a McDonalds on the left, take the first exit. Proceed over a double mini roundabout and then turn right into Swindon Lane. Go over the level crossing and straight over

the next roundabout (signposted Prestbury) passing the race course on your left. Turn right into Albert Road and at the bottom at the roundabout turn left into Prestbury Road, then right into Whaddon Road for the ground down on the left. The Club car park costs £5.

By train

Cheltenham Railway Station is over two miles from the Whaddon Road ground, so best to jump in a taxi. Phil Truscott advises; 'I caught Bus Service D from the Station Car park to the Town Centre (Clarence Street).

On Saturdays Service D runs every 10 minutes. It costs £3.40 for a "day-rider" ticket with unlimited travel in Cheltenham. From the Town centre it is a short walk to Whaddon Road down Prestbury Road.'

Proact Stadium
Sheffield Road, Chesterfield, S41 8NZ

What is the ground like?

On one side is the West Stand. This stand has a capacity of 2,902 seats on a single tier, with a glass fronted executive lounge at the rear. The players emerge from the tunnel at the centre of the stand, whilst the centre seating of the stand is taken up by the Directors Box, Sponsors and Legends seating areas, with the press seating situated towards the North end wing section. The stand has a graceful curved roof with white steelwork and a glazed windshield at the north end

Opposite is the East Stand which is similar in appearance, having a curved roof line and a capacity of 3,144 seats with glazed windshields on either side. The television camera gantry is situated in this stand below the roof steelwork.

Both ends are similar affairs, both being single tiered, covered and housing just over 2,000 supporters. Unlike the other stands the roofs on these ends are not curved, but again glass windshields are in place on both sides.

The stadium has a pleasing balanced feel with no single stand dominating the whole ground.

What is it like for visiting supporters?

Away supporters are housed in the North Stand at one end of the stadium, where up to 2,112 supporters can be seated. If demand requires it then additional seating can also be made available in the East Stand. Unlike most new stadiums the fans are housed pretty close to the pitch, ensuring good views of the playing action. The leg room is good too. The concourses are built to a high standard, with large flat screen televisions

Food on offer from the concourse includes the locally produced Jacksons Pies. The Peppered Steak and Brampton Ale Pie (£3) sounds particularly mouth watering! There are also Large Steak & Mushy Peas Pies (£3.50), Sausage Rolls (£3), Cheeseburgers

(£3.20), Burgers (£3), Rollover Hot Dogs (£3) Chicken Burgers (£3.20) and Mexican Chilli Bean Pies (£3). Pleasingly, the refreshment areas stay open throughout the match (although no alcohol is allowed to be served after 9pm for evening games).

The roof of the away end is quite low, which ensures that a relatively small number of away supporters can really make some noise. I noted that the stewards allowed standing at the back of the stand but not at the front.

Please note that cash is not accepted at the turnstiles, entrance is by ticket only. Away fans can purchase their tickets from the small portakabin located outside the North Stand.

Club nickname: Spireites	Ground name: Proact Stadium	Capacity: 10,400 (all seated)	Opened: 2010
Pitch size: 111 x 71 yards	Undersoil heating: No	Record attendance: 10,089 v Rotherham League Two March 18th, 2011	Home kit: Blue and White
Telephone: 01246 269300	Ticket Office: 01246 269300 (Option 1)	Website: chesterfield-fc.co.uk	Programme: £3

Pubs for away fans

Just across Sheffield Road from the Proact Stadium is the Spireite Pub. This pub has been recently refurbished and has up to six real ales on tap. It welcomes both home and way supporters. Further up Sheffield Road (a five minute walk, passing a handy Chinese/ Fish & Chip shop on the way) is the Derby Tup. This pub normally has ten ales available. Although the pub does not sell food, the landlord allows customers to bring in food from outside.

Further on up Sheffield Road on the right is the well placed North Sea Fish and Chip shop, which was doing a brisk trade on my last visit. Whilst up on the left is the Red Lion pub, which is serves beers from the Old Mill Brewery and shows Sky Sports.

If walking up to the stadium from Chesterfield Railway Station and you like good ale, then you may wish to make a small detour to the Chesterfield Arms. The pub which is situated on Newbold Road, is listed in the CAMRA Good Beer Guide and has normally ten ales and six ciders available. Alcohol is also available inside the ground.

Directions & Car Parking

Leave the M1 at Junction 29 and take the A617 towards Chesterfield. At the end of the dual carriageway at the edge of the town centre, turn right onto the A61 towards Sheffield. At the first roundabout turn left and the stadium is down on the right. For the main entrance turn right into Sheffield Road and then right again for the stadium. However the club car park is for permit holders only. There is nearby street parking available on side roads off the Sheffield Road, if you arrive early enough.

By train

Chesterfield Railway Station is walkable from the Proact Stadium, although it will take you between 20 and 30 minutes to walk to do so. Alternatively, there is a taxi rank outside the station. However as traffic is likely to be slow going along Sheffield Road on a matchday this could end up not being as quick as you thought.

Weston Homes Community Stadium

United Way, Colchester, CO4 5UP

What is the ground like?

In 2008 the Club left their Layer Road ground, their home for 71 years, and moved to a new stadium on the edge of town. The new Weston Homes Community Stadium as it has been named in a corporate sponsorship deal, was built by Barr Construction and the cost of £14m, was largely met by Colchester Borough Council, who own the stadium.

The stadium is functional and well presented, but as with a number of new stadiums built in recent years, it lacks character and is nothing 'out of the ordinary.' The ground is comprised of four separate stands. The Main (West)

Stand on one side of the pitch is a little taller than the other three stands, which are the same height. All the stands are covered single tiered, all seated stands. The Main Stand has a row of executive boxes/corporate hospitality areas running across the top of it, whilst the others are simply seating areas. The Weston Homes Stand though, at the South end of the stadium, does have a Police Control Box incorporated into it, on one side beneath the roof. All the stands have translucent panels built into their roofs as well as a perspex strip just below them, which allows more light and facilitates pitch growth.

What is it like for visiting supporters?

Away fans are normally housed in the northern part of the JobServe Stand, which is situated on one side of the stadium. Around a thousand supporters can be accommodated in this area. For Clubs with a larger travelling support then the North Stand at one end is given instead, where up to 2,000 supporters can be seated.

As you would expect from a modern stadium the facilities and view of the playing action are good. The stands are particularly steep, meaning that fans are kept close to the pitch and resulting in good sight lines. Entrance to the stadium is via automated turnstiles, where you need to insert your ticket into a electronic reader to gain entry.

A varied range of food is available on the concourses, including Cheesburgers (£3.40), Hot Dogs (£3.30), Cornish Pasties (£3.10), Chicken Balti Pies (£2.90), Steak & Ale Pies (£2.90), Cheese & Onion Pasties (£2.90) and Sausage Rolls (£2.90).

John Hill a visiting Huddersfield Town fan adds; 'One pleasing feature was that at 6'2", I was still okay for leg room, which is not always the case at some other grounds. We caught the shuttle bus from the station and it worked surprisingly well. We got to the ground easily, and afterwards they let the buses out of the car park before cars, which led to a fairly swift return to the station and an easy getaway.'

Club nickname:	Ground name:	Capacity:	Opened:
The U's	Weston Homes Community Stadium	10,105 (all seated)	2008

Pitch size:	Undersoil heating:	Record attendance:	Home kit:
110 x 70 yards	No	10,064 v Norwich League One January 16th 2010	Blue and White

Telephone:	Ticket Office:	Website:	Programme:
01206 755 100	01206 755 161	www.cu-fc.com	£3

Pubs for away fans

With the stadium being on the very outskirts of Colchester, then there is little in the choice of pubs and as you would expect what one there are tend to be for home supporters only.

Before the game the Club allow access to the bar and toilets located on the concourse area of the Weston Homes Stand. The bar opens at 12.15pm for a 3pm Kick-Off. Drinks can be taken back outside the stadium to enjoy the pre-match entertainment such as live bands which are often playing under the marquee. This bar is available to both home and away supporters.

Near Colchester North Station and where the stadium shuttle bus operates from in Bruff Close, there is the Norfolk Arms on North Station Road. This pub admits away fans. It offers real ale, serves food and has both BT and Sky Sports.

Inside the stadium alcohol is also available in the away sections.

Directions & Car Parking

Leave the A12 at Junction 28. Turn right at the first roundabout. Go across the bridge and then go straight over the second roundabout, before turning right into United Way at the third roundabout.

There are 700 car parking spaces at the stadium which cost from £6 to £10, depending on how close to the exit you are parked. It is essential that you pre-book your car parking space in advance via the Colchester United FC website.

By train

Colchester North is located just under two miles away from the stadium. Near to the station at Bruff Close is a shuttle bus service that will take you to the ground. The cost of the bus is £2 return, but it is free for OAP's.

The journey time is around 10 minutes. For 3pm kick offs it runs from 1pm, with the last bus returning from the stadium at 6pm. For 7.45pm kick offs, the service commences at 6pm with the last bus back at 10.15pm.

Ricoh Arena
Phoenix Way, Coventry, CV6 6GE

What is the ground like?

Like many grounds built in this country in recent years, the Ricoh Arena is functional and fairly conservative in its design. Three sides of the stadium, which are large single tiered stands, are fairly bland affairs. Happily, the complex has an exhibition centre attached to its West side, resulting in a unique looking stand that gives more of a continental feel. This stand has a small tier of seats overhanging the larger lower tier, with a row of corporate hospitality boxes, running along the back of the lower section. Along the top of the stand is a large area of white panelling, adorned with the logo of the stadium

sponsors, that runs along the length of the stand and around the corners of either side of it. In one of these corners is located a Police Control box. Below the white panelling is a large windowed corporate hospitality area.

The stadium is fully enclosed with all corners of the stadium being filled with spectator seating and all the stands are of the same height, giving it a symmetrical look. There is also a large video screen type scoreboard located in one corner of the stadium between the South and East Stands. The stadium is owned by Wasps Rugby who also play there.

What is it like for visiting supporters?

Away supporters are accommodated to one side of the South Stand (Blocks 6 & 7) towards the corner with the West Stand. Around 3,000 supporters can be seated in this area. The angle of the stand is quite steep, meaning a fair bit of effort to climb to the top. Normally a steep stand means that fans are close to the playing action, but not here. Not only is there a sizeable red coloured track surrounding the playing area, but the stand itself is further set-back from the pitch. This does lead to some viewing problems, especially when the action is taking place at the other end. The leg room is adequate for most and the stadium does have good acoustics, which helps boost the atmosphere.

Entrance to the stadium is through automatic turnstiles, where you have to put your ticket (which has a bar code on it) into a slot reader, which then allows the turnstiles admit you.

Behind the stands there are spacious concourses and a number of food and drink outlets. Food on offer includes; Steak Pie (£3.50), Chicken Curry Pie (£3.50), Cheese and Onion Pie (£3.50) and Sausage Rolls (£3). The concourses also have a number of televisions which show the game being played inside.

Club nickname:	Ground name:	Capacity:	Opened:
The Sky Blues	Ricoh Arena	32,500 (all seated)	2005

Pitch size:	Undersoil heating:	Record attendance:	Home kit:
115 x 74 yards	Yes	31,407 v Chelsea FA Cup 6th Round March 7th 2009	White and Sky Blue Stripes

Ticket Office:	Website:	Programme:	
024 7699 1987	www.ccfc.co.uk	£3	

Pubs for away fans

On one corner of the stadium, near to the Club Shop, is the Grosvenor Casino. This has bars inside and also shows televised sport. Both home and away fans are admitted on matchdays. Craig Woollaston adds; "Please note that the Grosvenor Casino has a strict over 18's policy, so is not suitable for families. In fact anyone who looks under 25 should make sure they have photo ID. Inside the casino, there are two bars, plus a number of pop-up bars depending on the anticipated attendance. The atmosphere is always relaxed. For families then there is an alternative; the Hilton Double Tree Hotel, which is also located at the stadium and has as a bar inside called The Mill. It has lots of screens showing the televised match and away fans welcome. However, being a hotel bar it is a bit pricey".

On Longford Road are the Longford Engine and Coach & Horses pubs which both welcome away fans. There is also a handily placed fish and chip shop located across the road from the Longford Engine. The visitors turnstiles are around a 15 minute walk away. Otherwise alcohol can be purchased inside the stadium.

Directions & Car Parking

Leave the M6 at Junction 3. Take the A444 towards the city centre and after one mile you will reach the stadium on your left. There is normally parking available at the stadium at a cost of £10 per car, although it is best to book a space in advance online via www.ricoharenaparking.co.uk. The Club also utilise a number of car parks within walking distance of the stadium, in such places as factory units and local schools. The cost of these car parks varies between venues but is around £3-£5 per vehicle.

By train

The stadium has its own Coventry Arena Station, however there is only an hourly service in operation, with a limited capacity train (2 carriages on Saturdays and only a single carriage in the Evenings) so I personally wouldn't rely on it to get to the Arena. Coventry Railway Station is about three and half miles away from the stadium and is really too far to walk. A taxi from the station costs around £12 to the Ricoh Arena.

Checkatrade.com Stadium

Winfield Way, Crawley, RH11 9RX

What is the ground like?

This relatively new stadium was opened in 1997, the Club moving there from their old Town Mead ground. The stadium looks to be a quality one in terms of standard of build. It is dominated by the good sized West Stand on one side. This smart looking stand, is covered, all seated and runs for about two thirds the length of the pitch. It is raised above pitch level meaning that fans have to climb a small flight of stairs at the front to enter the seated area. The stand also has windshields to either side, plus three unusual looking floodlight pylons on its roof. It has a capacity of 1,150 seats. Opposite is the new East Stand which was opened in April 2012. This semi-permanent all seated stand, accommodates 2,145 spectators in 12 rows of seating. The stand does though have a fair few supporting pillars running across the front of it that could impede your view. A pair of new floodlight pylons have also been erected to either side of the stand. Both ends are virtually identical, being small covered terraces that extend around both corners of the ground towards the West Stand, enclosing the stadium at those points. The stadium perimeter is surrounded on two sides by a number of trees, giving a rural look.

What is it like for visiting supporters?

Away fans are primarily housed in the North Stand at one end of the ground. This mostly covered terrace can accommodate up to 1,600 fans. A small number of seats are also available to away supporters in the West Stand. The segregation of the terrace can be adjusted depending on the size of the away following. For example clubs will a small following will be given only the North West area up to the corner flag, whilst the largest will be allocated that corner plus the whole of that end.

The facilities inside the stadium are pretty good and the atmosphere in the away end is boosted its low roof. However for those seated in the East Stand then the temporary nature of this stand is shown by a number of supporting pillars running across the front of it that may impede your view. A visit to the Broadfield Stadium, as it is still known to many, is normally a relaxed and enjoyable day out.

Food on offer inside includes a range of Pies from the local supplier "The Real Pie Company". Priced at £3, they include a Chicken Balti Pie, Steak & Guinness Pie and a 'Monthly special' pie. There are also Meat Pasties (£2.50), plus Cheese and Onion Pasties (£2.50). Also there are Bacon Burgers (£4), Double Burgers (£4), Burgers (£3), Veggie Burgers (£3), Hot Dogs (£2.50), Sausage Rols (£2.50), Bacon Rolls (£2.50) and Chips (£2.50).

Club nickname:	Ground name:	Capacity:	Opened:
The Red Devils	Checkatrade.com Stadium	5,996	1997

Pitch size:	Undersoil heating:	Record attendance:	Home kit:
110 x 72 yards	No	5,880 v Reading FA Cup 3rd Round January 5th 2013	Red and White

Telephone:	Ticket Office:	Website:	Programme:
01293 410 000	01293 410 005	crawleytownfc.com	£3

Pubs for away fans

There is a bar at the stadium at the back of the Bruce Winfield Stand called the "Redz Bar", which allows in away fans. Entrance to this bar is gained from outside the stadium. Peter Bellamy informs me, 'The closest pub to the stadium is the New Moon on Brighton Road (A2219). This is about a five minute walk away going towards the town centre. Another pub close by is The Downsman, which is on Wakehurst Drive, just off Southgate Avenue.'

To find these pubs, come out of the stadium car park entrance and turn right and go back up to the main roundabout. Cross the dual carriageway using the underpass and go straight on into Southgate Avenue (A2004). For the Half Moon take the first left off Southgate Avenue into Brighton Road (A2219) and the pub is further up the road on the right. For the Downsman also go to Brighton Road, then take the first right in to Wakehurst Drive. Continue along Wakehurst Drive to find the pub on the left. Otherwise alcohol is available to away fans inside the ground, albeit in a small area where a maximum of 60 fans are allowed in at any one time.

Directions & Car Parking

Leave M23 at Junction 11 (sign posted A264 Horsham, Pease Pottage Services) and take the A23 going towards Crawley. The ground is down on the left just before the next roundabout. It is a little obscured by trees, so look for the large red and white football on the roundabout itself and you will see the stadium entrance. Turn left at the roundabout and then left again for the stadium car park (£5). Peter Bellamy adds; 'There is a free overflow car park at Broadfield Park, which is accessible from the A23 and is signposted.'

By train

Crawley Railway Station is just over a mile away. You can either take a taxi (about £6), or from the bus station across the road, you can take a Fastway number 10 bus to the ground.. Otherwise it is about a 20 minute walk. As you come out of the station turn left and walk down to the T-junction. At the junction turn left into Brighton Road. Keep on Brighton Road for just under a mile and at its end turn right, the stadium is now visible.

Alexandra Stadium
Gresty Road, Crewe, Cheshire, CW2 6EB

What is the ground like?

The ground is officially known as the Alexandra Stadium, but it is more widely referred to as Gresty Road, the street which it is located on. The opening of the new Main Stand in 1999 changed forever the look and feel of the ground. Before, it had always been small and homely, but the addition of the Main Stand has drastically changed the overall scene. The stand, which sits proudly along one side of the pitch, is a single tier cantilever holding just under 7,000 people. The other three stands are roughly of the same height, but are rather small when compared to the Main Stand. So much so, that balls are regularly kicked out of the ground during a game. The newest of these smaller stands is the Gresty Road End, which is the home end of the ground and seats around 900. Opposite is the Railway End. This has some executive boxes at the rear, but the seating area is only opened for the bigger games. The Whitby Morrison Ice Cream Van Stand at one side of the ground, has an unusual television/press gantry on its roof. An unusual feature is the absence of dugouts, the teams instead are given a section of seating at the front of the Main Stand. You will also notice that the pitch is slightly raised above ground level.

What is it like for visiting supporters?

Away fans are housed in the Whitby Morrison Ice Cream Van Stand at one side of the ground. The whole of this stand is given to away supporters and houses 1,680 fans, though if required the Railway End can also be allocated to away fans. Entrance to the away stand is by ticket only, (no cash is accepted at ironically some of the oldest turnstiles I have ever seen at a League Ground). Tickets need to be purchased from the ticket booth next to the supporters club at the entrance to this stand. Please also note that alcohol is not available in this stand.

I found Crewe to be relaxed and friendly, making for a good day out. There was a large away support on my last visit which boosted the atmosphere of the ground, however I have heard reports that it can be a bit flat at certain games, even with the efforts of a drummer in the home end. There are a couple of supporting pillars in the Whitby Morrison Ice Cream Van Stand which if you are unlucky could affect your view of the playing action. There is a popular fish and chip shop just outside of the stadium, the smell of which, early in the game, wafts across the ground. Food on offer inside the stadium includes a range of Holland's Pies; Chicken Balti, Potato & Meat, Cheese & Onion, Peppered Steak (All £2.90), Beef and Vegetable Pasty (£2.90), Sausage Rolls (£2.20), Hot Dogs (£2.90), Cheeseburgers (£2.90) and the 'Alex Whopper' Cheeseburger (£3.70).

Club nickname:	Ground name:	Capacity:	Opened:
The Railwaymen	Alexandra Stadium	10,066 (all seated)	1898
Pitch size:	Undersoil heating:	Record attendance:	Home kit:
100 x 66 yards	No	20,000 v Tottenham FA Cup 4th Round January 6th, 1960	Red, White & Blue
Telephone:	Ticket Office:	Website:	Programme:
01270 213 014	01270 252 610	www.crewealex.net	£3

Pubs for away fans

If you get there early before the game, the supporters club at the ground allows small numbers of away fans in. There are also a number of pubs within easy walking distance of the ground. The pick of these, is probably Bar 7 at the Royal Hotel on Nantwich Road. As Barry Cutts a visiting Coventry City supporter adds; 'I found the Royal Hotel to be a warm and welcoming drinking house. Turn left out of the railway station & the pub is 50 yards down this road on the right hand side. There is also a fantastic chippie opposite.' Although the pub does not look that welcoming, with a number of bouncers on the door, once inside you will find it okay. Zane Alpine a visiting Walsall supporter adds;

'We went to the Cheshire Inn pub a little further along Nantwich Road. It was popular with away fans and was showing the early kick off on large television screens.'

If you park on the industrial estate just off Weston Road, then on your way to the ground you will pass the Brocklebank Pub, a Brewers Fayre outlet, which is very popular with away fans. Otherwise alcohol is available inside the stadium to away fans, albeit only plastic bottles of Carlsberg at £3 each.

Directions & Car Parking

Leave the M6 at Junction 16 and take the A5020 towards Crewe. Follow this road right into Crewe. At the roundabout junction with the A534, Nantwich Road, take the first exit. After passing the Railway Station on the left, turn left into Gresty Road. The ground is

down on the left. There is a pay and display car park at the ground which costs £3.50. Or street parking is available on an industrial estate on Weston Road (signposted; 'Away Supporters On Street Parking'). It then takes about 15 minutes to walk to Gresty Road.

By train

Crewe Railway Station is located around a quarter of a mile away from the ground and is only a five minute walk.

As you come out of the Railway Station turn

left and proceed down the hill. Then take the next left into Gresty Road. Alexandra Stadium is further down this road on the left.

Selhurst Park
London, SE25 6PU

What is the ground like?

Selhurst Park is a mixture of the modern and the old, with two old side stands and two more modern looking end stands. The newest edition is the two-tiered Holmesdale Road Stand at one end, which was opened in 1995. This stand has a large lower tier, with a smaller upper tier that overhangs it. The stand looks impressive and has a large curved roof, as well as windshields on either side of the upper tier.

Opposite is the Whitehorse Lane Stand. This stand has an interesting look, with visible tubular steelwork with floodlights, encasing a single tier of seating that also has a double row of executive boxes located above. There is a large video screen installed upon its roof.

One side is the large, covered, single tiered Arthur Wait stand, which was built in 1969, while on the other side the Main Stand, which dates back to when the ground opened in 1924, is also single tiered. Both stands are now beginning to show their age; with a number of supporting pillars. The Arthur Wait Stand has a TV gantry suspended beneath its roof, whilst the Main Stand has a number of old looking floodlights on its roof.

What is it like for visiting supporters?

Away are housed on one side of the Arthur Wait Stand, towards the Whitehorse Lane Stand, where just over 2,000 away supporters can be accommodated. The views of the playing action are not particularly great from the back of the stand, due to the overhang of the roof and television gantry. There is also one supporting pillar to contend with too. So if possible try to buy tickets for the lower portion of this stand.

On my last visit there was a particularly good atmosphere within the ground, especially from the home fans in the Holmesdale Road End. I was impressed with the Palace fans, who clearly were passionate about their Club, but in a non-intimidatory manner, towards away fans. In fact there was plenty of good banter going on between the two sets of supporters. There are plenty of refreshments available, however, if you if there is a sizeable away support, then getting food and drink could be a problem because there is only one small refreshment area to cater for the whole away support. However there are queuing barriers in place to prevent the obligatory scrum that inevitably ensues at some other grounds.

There is a wide choice of food on offer, including handmade Goddard's Pies such as; Steak and Cronx Ale (£4). You can also enjoy a "Mighty Burger" which comes at a "Mighty Price" of £10 or "normal" burgers at £4.50.

Club nickname: The Eagles	Ground name: Selhurst Park	Capacity: 26,309 (all seated)	Opened: 1924
Pitch size: 110 x 74 yards	Undersoil heating: Yes	Record attendance: 51,482 v Burnley Division 2 May 11th 1979	Home kit: Red and Blue
Telephone: 0208 768 6000	Ticket Office: 0871 2000 071	Website: www.cpfc.co.uk	Programme: £3.50

Pubs for away fans

Opposite Thornton Heath Railway Station there is a Wetherspoon pub, called the 'The Flora Sandes" which is popular with both home and away supporters.

Also close by is 'The Railway Telegraph' on Brigstock Road (as you come out of Thornton Heath station turn right and the pub is further down on the left). This pub serves Youngs beers and is quite spacious. It is then about a 15 minute walk from here to Selhurst Park (as you come out of the pubs turn right and follow the other fans). There are also plenty of Kebab and Chip shops available on the route to Selhurst Park.

Generally beer and lager are served inside the ground, although for certain high profile games, the Club choose not to serve alcohol to away supporters. The choice of alcohol includes; Carlsberg Lager (Bottle £4.50), Somersby Cider (Bottle £4.50) and Wine (Small Bottle £4.50).

Alas away fans don't get to enjoy the 'Palace Ale' which is produced by a craft brewery owned by Neil Morrissey for the Club and is available in the home sections.

Directions & Car Parking

Leave the M25 at J7 and follow the signs for A23 Croydon. At Purley bear left onto the A23 at its junction with the A235 (to Croydon). As you pass Croydon, after which the A23 bears left at Thornton Heath (at the Horseshoe pub roundabout). Go straight over, into Brigstock

Road (B266), passing Thornton Heath Station on your left and bearing right on to the High Street. At the next mini roundabout, go left into Whitehorse Lane for the ground. Street parking, but beware of residents only restrictions on some streets.

By train

The nearest railway stations are Selhurst, Thornton Heath or Norwood Junction, all of which are served by London Victoria main line station. Both Thornton Heath and Norwood Junction are also served by trains

from London Bridge. From each of these local stations it is then a 10-15 minute walk to Selhurst Park. Thornton Heath tends to be more popular with away fans as there are a few pubs for visiting supporters nearby.

Pride Park
Derby, DE24 8XL

What is the ground like?

The Club moved to Pride Park in 1997 after spending 102 years at their former Baseball Ground home. The stadium which was opened by Her Majesty the Queen, is totally enclosed with all corners being filled. One corner is filled with executive boxes, giving the stadium a continental touch.

The large West Stand which runs down one side of the pitch is two tiered, complete with a row of executive boxes. The rest of the ground is smaller in size than the West Stand, as the roof drops a tier to the other sides, making it look unbalanced. It is a pity that the West Stand could not be replicated throughout the rest of the stadium as this would have made it truly magnificent.

An unusual feature inside the stadium is next to the home dugout there is a statue of former player Steve Bloomer who overlooks the pitch. Outside the stadium on one corner is a statue of Brian Clough and Peter Taylor.

What is it like for visiting supporters?

Away fans are located in one corner of the stadium, between the East and South Stands, where up to 2,700 fans can be housed. The facilities within the stadium and view of the playing action are both very good. This coupled with normally a great atmosphere and a deafening PA system, make for a memorable experience. I have visited Pride Park a number of times now and have found the Derby supporters to be friendly and have not experienced any problems. Entrance to the stadium is via electronic turnstiles, meaning that you have to insert your ticket into an electronic reader to gain entry.

Available on the concourse are a selection of Pukka Pies (Chicken Balti, Meat and Potato,

Cheese and Onion) all at £3.80, plus a 'Stand Up Pastie' (I wonder if it tells jokes?) at £3.80.

At half time fans are allowed outside the stadium into a cordoned off area; where there is a catering unit selling Burgers, Hot Dogs etc... It also provides an opportunity for those who smoke to have a cigarette outside. There are televisions on the concourses showing the game going on inside, with commentary, so that you don't have to miss anything while waiting for your half time cuppa.

Club nickname:	Ground name:	Capacity:	Opened:
The Rams	Pride Park	33,597 (all seated)	1997

Pitch size:	Undersoil heating:	Record attendance:	Home kit:
105 x 68 metres	Yes	33,475 v Glasgow Rangers, Friendly May 1st 2006	White and Black

Telephone:	Ticket Office:	Website:	Programme:
0871 472 1884	0871 472 1884 (Option 1)	www.dcfc.co.uk	£3

Pubs for away fans

Pete Stump informs me; "On a recent visit, the police directed us to a 'Harvester' pub about five minutes walk away from the stadium. It was full of away fans, however we were told that for some matches they don't admit visiting supporters."

Nigel Summers a visiting Brighton fan adds; 'The Navigation Inn on London Road, is okay for away supporters. It has free street parking outside, is on the A6 (so an easy get away after the game) and it is just a ten minute walk away from the stadium. It shows televised sports and although home fans frequent the pub too it was friendly enough.' Near to the railway station the Brunswick and the Alexandra Hotel. Both these pubs are listed in the CAMRA Good Beer Guide. Although they both have bouncers on the doors away fans are normally let in as long as there is no singing. The Brunswick though does revert to a home fans only pub for local derbies.

There are bars at the back of the stands, offering pints of Lager or Cider (both £4.10), however they do get quite crowded.

Directions & Car Parking

From the M1, exit at Junction 25 and take the A52 towards Derby. The ground is signposted off the A52 after about seven miles. There are a couple of fair sized parks at the new Velodrome which is situated next to Pride Park and is convenient for the away supporters entrance, being at that end of the stadium. The cost of parking is £8 per car, or £6 if the car has four or more people in it. There is also the Cattle Market 'pay and display' car park. It is just off the A52 & costs £6. It is about a 20mins walk to the ground.

By train

Pride Park is about a 10 minute walk away from Derby Railway Station and is signposted. Dave Plunkett adds; 'Go up the stairs from the platform, turn right and walk to the end of the bridge. Go down the stairs, exit and turn right down Roundhouse Road. Bear left at the roundabout, go straight down Riverside Road or turn right to go down Pride Parkway where there are couple of places to eat and drink. The ground is in front of you.'

Keepmoat Stadium
Stadium Way, Doncaster, DN4 5JW

What is the ground like?

To be honest the Keepmoat Stadium, in common with a number of new stadiums, looks far more interesting from the outside that it does on the inside. The stadium is situated next to a lake (which I believe makes Doncaster the only league ground to do so) and looks smart with four interesting looking floodlights, protruding at an angle from the stadium roof. However, on the inside the stadium is rather non-descript. Yes it looks tidy, the stadium is completely enclosed and all the covered stands are of the same height. But it lacks character and it is rather similar to other new stadiums that have been built, except that it is on a smaller scale.

On one side is the West Stand, which is the Main Stand, containing the teams' dressing rooms and having the players tunnel and team dugouts at its front. Opposite is the East Stand which contains a row of 16 executive boxes, outside which patrons can sit. These run across the back of the stand. Both ends are identical, both being single-tiered and all seated. There is a large video screen located in the South West corner of the stadium.

What is it like for visiting supporters?

Away fans are located in the North Stand at one end of the stadium, where around 3,344 fans can be accommodated. If demand requires it then a portion of the East Stand can also be allocated. The view of the playing action, leg room, and facilities are all good, although fans are set well back from the pitch.

The concourses are a good size and there are a number of televisions on view to keep supporters entertained. Food included a selection of pies (including the Chicken Balti pie) and pasties at £3.10 each, plus burgers and hot dogs.

I found the stadium to be more atmospheric than the Belle Vue ground which was largely open to the elements. This is a bit unusual as most clubs that move to new grounds usually complain that the atmosphere suffers in the new arena, however at the Keepmoat this is not the case. The stewarding was relaxed on my visit and no problems were experienced. The pitch also looked in top condition, although you could still see the lines of a previous rugby league game.

Mark Chatterton a visiting Southend United supporter adds; 'It poured down with rain at our last match and it was noticeable around the stadium that those people sitting in the front rows of the stands, got particularly wet.'

Club nickname:	Ground name:	Capacity:	Opened:
Rovers	Keepmoat Stadium	15,231 (All seated)	2007

Pitch size:	Undersoil heating:	Record attendance:	Home kit:
109 x 76 yards	No	15,001 v Leeds Utd League One April 1st 2008	Red and White Hoops

Telephone:	Ticket Office:	Website:	Programme:
01302 764 664	01302 762 576	doncasterroversfc .co.uk	£3

Pubs for away fans

As the stadium is on the outskirts of town, then there is not much choice in the way of pubs. There is though the Lakeside, a Beefeater outlet near Stadium Way (you should catch sight of it, if you drive towards the stadium from Junction 3 of the M18). Chris Parkes a visiting Nottingham Forest supporter informs me; 'I had no problems with getting a drink in the Lakeside Beefeater, in fact there were more Forest fans in there than home fans before the game. We were also allowed in after the game for a pint or two while the traffic cleared' The pub also has a separate restaurant section. Whilst

David Rose adds; "There is a bar in the bowling alley next to the Vue Cinema, which is situated on the other side of the lake."

Dave a Norwich City fan tells me; 'There is the Belle Vue bar at the stadium itself, which we were allowed to go into. It does get very busy in the hour up to kick off but if you get in early, as we did, you should be okay. The bar has plenty of seating, as well as an organised queuing system.' plus large television screens showing televised football. Alcohol is also available inside the stadium to away fans.

Directions & Car Parking

Leave the M18 at J3 and take the A6182 towards Doncaster (the stadium is well signposted from this point). You will pass a retail park on your left and then at the next roundabout turn left onto White Rose Way. The Lakeside Shopping Centre is now on

your right (the stadium is located directly behind the shopping centre). At the next island turn right onto Middle Bank and then turn right at the bottom of this road onto Stadium Way for the ground. There is a large car park at the stadium which costs £5.

By train

Doncaster Railway Station is around 2 miles away, so you are probably best taking a taxi. If you do fancy the long walk (around 25-30 minutes) then as you come out of the station turn right and then keep straight on this

road (the A 6182 Trafford Way) and you will eventually reach the stadium on your left. There is a matchday shuttle bus 75X running from Stand C6 in the nearby Interchange bus station, which takes 10mins and costs £1.10.

Goodison Park
Goodison Road, Liverpool, L4 4EL

What is the ground like?

Looking from the outside, Goodison Park, with its tall stands seems huge. The crowds filling the narrow streets around the ground on matchday, make you feel that you are going back in time, to when the outside of every football ground appeared like this. However, that's Goodison's problem. Apart from the modern Park Stand (which has an electric scoreboard on its roof and was opened in 1994), the rest of the ground looks tired. Yes the ground is still large, but it needs modernising and hence the Club's desire to build a new stadium elsewhere. Nevertheless unlike some new grounds, Goodison oozes character and the three tiered Main Stand, which was opened in 1971, is still an impressive sight. There are two large video screens at opposite corners of the ground. A unique feature of the stadium is a church called St Lukes which sits just beyond the video screen in one corner of the ground.

If you have time before the game look out for the statue behind the Park Stand; a tribute to the legend that was Dixie Dean. After all these years, the Everton team still come out to the theme tune of the old police television series, Z Cars.

What is it like for visiting supporters?

Away fans are located in one corner of the two tiered, Bullens Road Stand, which is at the side of the pitch, where just over 3,000 away fans can be accommodated. If a small following is expected, then only the lower tier is allocated, which holds 1,700. For larger followings the upper tier is also made available. If you can, try to avoid getting get tickets for the rear sections of both the upper and lower tiers, as the view can be quite poor. For example, in the rear of the lower tier there are a number of supporting pillars that can hinder your view, the seating is of the old wooden type and the gap between rows is tight. The front of the lower tier is a lot better having newer seats and no supporting pillars to contend with.

The facilities within the stand are basic and it is really showing its age (the stand was first opened in 1926). However, away fans can generate some noise from this area, making for a great atmosphere. The catering from the small concourse area, includes amongst other things; a Scouse Pie, which apparently is a kind of meat stew in pastry.

I have enjoyed a number of good days out at Goodison. The atmosphere was relaxed and friendly, with both sets of fans mixing freely before the game. If you arrive at the ground early then there is a small fanzone located in the car park behind the Park Stand. It has entertainment as well as eating and drinking outlets and away fans are able to gain entry.

Club nickname:	Ground name:	Capacity:	Opened:
The Toffees	Goodison Park	39,572 (all seated)	1892

Pitch size:	Undersoil heating:	Record attendance:	Home kit:
112 x 78 yards	Yes	78,299 v Liverpool Division One Sept 18th, 1948	Royal Blue & White

Telephone:	Ticket Office:	Website:	Programme:
0151 556 1878	0151 556 1878 (Option 1)	www.evertonfc.com	£3.50

Pubs for away fans

Behind the Park Stand is a small outdoor fanzone which serves alcohol. About a 15 minute walk away from the visiting supporters entrance, is the Thomas Frost pub on Walton Road. This Wetherspoon outlet, is a fair sized pub, that had a good mixture of home and away supporters, when I last visited. Rob Elmour adds; 'We tried the Bradleys Wine Bar, which is just further down and across the road from Wetherspoons. It had a good mix of fans all very friendly.'

John Ellis a visiting fan informs me; 'Along Walton Lane, on the corner of Cherry Lane is the Liverpool Taxi Cab Drivers, Sports and Social Club. On our visit there was a good mix of home and away supporters. The Club charges a £1 entry fee.'

Otherwise you can walk along Priory Road (where the away coaches drop off and park) or across Stanley Park, going away from Goodison over towards Anfield. The Arkles pub, the usual haunt of away fans visiting Anfield is also popular with away fans going to Goodison. It is about a 15 minute walk. Alcohol is also served inside Goodison to away fans.

Directions & Car Parking

At the end of the M62 keep right and take the A5058 Ring Road North, signposted Football Stadia. After three miles turn left at the traffic lights into Utting Avenue (there is a McDonalds on the corner of this junction). Proceed for one mile and then turn right at the corner of Stanley Park into Priory Road. Goodison is at the end of this road. There is a car park in nearby Stanley Park which costs £10. The entrance to the car park is in Priory Road. There is also the Walton Lifestyles Sports Centre (L4 9XP) which costs £7.

By train

Kirkdale Railway Station is the closest to the ground (just under a mile away). However, it may be more advisable to go to Sandhills Railway Station as this has the benefit of a bus service to the ground, which runs for a couple of hours before the game and around 50 minutes after the final whistle. The bus drops you off within easy walking distance of Goodison Park. It costs £2.

St James' Park
Stadium Way, Exeter, Devon, EX4 6PX

What is the ground like?

The ground is a mixture of the old and the modern. On one side is the old Grandstand that was originally opened in 1926. It is all seated, covered and has windshields to either side. However, it is in size about half the length of the pitch and although part of it straddles the half way line, it mostly sits to one side towards the St James' Terrace End. This stand is due to be demolished in November 2017 to make way for a new 2,800 single-tiered stand.

Opposite is the Main Stand which is the newest addition to the ground and was opened in 2001. This smart looking all seater stand, is single tiered, with some executive boxes located in the middle to the rear.

At one end is the Thatchers 'Big Bank' covered terrace, which was opened in February 2000 and replaced a former open terrace. This stand is quite impressive looking and with a capacity of just under 4,000, means it is now the largest terrace left in the Football League. The other end is a very small open terrace. It is that small, you can clearly see a row of houses beyond it, from which the residents get free view of the game.

What is it like for visiting supporters?

Away fans are mostly housed in the St James' Road terrace at one end of the ground, where just over 1,000 fans can be accommodated.

The facilities in the St James' Road Terrace are rather basic. Also the views from the St James' Road terrace are not great, as due to its limited size (it has only four steps of terrace), fans are situated quite low down and close to the pitch. It is also does not have any cover and is open to the elements. As this end does not have a roof, then it is difficult for the visiting fans to generate atmosphere from this area.

Instead it may be a better idea to head for one of the seats that the Club make available to visiting supporters in Blocks L & M of the Main Stand. The Main Stand is not only more modern and covered, it affords better views of the playing action and has better facilities for fans.

I personally have enjoyed my visits to St James' Park, with no problems experienced.

Club nickname: The Grecians	Ground name: St James' Park	Capacity: 8,830	Opened: 1904
Pitch size: 114 x 73 yards	Undersoil heating: No	Record attendance: 21,014 v Sunderland FA Cup 6th Round March 4th, 1931	Home kit: Red and White
Telephone: 01392 411 243	Ticket Office: 01392 411 243 (Option 3)	Website: exetercityfc.co.uk	Programme: £3

Pubs for away fans

There is a Social Club at the ground itself, which allows in away supporters. Paul Stillwell a visiting Luton Fan informs me; 'Just a minute walk from the away end of the ground is the St Anne's Well on Well Street. Local ales, nicely cooked food, Wifi, BT and Sky Sports and friendly bar staff. It is very popular with away fans.' About a ten minute walk away on Stoke Hill, is the Stoke Arms, which also has BT and Sky Sports.

Otherwise, the ground is walkable from the city centre where there are plenty of pubs. Mike Faulkner from Somerset, recommends the Duke Of York and the Amber Rooms in Sidwell Street.

Whilst Tony Fort recommends "The Victoria" on Victoria Road (follow Victoria Street from the back of the Grandstand). As Tony says 'You can park here (for free) but it is a good 10-15 minutes walk from the ground and steep! The pub is great, very "studenty", but full of friendly Exeter supporters. Both the food and ale were excellent both from a quality and value perspective.'

Directions & Car Parking

Leave the M5 at Junction 30 and follow signs for Exeter city centre along the A379 and then onto Rydon Lane (A3015). Take the Sidmouth Road turn off (B3183) towards the city centre. Keep going towards the town centre as the road becomes Heavitree Road.

On nearing the city centre take the fourth exit at the large roundabout onto Western Way. At the next roundabout take the second exit onto Old Tiverton Road, then turn left into St James Road for the ground. There is street parking, but check for restrictions.

By train

The nearest railway station is St James Park, which is adjacent to the ground and only a short walk away, However this station is on a local line and most fans will arrive first into the mainline stations of Exeter St Davids or Exeter Central, from which you can then get a local train to St James Park. Exeter Central is the closer of the two mainline stations is just under a mile away from the ground and should take around 20 minutes to walk.

Highbury Stadium
Park Avenue, Fleetwood, FY7 6TX

What is the ground like?

On one side of the ground is the very impressive looking Parkside Stand which was first opened to spectators in March 2011. This 2,000 capacity all seated stand has a single tier of seating, whilst above are offices and hospitality areas. These are covered by an eye catching semi-circular roof, with large glassed areas to either side.

Opposite is the Highbury Stand, which is a small all-seated covered stand, which was opened in 2008. It is only six rows high, has a capacity of 550 and runs for only half the length of the pitch, meaning that there is a large open area next to it, For the 'eagle eyed' then directly behind it you can see a small roof which is the roof the old Main Stand which is still in existence having had the new stand built in front of it.

Both ends are covered terraces, which are similar in size in terms of height. The Percy Ronson Terrace runs for around 2/3rds of the width of the pitch. Whilst the home end, the Memorial Stand, is larger extending the full width of the pitch and housing just under 1,500 supporters. In one corner of the stadium is a large video screen.

What is it like for visiting supporters?

Away fans are mostly housed in the Percy Ronson terrace at one end of the stadium, where 831 fans can be accommodated. This terrace which was opened in 2007, is covered, free from supporting pillars and affords a good view of the playing action. The Club have recently improved the facilities in this area with a new snack bar and toilet block. The terrace capacity also includes an open flat standing area on the Highbury Stand side. The official capacities are 621 for the Percy Ronson Terrace and 210 for the Highbury side standing area.

Visiting supporters are also allocated 300 seats in the Parkside Stand and this can be increased if required. The facilities in this stand are far better than the terrace with alcoholic drinks available to purchase and there are large screens on the concourse showing Sky Sports. For teams with a smaller following then only the Parkside seats will be made available and not the Percy Ronson Terrace.

Food on offer inside the Highbury Stadium includes; Cheeseburgers (£3), Hot Dogs (£3) and a range of Hollands Pies (£3).

There is an away fans ticket office and programme booth situated outside the visiting supporters entrance. Also listen out for the old sea shanty music which is played when Fleetwood score.

Club nickname:	Ground name:	Capacity:	Opened:
Cod Army	Highbury Stadium	5,311	1939

Pitch size:	Undersoil heating:	Record attendance:	Home kit:
112 x 74 yards	No	6,150 v Rochdale FA Cup First Round 13th November 1965	Red and White

Telephone:	Ticket Office:	Website:	Programme:
01253 775080	01253 775080 (Option 1)	fleetwoodtownfc. com	£1

Pubs for away fans

There is Jim's Sports Bar at the ground, which normally admits away fans. The facilities in this bar are excellent, but get there early as it is very popular on matchdays. It is located at the back of the Memorial Stand and can be accessed from the park pathway that runs along that side of the ground. It also shows BT and Sky Sports on a large number of televisions.

Martin Crimp a visiting Southport fan informs me; 'We were directed to the Queens Hotel, on Poulton Road, about a 15 minute walk away. It has Sky Sports on multi screens along with a decent pint of Thwaites. Go up Highbury Avenue then left at the St Nicholas church into Poulton Road. The Queens is about 300 yards along this road on the left.'

Otherwise take a 10-15 minute stroll into Fleetwood itself where there are plenty of pubs to be found, including the Wetherspoon outlet called the Thomas Drummond on London Street (off Lord Street) and the Strawberry Gardens pub on Poulton Road. Alcohol is also available inside the stadium but only to away fans who are seated in the Parkside Stand.

Directions & Car Parking

Leave the M6 at J32 and take the M55 towards Blackpool. Leave the M55 at J3 and take the A585 towards Fleetwood. On the outskirts of Fleetwood you will come to a roundabout with Blackpool and Fylde college on your left. Continue straight across and then take the first left into Copse Road. After about a mile and as you pass Fleetwood Fire station on your left then branch left and turn left onto Radcliffe Road. Then next right into Stanley Road for the stadium. There is plenty of street parking available in the area.

By train

There is no railway station in Fleetwood itself. The closest is at Poulton-le-Fylde, which is just over five miles away. However it is more likely that fans will head to Blackpool North station which is around seven miles away. A taxi from the station to Fleetwood will cost you the best part of £20. It may be better to catch a bus to Fleetwood, Service numbers 1 and 14, run from Blackpool, or take a tram up to Fleetwood from the sea front.

The New Lawn
Nympsfield Road, Nailsworth, GL6 0ET

What is the ground like?

The club moved a short distance to their new ground at beginning of the 2006/07 season. Now when I mean a 'short distance' then I literally mean only a few hundred yards up the road from their old Lawn Ground which is has now been redeveloped for housing.

The stadium is dominated by the smart looking Main Stand at one side of the pitch. This 2,000 all seated capacity stand, has a cantilever roof as well as row of executive boxes running across the back of it. The team dugout areas are located at the front of this stand. Opposite is a small open terrace, which is only seven steps high. Running along the back of this terrace are 4 floodlight pylons. Interestingly both ends have to different degrees been relocated from the old Lawn to the new ground. At the Nympsfield Road end of the ground, is a covered terrace, the roof of which came from the Barnfield Road side of the old ground. Opposite is the South Stand, which until recently was a covered all seated stand, but has now had the seats removed to make it a terrace for home fans. This stand is of interest as it was the Trevor Horsley Stand which was transported from the Club's old ground and re-erected at the New Lawn.

What is it like for visiting supporters?

Away fans are mostly housed in the West Terrace on one side of the ground. This terrace has a capacity of around 1,150 fans and runs the full length of the pitch. The terrace is uncovered, so hope that it doesn't rain. In addition, around 250 seats are made available to visiting fans in Block A of the Main Stand opposite. Located towards the North End, this area does have roof cover. Entrance to the ground is via electronic turnstiles, meaning that you need to scan your ticket to gain admittance.

My visits to The New Lawn (and the old ground for that matter) have been most enjoyable and it would be difficult to find a more friendly and welcoming club than this one. If the chance arises, a visit to this Gloucestershire ground is a pleasant days outing in a unique setting.

If you are looking for a Meat Pie, Beef Burger or Hot Dog to buy inside the ground, then you will be disappointed, as the Club has decided not to sell any meat products. Instead, there are Veggie Burgers (£3), Veggie Cheeseburgers (£3.50) and Falafel Wraps (£2.50) on offer, as well as Chips and Curry Sauce (£2.70) and Chip Butties (£2.70). I guess as a bit of a 'tongue in cheek' the club also sell a vegetable pasty called the Badger pasty! (£3.50).

Club nickname:	Ground name:	Capacity:	Opened:
The Rovers	The New Lawn	4,803	2006

Pitch size:	Undersoil heating:	Record attendance:	Home kit:
110 x 70 yards	No	4,836 v Derby County FA Cup 3rd Round January 3rd 2009	Green and Black

Telephone:	Ticket Office:	Website:	Programme:
01453 834 860	01453 834 860 (Option 1)	forestgreenroversfc. com	£3

Pubs for away fans

The best option for a drink though is in the clubs own bar, the Green Man, which is built into the back of the Main Stand. This bar serves real ale, hot food and has a number of televisions showing televised sports. However, when a large away following is expected, then the Club reverts to allowing only home fans entrance to it.

If you have a bit of time on your hands then there is the Village Inn on the A46 on the North side of the town. This former CAMRA Good Beer Guide listed pub is also home to the Nailsworth Brewery.

There are some other pubs and food outlets are at the bottom of the hill in Nailsworth, which is about a 15 minute walk down the hill. But unless you are rather fit then the walk back up to the ground is not for the faint hearted as it is mostly up a very steep incline.

Directions & Car Parking

Leave the M5 at junction 13 and head for Stroud on the A419. At Stroud turn onto the A46 towards Nailsworth. This will bring you into the centre of the town, when you reach the Information Centre take the first right at the mini roundabout into Spring Hill, which

goes up a steep hill sign posted Forest Green. Turn left at the roundabout at the top of the hill into the Club car park, which holds 250 cars (£4) Also nearby Nailsworth Primary School also offers matchday parking at a cost of £4.

By train

There is no railway station in Nailsworth. The nearest is in Stroud which is three miles away. Either take a taxi from the station to the ground or as John Aitken informs me; 'You can also take a bus from Stroud to

Nailsworth. Stagecoach numbers 93 & 46 both operate from Stroud Bus Station to Nailsworth. Ask the driver to let you off at Beechwood Close in Nailsworth, just a short walk from the ground.'

Craven Cottage

Stevenage Road, London, SW6 6HH

What is the ground like?

On one side of the ground is the Johnny Haynes Stand named after the former Fulham great. This covered all-seated stand dates back to 1905 and was originally designed by the then famous football ground architect, Archibald Leitch. Considering its age, it can be forgiven for having a number of supporting pillars and old wooden seating in its upper tier. It does though have a fine classic looking gable on its roof.

Opposite is the aptly named Riverside Stand. which sits on the banks of the River Thames. This all seated, covered stand was opened in 1972. It was slightly raised above pitch level. It also has a row of executive boxes running across the back of it and also houses a television gantry.

Both ends are large modern all seated, covered stands, that look fairly similar in design. They both though have some supporting pillars which is disappointing.

In one corner of the ground is the unique Pavilion building, which many fans refer to as 'the Cottage', giving the ground further character.

What is it like for visiting supporters?

Away fans are housed to one side of the Putney End Stand on the river side of the ground. This stand is shared with 'neutral' supporters, with away fans being allocated around 3,000 seats, which is just under half of the overall capacity of this stand. There are a couple of supporting pillars that could impede your view, but this only applies to certain seats in Row DD and above. The leg room is ample and as the rows of the stand seem to have been constructed from metal and plywood, rather than concrete, fans can't resist making some noise, by stamping up and down on it.

Food and drink are served from a number of outlets and stalls situated behind the stands.

These areas although mostly covered are not enclosed, which is great in the Summer but can be rather cold in Winter. However if you go to the outlets around to the left of the stand then you can enjoy some nice views of the Thames, whilst having your beer. Around the concourses are flat screen televisions showing the game being played inside.

I have been previously to Craven Cottage on a number of occasions and on a nice summer day, this is one of my favourite grounds. From the walk from the tube station through a park, to having a pint overlooking the River Thames, this can be quite an enjoyable experience and I have never had any problems there.

Club nickname:	Ground name:	Capacity:	Opened:
The Cottagers or The Whites	Craven Cottage	25,678 (all seated)	1896
Pitch size:	Undersoil heating:	Record attendance:	Home kit:
109 x 71 yards	Yes	49,335 v Millwall Division Two October 8th, 1938	White With Black Trim
Telephone:	Ticket Office:	Website:	Programme:
0843 208 1222	0843 208 1234	www.fulhamfc.com	£3.50

Pubs for away fans

Near to the tube station is the 'Eight Bells' which is popular with away fans. James Merrick a visiting Ipswich Town fan adds; 'We arrived at the Eight Bells at 1pm, to find it was already full but was advised to head for the 'The Temperance" which is only a few minutes walk away. They have a round bar in the centre of their main room, there is ample seating and the football was being screened on a large projector with other televisions placed around the room. Prices were reasonable and the service excellent. There was a mix of home and away fans in there, but there were no problems whatsoever, in fact we spent a bit of time talking to some very nice Fulham fans about the game and their season as a whole.' Opposite the Temperance on the same road is the King's Arms, which is also popular with visiting supporters. It also shows televised sport.

David Frear recommends; 'The Crabtree on Rainville Road (10 minutes walk from the ground) welcomes all away supporters and as a Fulham season ticket holder I can tell you that as long as you don't watch your football at Loftus Road you can be assured of a warm welcome.'

Directions & Car Parking

Leave the M25 at J15 and take the M4, which leads onto the A4, towards Central London. After around two miles branch off left into Hammersmith Broadway (before the flyover). Go around the ring road around central Hammersmith, keeping to the right. Then take the A219 Fulham Palace Road. Keep straight on this road, passing Charing Cross Hospital on your left. After about another half a mile, take one of the right hand turns for the ground. Metered paid street parking, but not on the roads closest to the stadium.

By tube

The nearest tube station is Putney Bridge, on the District Line. The ground is about a 15 minute walk. Turn left out of the station and then turn right into Ranelagh Gardens. After passing the Eight Bells pub on your right, turn left after the pub onto the main road and then cross over to the other side. Before the bridge turn right to enter into Bishops Park. Just proceed on through the park to the ground (you can see the floodlights).

MEMS Priestfield Stadium
Redfern Avenue, Gillingham, ME7 4DD

What is the ground like?

Priestfield Stadium has been virtually re-built since the current Chairman Paul Scally took over in 1995. On one side of the ground is the impressive looking Medway Stand. Opened in 2000, it is two-tiered, with a large lower tier and a small upper tier. In-between these tiers are a row of executive boxes, which also have seating outside. Opposite is the Gordon Road Stand. Opened in 1997, this is a much smaller single tiered stand, which is partly covered (to the rear). It contains a number of supporting pillars running across the back of it, plus it also has an unusual looking TV gantry perched on its roof.

The Rainham End was opened in 1999. It is a single tier cantilevered stand, which replaced a former terrace. Opposite is the Brian Moore Stand. This is in fact a temporary seated stand that has been situated on top of an existing terrace. When I say temporary (considering that it has been there since 2003) I mean that the stand can be easily dismantled and re-assembled. This is the only open area at the stadium. This stand is named in memory of the legendary commentator and lifelong Gills fan, Brian Moore.

What is it like for visiting supporters?

Away fans are housed on one side of the Brian Moore Stand (on the Medway Stand side) where around 1,500 supporters can be accommodated. The stand is largely constructed from scaffolding and is temporary in nature. It is of a good size and height (you can get some great views of the surrounding area at the very top of it), plus the views of the playing action are fine.

Unlike most temporary stands though the facilities are surprisingly good, being of a more permanent nature behind the structure. However the stand is uncovered, so although the Club hand out free rain macs if it rains, still be prepared to get wet! The absence of a roof also dampens the atmosphere

somewhat, even considering that the end is shared with home fans. However supporters in this area do try to make some noise by stamping on the metal rows of the stand.

One unusual aspect of visiting Priestfield Stadium is that away supporters have to walk down a very narrow terraced street to reach the away entrance, or if coming from adjacent streets down very tight alleys. However, there is never normally any problems with this although after the game the Police sometimes close of some of the surrounding streets and alleyways to keep fans apart.

Club nickname: The Gills	Ground name: MEMS Priestfield Stadium	Capacity: 11,582 (all seated)	Opened: 1893
Pitch size: 114 x 75 yards	Undersoil heating: No	Record attendance: 23,002 v QPR FA Cup 3rd Round January 10th 1948	Home kit: Blue With White Trim
Telephone: 01634 300 000	Ticket Office: 01634 300 000 (Option 3)	Website: gillinghamfootball club.com	Programme: £3

Pubs for away fans

The Fleur De Lis pub on Gillingham Road, which is around a ten minute walk away from the stadium, has been designated by the local Police as an away fans pub. This pub shows BT Sports, has hot and cold snacks and is family friendly. To find this pub, then with away entrance behind you, walk down to the bottom of the street. Turn left and on reaching a roundabout (where the Livingstone Arms used to be and where there is a handy fish & chip shop) turn right onto Gillingham Road. The pub is up on the right.

Otherwise, the ground is walkable from the town centre, where there are a fair few pubs to be found. Paul Kelly a visiting Preston fan adds; 'We have used the 'Will Adams' in the town centre. The pub is in the CAMRA Good Beer Guide and does good cheap food. Plus a very friendly crowd of football locals happy to indulge in friendly banter - the landlord is a Gill fan too!' Robert Donaldson recommends the "Southern Belle" opposite the railway station, which also has a cafe located next door.

As far as I am aware alcohol is not on sale to away fans inside the stadium.

Directions & Car Parking

Leave the M2 at Junction 4 and take the A278 towards Gillingham, going straight across two roundabouts. At the third roundabout turn left onto the A2 towards Gillingham town centre. At the traffic light junction with the A231, turn right into Nelson Road and passing the small bus station take a right turn into Gillingham Road, the ground is down on your right. Residents only parking scheme near to the ground. Parking is also available at a cost of £3 at the Our Lady Of Gillingham Catholic Church on Ingram Street (ME7 1YL).

By train

Priestfield Stadium is about a ten minute walk away from Gillingham Railway Station, which is served by trains from London Victoria (every 15mins), Charing Cross (every 30mins), St Pancras and Stratford International (both located on the same line, every 30mins). It is worth noting that the quickest trains leave from St Pancras (journey time around 45mins) and Stratford International (journey time 37mins).

Blundell Park
Cleethorpes, DN35 7PY

What is the ground like?

At one side of the ground is the Findus Stand, which is the tallest stand and is two tiered and covered. The lower tier, which was originally terracing, has only seven rows of seating whilst the upper tier is much larger. However this stand only runs half the length of the pitch, straddling the half way line. Running in-between the two tiers is a row of executive boxes.

Opposite is the old Main Stand, which is small covered all seated stand and has a large number of supporting pillars running across the front of it. Part of this stand dates back to

1901. This possibly makes it one of the oldest surviving stands in the country.

Both ends are small covered affairs. The Pontoon Stand is the traditional home end, whilst the away fans are housed in the Osmond Stand opposite. The corner between this stand and the Main Stand is also filled, as the stands are joined at this point, though this is unused for supporters. There is a Police Control box located on one side of the Main Stand and a large video screen in one corner of the ground.

What is it like for visiting supporters?

Away fans are located in one corner of the Osmond Stand, at one end of the ground, where just under 600 supporters can be accommodated. For teams with a larger following then the whole of the stand can be given to away fans increasing the allocation to 2,200. One downside of this stand is that there are a couple of supporting pillars which could impede your view of the game, especially if you are located towards the back of the stand.

Food on offer inside the ground include a range of Pies; Steak, Chicken Balti and Cheese and Onion (all £3). Pukka Pasties (£3), Jumbo Sausage Rolls (£2.50), Cheeseburgers (£3.80), Burgers (£3.50) and Jumbo Hot Dogs (£3.50).

Blundell Park is a rather small ground and sometimes gets over criticised by visiting fans. However it is a proper traditional football ground the likes of which are fast disappearing, so enjoy it before it goes too!

Also normally there is a passionate home crowd, which contributes to a good atmosphere. The low roof in the away end, helps this as well.

Remember though to wrap up warm as there can be a biting wind coming off the North Sea.

Club nickname:	Ground name:	Capacity:	Opened:
The Mariners	Blundell Park	9,052 (all seated)	1899

Pitch size:	Undersoil heating:	Record attendance:	Home kit:
111 x 75 yards	No	31,651 v Wolves FA Cup 5th Round February 20th, 1937	Black and White Stripes

Telephone:	Ticket Office:	Website:	Programme:
01472 605 050	01472 605 050 (Option 4)	grimsby-townfc. co.uk	£3

Pubs for away fans

Inside Blundell Park, away fans are treated to their own bar called Scotties. The bar is of a fair size, has seating, plus it shows Sky Sports television. This is being run by the Mariners Trust, a supporters organisation with has the aim of raising money for the Club. Please note that entrance to Scotties Bar can only be gained from inside the ground, once you have entered through the away turnstiles.

Dave Peasgood recommends the Blundell Park Hotel, which is located just across the road from the ground. However as you would expect it can get pretty full, so it is advised to arrive early. It also serves some good food at reasonable prices (expect to pay around £5 for a good portion of fish and chips).

The Rutland Arms has also been recommended to me. It normally has a mixture of both home and away fans and is family friendly. However the pub is some distance from the ground, being located around half a mile before Blundell Park, just off the main Grimsby Road.

Directions & Car Parking

On reaching the end of the M180 continue along the A180 towards Grimsby. After around 14 miles you will near Grimsby town centre. Continue along the A180 following signs for Cleethorpes. On reaching a McDonalds sign on your left and the Blundell Park Hotel on your right, turn left into Imperial Avenue for the Club entrance.

There is no car park at the ground, therefore it is a case of finding some street parking.

By train

Cleethorpes Railway Station is about a mile from the ground and takes around 15-20 minutes to walk. Exit the station and turn right; then turn left onto Station Road. At the end of Station Road turn right onto the High Street. Follow this road down to the roundabout; where you turn right onto the Grimsby road (A180). Continue straight for approximately half a mile and you will see the floodlights of the ground on your right.

John Smith's Stadium
Huddersfield, HD1 6PX

What is the ground like?

Most modern stadiums in this country are rather boring affairs with little character, but the John Smith's Stadium does not fall into this category. Each stand is semi-circular rather than rectangular, and is further enhanced with large white steel tubing above the contours. In fact from the car park I first thought it looked like a new ride at Alton Towers! It is good to see something different from the architects for a change. The ground has won many design awards and is well worth a visit.

The only disappointment is that the corners of the ground are open. The Fantastic Media (North) Stand at one end and the Revell Ward Stand at one side are both two tiered stands, each with a row of executive boxes running across the middle. The other two sides of the ground are large single tiered affairs. One of these the Britannia Rescue Stand, at one side of the pitch, can accommodate 7,000 supporters. There is an electric scoreboard at the back of the away end. The stadium is completed with a striking set of four floodlights. The stadium is also shared with Huddersfield Giants Rugby League Club.

What is it like for visiting supporters?

Away fans are located at one end of the ground in the Chadwick Lawrence (South) Stand. Up to 4,000 supporters can be accommodated in this area. The facilities in this stand and the view of the playing action are both good. The acoustics of the stand are good also, meaning that a relative small number of fans can really make some noise, contributing to what is normally a good atmosphere within the stadium.

There is also a betting outlet and a bar serving alcoholic drinks at the back of the stand, which remains open during the first half and half time. Stewarding is normally amicable and relaxed.

Food on offer inside the stadium, includes; Cheeseburgers (£3.50), Hamburgers (£3.20), Hot Dogs (£3.20), Peppered Steak Pie (£3.50), Meat and Potato Pie (£3), Chicken Balti Pie (£3), Cheese and Onion Pie (£3) and Sausage Rolls (£3)

I have enjoyed my visits to the John Smith's Stadium, I have always been thoroughly impressed with the stadium and the general set-up.

Club nickname:	Ground name:	Capacity:	Opened:
The Terriers	John Smith's Stadium	24,500 (all seated)	1994
Pitch size:	**Undersoil heating:**	**Record attendance:**	**Home kit:**
115 x 76 yards	Yes	24,129 v Man City FA Cup 5th Round February 18th, 2017	Blue and White
Telephone:	**Ticket Office:**	**Website:**	**Programme:**
01484 484112	01484 484123	www.htafc.com	£3

Pubs for away fans

John Ellis a visiting Leicester City fan recommends the Gas Club on Gasworks Street, about five to ten minute walk from the Stadium. 'On our visit there was a good mix of home and away fans. The Club does charge a £1 entry fee, but both the drinks and food were reasonably priced. You can also park in their car park at a cost of £3.' Please note that after the game the Club reverts to being a 'home fans only' bar.

Tim Oscroft informs me; 'The Head of Steam pub at the railway station is pretty good and serves food too.' Also near to the railway station is the Cherry Tree pub.

This Wetherspoons outlet is located on John William Street and is popular with away fans.

There is also a cinema and entertainment complex behind the North Stand, which also contains the Rope Walk pub. Craig Murray a visiting AFC Bournemouth fan adds; 'We went for a pre-match pint at the Rope Walk. Inside it was a mixture of home and away fans and the locals were very friendly and happy to chat about footy.' Otherwise beer (including John Smith's!) is available inside the stadium.

Directions & Car Parking

Leave the M1 at Junction 38 and take the A637 towards and then the A642 into Huddersfield. As you approach the town centre try to keep to the right hand lane as you will turn right at the roundabout and onto the A62 Leeds Road.

The stadium is a short distance down this road on the right.

Parking at the ground costs £6 or alternatively on St Andrews Road there are a number of small businesses that offer parking for around £5.

By train

The John Smith's Stadium is walkable from Huddersfield Railway Station. it should take no more than 15 minutes at a comfortable pace. After coming out of the Railway Station, turn down past the front of The

George Hotel. Go straight over the crossroads into Northumberland Street and walk down across the Ring Road straight on into Leeds Road. Turn right down Gasworks Street, then straight over the crossroads to the ground.

KCOM Stadium
The Circle, Walton Street, Hull, HU3 6HU

What is the ground like?

The KCOM Stadium was opened in 2002 and from the inside the stadium looks very impressive, however from the exterior it looks a bit plain. It doesn't help that the most interesting part of the exterior, visually, around the main entrance, is mostly obscured by trees. However the stadium is set in a park land and can be seen for some distance around and has won a number of awards for its design.

The KCOM Stadium is totally enclosed, with the West Stand being around twice the size of the other three sides. The roof rises up and curves around the West Stand, giving the stadium an interesting look.

Inside the curves continue as each of the stands slightly bend around the playing area, drawing the eye to sweep panoramically around them. Apart from the West Stand, each of the other three stands is single tiered. The West Stand also benefits from having a row of executive boxes running across its middle. There is a large video screen at the North End of the stadium, where the Police Control Box is also situated. The P.A system within the stadium is also excellent. The KCOM Stadium is home to both Hull Football and Rugby League Clubs.

What is it like for visiting supporters?

Away fans are located in the North East corner of the stadium, where up to 2,510 supporters can be housed. This away section extends around the North East Corner into the first couple of blocks of the North Stand. The facilities available are good, plus you enjoy an unobstructed view of the playing action, although fans are a little set back from the pitch. I found the atmosphere to be also generally good within the stadium.

Dave Winsor a visiting Nottingham Forest fan adds; 'Our seats were roomy and comfortable with a raised behind the goal view. Plenty of leg room and helpful stewards along with a nice fat matchday programme and a really good selection of food and drink from the

concourse all contributed to the favourable impression. An interesting ground with much more to it than the usual depressing flat pack stadium of some other designs.'

For night games the stadium puts on a cracking light show, accompanied by music, which is put on for around five or six minutes before the teams come out onto the field of play. It is well worth watching.

Club nickname:	Ground name:	Capacity:	Opened:
The Tigers	KCOM Stadium	25,404 (all seated)	2002

Pitch size:	Undersoil heating:	Record attendance:	Home kit:
114 x 78 yards	Yes	25,030 v Liverpool Premier League May 10th 2010	Amber and Black

Telephone:	Ticket Office:	Website:	Programme:
01482 504 600	01482 505 600	hullcitytigers.com	£3

Pubs for away fans

Away supporters have their own bar called the Pitch Side located at the KCOM Stadium itself. Although not the most spacious of bars it does show live sports on a number of screens and also offers cold food and snacks, such as sandwiches. The entrance to the bar is located outside the stadium, next to the visiting fans turnstiles. However please note that the Pitch Side Bar stops serving alcohol 45 minutes before kick off. Tim Jones a visiting Aston Villa supporter informs me; 'The Park View pub virtually opposite the stadium car park entrance allows in away fans. It has a good atmosphere and the Hull fans there were friendly. It also has a big screen showing Sky Sports and a burger van outside.' Whilst fellow Villa fan Neil Tate adds; 'There is also the nearby Walton Street Social Club that also admits away supporters. Although it costs £1 to go in, it has good cheap beer, is of a good size and offers a separate area for sale of food such as burgers and chips etc.. There were plenty of fellow Villa fans in there during our recent visit. Turn right out of the main car park entrance and it is down the road on the left hand side.' Alcohol is also made available to visiting fans inside ground.

Directions & Car Parking

At the end of the M62, continue onto the A63 towards Hull. Stay on the A63 and the stadium is clearly signposted (KCOM Stadium and a football symbol) as you approach Hull. About one mile from the centre of Hull leave the A63 (just after you pass B&Q on the opposite side of the carriageway and is sign posted Local Infirmary) and take the second exit at the roundabout. Turn left at the lights and then over the flyover, right at the next lights and the ground is down on the right. There is a car park at the stadium (£5).

By tube

The KCOM Stadium is 20 minute walk away from Hull Paragon Station. Turn left at the end of the station platform and then left into the bus station. Exit the bus station at the far end. Walk past Tesco on your right, cross over Park Street at the traffic lights. Following blue pedestrian signs to KCOM Stadium go along Londisborough Street. Cross Argyle Street and onto pedestrian walkway and bridges over the railway lines to the stadium.

Portman Road
Ipswich, IP1 2DA

What is the ground like?

The overall look of the ground has greatly improved, with the re-development of both ends. Both these ends, the Sir Alf Ramsey Stand and the Sir Bobby Robson Stand, are similar in appearance and size, and dwarf the smaller older stands, located on each side of the ground. Unusually, both ends have a larger upper tier which overhangs slightly the smaller lower tier. Both have some spectacular looking floodlights perched on their roofs. They were both fully opened a year apart in 2001 and 2002.

Both sides are much older stands and now look quite tired in comparison. On one side, the fair sized East of England Co-operative Stand is a three tiered covered stand, with a row of executive boxes running across its middle. This stand was originally opened in 1957 and had an additional tier added along with a new roof in 1984. Opposite is the smaller Cobbold Stand. Again it is two tiered and has a row of executive boxes. This stand was first opened in 1971. Unusually the teams emerge onto the field from one corner of the ground. Outside are two statues of two former Ipswich Town and England managers; Sir Alf Ramsey and Sir Bobby Robson.

What is it like for visiting supporters?

Away fans are placed on one side of the upper tier of the Cobbold Stand at one side of the pitch, where up to 1,900 away supporters can be accommodated. Although the views from this area are generally not too bad (unless you are at the very back of the stand where there are some supporting pillars), the leg room is rather cramped and as with the rest of the stand the facilities are beginning to show their age.

On the plus side, away fans can really make some noise from this area, contributing to a good atmosphere. On my last visit I noticed that fans at the front of the upper tier were being asked to keep seated by stewards, whilst those at the back were allowed to stand.

The Cobbold Stand also has one of the poshest gents toilets that I have visited at a football ground (this was one of the two toilet blocks on the upper concourse). They wouldn't have looked out of place in a hotel.

Food on offer inside the ground include; Rollover Hot Dogs (£3.30), Various Pies & Pasties (£3), including the tasty Portman Steak & Ale Pie (£3.60) and Jumbo Sausage Rolls (£3). They also offer a Pie & Pint/Drink deal.

I have always found this to be a friendly place and pleasurable day out, even though I've never seen my team win there!

Club nickname: Blues or Tractor Boys	Ground name: Portman Road	Capacity: 30,300 (all seated)	Opened: 1888
Pitch size: 112 x 70 yards	Undersoil heating: No	Record attendance: 38,010 v Leeds Utd FA Cup 6th Round March 8th 1975	Home kit: Blue and White
Telephone: 01473 400 500	Ticket Office: 03330 050503	Website: www.itfc.co.uk	Programme: £3

Pubs for away fans

The main away supporters pub is the Riverside (Station) Hotel, which as the name suggests, backs onto a river and is located close to the railway station which is only a five minute walk away from Portman Road. Otherwise the Punch & Judy pub on Cardinal Park, which is close to the ground, has also been recommended to me as a pub which is family orientated and where both sets of fans can enjoy a drink.

If you arrive in good time then you can take the walk into the town centre where there are plenty of pubs to be found. Of particular note is the Lord Nelson in Fore Street, which is an interesting pub that sells Adnams beers. Also there is the Dove Street Inn on St Helens Street which is listed in the CAMRA Good Beer Guide which has up to 20 real ales and ciders on tap.

Liam Burgess adds; 'The waterfront area has recently been re-developed and has a number of bars and restaurants. This is visible from the train station and is a 10 minute walk from the ground. The Isaac Lord on the quay is a local favourite and serves various real ales.' Beer is also on sale inside the ground.

Directions & Car Parking

Follow the A14 around Ipswich from which the ground is well signposted. From the A14 take the A137 towards Ipswich. As you approach the town centre and as you cross the bridge over the river, stay in the left hand lane. Once over the river turn left at the roundabout (signposted Colchester). Continue along this road as it bends to the left into Commercial Road, you should be able to see the ground floodlights over to your right. On Portman Road there are Pay & Display car parks (£4 for four hours on Sat).

By train

Portman Road is only a quarter of a mile away from Ipswich Railway Station and is only a five minute walk away. You will see the Portman Road floodlights in the distance as your train comes into the station.

Ipswich Railway Station is served by trains from London Liverpool Street and Peterborough.

Elland Road
Leeds, LS11 0ES

What is the ground like?

The ground is dominated by the East Stand on one side of the stadium. This huge stand which holds around 15,000 supporters was opened in the 1992-93 season, and is at least twice the size of the other three stands at Elland Road. The East Stand is a two tier stand which has a large lower tier of seating with a smaller tier above. In-between the two tiers is a row of executive boxes. The stand is completed by a large imposing roof.

The good thing about the rest of the stadium is that it is totally enclosed, with the corners of the ground being filled with seating. The downside is that compared to the East Stand the other stands are looking rather tired and old in comparison. All the remaining stands have a number of supporting pillars and at the back of the John Charles Stand there are a number of old wooden seats, which look as if they have been there since the stand was first opened in 1957. This stand also houses the team dugouts and television gantry. There is an electric scoreboard in one corner of the ground between the South and John Charles Stands. Outside the stadium there are statues of Billy Bremner and Don Revie.

What is it like for visiting supporters?

Away fans are housed on one side of the John Charles Stand (towards the South Stand), in the upper tier where up to 3,000 supporters can be housed. The seating is a mixture of old wooden and plastic seats, the leg room sparse, plus there are a number of supporting pillars running along the front of the upper tier which could impede your view. So if you can you may be better getting a ticket for the lower tier where your view is unobstructed. The facilities within the stand are very good and there is normally an excellent atmosphere.

Food on offer on the concourse includes; Cheeseburgers (£3.90), Burgers (£3.70), Peppered Steak Pies (£3.80), Chicken Balti Pies (£3.80) Potato and Meat Pies (£3.80) and Cheese, Onion and Potato Pies (£3.80). On previous visits, I have seen a number of away fans being ejected (without warning) for swearing. So be on your best behaviour.

Although I my visits I have not had any problems around the stadium, I have received reports of others who have. So I would exercise caution and keep colours covered outside the ground and in the city centre. Also on previous visits, I have seen a number of away fans being ejected (without warning) for swearing. So be on your best behaviour.

Club nickname:	Ground name:	Capacity:	Opened:
United, Whites or Peacocks	Elland Road	37,900 (all seated)	1919

Pitch size:	Undersoil heating:	Record attendance:	Home kit:
117 x 76 yards	Yes	57,892 FA Cup 5th Rd v Sunderland March 15th 1967	White With Blue Trim

Telephone:	Ticket Office:	Website:	Programme:
0871 334 1919	0871 334 1992	leedsunited.com	£3

Pubs for away fans

At the ground itself on the corner of the South and West Stands is Howards, a dedicated bar for away supporters. Opening two hours before kick off, you need to show your away ticket to gain entrance.

There is also the Drysalters pub which is about a ten minute walk away from the ground. On my last visit it had a good mix of home and away supporters, real ale and large screen SKY TV. To find this pub; with the Old Peacock pub behind you, turn left and follow the road down to the very end. Pass the entrances to a number of car parks and go under a railway bridge. At the end of the road, turn left along the dual carriageway and the pub is a short way down 'tucked in' on the left. Otherwise alcohol is served within the ground in the form of draught Fosters Lager, John Smith's Bitter and Strongbow Cider, plus small bottles of red and white wine.

Just a few doors down from the Old Peacock pub (which is behind the South Stand and is not recommended for away supporters) is the Graveleys chippy, which does brisk business on matchdays.

Directions & Car Parking

Leave the M1 at Junction 43 and take the M621, towards Leeds City Centre. You will pass the ground on your left and then you need to leave at the next Junction 1 and turn left onto the A6110 ring road. Take the next left onto Elland Road for the ground.

Just as you go under a railway bridge there are entrances on either side to a couple of very large car parks run by the club which cost £6.

By train

Leeds Railway Station is around a 35 minute walk from Elland Road. Probably best to either take a taxi or one of the shuttle buses that run from near the station to the ground. Franklin Delvael informs me; 'The shuttle buses cost £2.50 return. The pick-up point is in Sovereign Street, opposite the Hilton Hotel (on Neville Street), about a two minute walk from Leeds train station. The buses drop you off at the ground on Lowfields Road.'

King Power Stadium
Filbert Way, Leicester, LE2 ZFL

What is the ground like?

The stadium which was opened in 2002 is completely enclosed with all corners being filled with seating. The sides are of a good size, all single tiered and built in the same style and height. The West Stand on one side of the ground is slightly different having a row of executive boxes, at the rear, plus the team dug outs are also located at the front of this stand. Running around three sides of the stadium, just below the roof, is a transparent perspex strip, which allows more light and facilitates pitch growth. There are also two large video screens located in opposite corners of the stadium.

Like most new stadiums, the King Power Stadium is functional but lacks character. I don't know whether I'm starting to suffer from 'new stadium fatigue' having visited so many in the last few years, but to me it seemed somewhat bland looking both inside and out. Unusually the public address system is also broadcast on the speakers around the outside of the stadium. The King Power Stadium does though have one redeeming feature - atmosphere. The acoustics are very good and both sets of supporters can really make some noise, making for an enjoyable visit.

What is it like for visiting supporters?

Away supporters are housed in the North East corner of the stadium, where just over 3,000 fans can be accommodated. The view of the playing action is good (although you are set well back from the pitch) as well as the facilities available. The concourse is comfortable with television screens showing the game going on within the stadium. My only slight grumble was that the gents toilets are poorly designed. They have a narrow 'zig zag corridor' of an entrance which hindered people coming in or out and didn't help the major traffic flow at half time! On the positive side though, the atmosphere within the stadium was good, with the home fans singing on both sides of the away section. The atmosphere is further boosted by a huge

bare chested drummer, who is located at the back of the home section, immediately to the left of the away fans. The stewarding was also pretty relaxed. The teams come out to the Post Horn Gallop tune, reminiscent of fox hunting! (Leicester are nicknamed the Foxes).

Paul Groombridge a visiting Gillingham fan adds; 'From the far upper seats of the away section, the view was pretty good, though from there, you'd probably complain of being too far away from the action (I thought it was okay). One good thing about being at the top of the away section - you can use the plastic transparent panels as pretty good drums when singing!'

Club nickname:	Ground name:	Capacity:	Opened:
The Foxes	King Power Stadium	32,500 (all seated)	2002

Pitch size:	Undersoil heating:	Record attendance:	Home kit:
110 x 76 yards	Yes	32,242 v Sunderland Premier League August 8th, 2015	Blue and White

Telephone:	Ticket Office:	Website:	Programme:
0344 815 5000	0344 815 5000 (Option 1)	www.lcfc.co.uk	£3.50

Pubs for away fans

Andy Jobson a visiting Southampton fan informs me; 'Probably the best bet for away fans is the Counting House pub on Freemens Common Road. It has a good mix of both sets of supporters, with all the normal facilities on offer. It does though exclude away supporters when the game is deemed to be a "high profile" one.' John Ellis adds; 'Away fans are welcomed at the Huntsman pub on Narborough Road (next to Iceland supermarket) about a 15 minute walk away from the King Power Stadium. It shows BT televised sports and offers car parking at a cost of £5.'

David Moore informs me; 'If away fans fancy a quiet drink in a CAMRA Good Beer Guide listed pub then the Swan & Rushes (on Infirmary Square, near the Royal Infirmary) always has excellent guest ales on.'

For those arriving by train, then as you come out of the main entrance turn left and cross to the other side and there you will find "The Hind" which is rather a basic pub, but does have real ales. A better bet may be the Wetherspoons pub called the "Last Plantagenet" which is nearby in Granby Street.

Directions & Car Parking

Leave the M1 at Junction 21 and take the A5460 towards Leicester city centre. Continue on this road, until you go under a railway bridge. Carry on for another 200 yards and turn right at the traffic lights into Upperton Road (sign posted Royal Infirmary)

and then right again into Filbert Street for the stadium. Street parking but not close to the ground due to parking restrictions on matchdays. Alternatively you can park at Leicester Rugby Club (£10) which is a ten minute walk away from the stadium.

By train

Leicester Railway Station is located in the City Centre, around one and a half miles away from the King Power Stadium. This should take you around 25-30 minutes to walk.

A walking route to the King Power Stadium is signposted from across the road from the railway station entrance.

Sincil Bank Stadium
Lincoln, LN5 8LD

What is the ground like?

On one side is the large all seater Co-op Community Stand. This large single tiered covered stand opened in 1995 and has a capacity of 5,700. Opposite is the Lincolnshire Echo Stand. This old looking covered seated stand (although in fact it is comparatively modern being built in 1987), is the tallest at the stadium. However it only runs half the length of the pitch, straddling the half way line and hence there are gaps at either side. One gap has now been partly filled by a tiny covered Family Stand.

Both ends are small covered affairs. The Bridge McFarland Stand is all seated and has a row of executive boxes running across the back. This stand has a couple of supporting pillars at the front. The other end is the 'Stacey West' is a single tier, all seated, covered stand, for home supporters. It was named in memory of the two Lincoln supporters who lost their lives in the Bradford City Fire at Valley Parade in 1985.

What is it like for visiting supporters?

Away fans are located in the Stacey West Stand at one end of the ground, where up to 2,000 fans can be accommodated. This covered, all seated stand, generally has good views of the playing action, although it does have a couple of supporting pillars at the front of the stand that could affect your view, especially if your team has a very large following and you are unable to move seats.

On the plus side, the acoustics of this stand are very good, meaning that even a relatively few travelling fans can really make some noise. The facilities are also okay and food on offer inside includes Lincolnshire sausage and bacon rolls. I had an enjoyable day at Lincoln. There was generally a good atmosphere

inside the ground, with plenty of noise being created by the local home supporters band in the Co-op Stand.

Jason Adderley a visiting West Brom supporter adds; 'Lincoln's small band of fans are passionate about their team and are one of the friendliest bunches I've met on my travels. The atmosphere was great and the drums were rousing, leading the chants of the Lincoln supporters.'

Club nickname: The Imps	Ground name: Sincil Bank Stadium	Capacity: 10,130 (all seated)	Opened: 1895
Pitch size: 110 x 73 yards	Undersoil heating: No	Record attendance: 23,196 v Derby League Cup 4th Rd November 15th, 1967	Home kit: Red, White and Black
Telephone: 01522 880011	Ticket Office: 01522 880011 (Option 1)	Website: www.redimps.com	Programme: £3

Pubs for away fans

Neil Le Milliere a visiting Exeter City fan informs me; "Away supporters are admitted to the Supporters Club at the Club (called the Trust Suite) behind the South Park Stand".

Otherwise there are plenty of good pubs to be found if you head along the High Street towards the town centre. Close to Sincil Bank on the High Street is the Hop and Barley micropub. John Bennett a visiting Bristol Rovers supporter recommends the Golden Eagle, which is listed in the CAMRA Good Beer Guide. Whilst Jon Morley adds; 'The Wetherspoon's pub called 'The Ritz" serves

reasonably priced food and ales.' Not far from Lincoln Railway Station is the Treaty of Commerce, which serves Batemans Beers.

Also near to Sincil Bank on Scorer Street is the handy "Back of the Net" Fish and Chip Shop.

Directions & Car Parking

Follow the A46 into Lincoln, which leads onto the High Street and the ground is indicated from there. If you follow the signs for 'away coaches' then this leads you onto the A158 South Park Avenue, where there is plenty of street parking to be found (although

it is a ten minute walk around to the ground). Otherwise the signs lead you to Sincil Bank, where if you arrive early then you can park behind the Stacey West Stand (cost £4), Ian Gibson adds; 'South Common car park is free at the beginning of South Park Avenue.'

By train

Lincoln Central Railway Station is around a 15 minute away from Sincil Bank. Ben Schofield informs me; 'Come out of the station and turn right to go down the road. About 30 yards ahead on your right you will see some

steps and a bridge over the railway. Go over the bridge and once on the other side follow the road down to the ground.'

Anfield

Anfield Road, Liverpool, L4 0TH

What is the ground like?

During 2016 two additional tiers were added above the Main Stand. These extra tiers have made this stand simply huge, having increased the capacity of the stand from 12,000 to 20,500 and increased the overall capacity of Anfield to over 54,000. The expanded Main Stand now towers of the rest of the stadium and even makes the Kop Stand (with a capacity of 13,000) look rather small. The Main Stand itself looks smart with a row of executive boxes located between each of the tiers and having the players tunnel and team dugouts located at out front. Its' most striking feature though is its roof. Mostly made up of transparent panels to allow more light to the pitch, it protrudes out over the stand by quite some distance.

The famous Kop End at one end of the ground, replaced the former terrace in 1994. Designed to emulate the shape of the old Kop, it has a semi-circular look and large single tier. The other end, the Anfield Road Stand, opened in 1998. is a two tiered with a smaller upper tier overhanging a larger lower one. On the remaining side of the stadium is the fair sized, two tiered, Centenary Stand. It has a capacity of just under 12,000.

What is it like for visiting supporters?

Away fans are located in the Anfield Road Stand at one end of the ground, where just under 3,000 seats are available, although this can be increased for cup games. This stand is also shared with home supporters, some of whom will be sitting in the small seated tier above the away fans. Malcolm Dawson a travelling Sunderland supporter adds; 'Try to avoid getting tickets sold as restricted view, for the rear rows of the Anfield Road Stand as it can be difficult to see the goals with people standing up in front of you'.

Kimberly Hill adds; 'Restricted view doesn't even begin to describe what it was like. The Wolves fans insisted on standing so it was like trying to watch the game through a letterbox!' The facilities within the stand are not bad. There is a betting outlet and the refreshment kiosks sell a wide variety of Pies including a 'Scouse Pie' (£3.50), Potato and Meat, Potato and Butter, Cheese Slices and Sausage Rolls (all £3.40).

I have always found it to be a good day out at Anfield, getting the feeling that you are visiting one of the legendary venues in world football. This is enhanced with the teams coming out to 'You'll Never Walk Alone' reverberating around the ground, with the red and white scarves and flags of the fans displayed across the Kop, at the beginning of the match. The atmosphere is normally good, so sit back and enjoy the experience.

Club nickname:	Ground name:	Capacity:	Opened:
The Reds	Anfield	54,074 (all seated)	1884
Pitch size:	Undersoil heating:	Record attendance:	Home kit:
110 x 75 yards	Yes	61,905 v Wolves FA Cup 4th Round February 2nd, 1952	All Red With White Trim
Telephone:	Ticket Office:	Website:	Programme:
0151 264 2500	0843 170 5555	liverpoolfc.com	£3.50

Pubs for away fans

The Arkles pub near to the ground (see Directions & Car Parking below for directions), is known as the away fans pub, but as can be expected it can get extremely crowded. It also has a handy fish and chip shop located just around the corner from it.

Mark Parsons a visiting Aston Villa fan adds; 'We arrived at the Arkles at about 1.15pm and already found it packed out, with fans queuing outside to get in. We asked a very helpful WPC for any other away friendly pubs and were told to go to the Flat Iron which was a five minute walk away. Although the

pub was mostly full of Liverpool fans, the bars were mixed and all were very friendly. To find this pub, turn left at the junction where Arkles is (opposite direction to where Anfield is over to your right) onto Anfield Road. Head away from the ground and the pub is down at the bottom of this road on the right hand side.'

Otherwise located near to the away turnstiles is a small Fanzone, which admits away fans and serves food and drink, including alcohol too. Bottles of Carlsberg are also available inside the stadium (£3.90 each).

Directions & Car Parking

Follow the M62 until you reach the end of the motorway. Then keep right and take the A5058 Ring Road North, signposted Football Stadia. After three miles turn left at the traffic lights into Utting Avenue (there is a McDonalds on the corner of this junction).

Proceed for one mile and then turn right at the Arkles pub for Anfield. Parking is available at nearby Goodison Park which costs £10. Rob Campion adds; "I parked at The Dockers Club on Townsend Lane (A580) at a cost of £5. It's a 15 minute walk to Anfield".

By train

Kirkdale Railway Station is the closest to the ground (just under a mile away). However, it may be more advisable to go to Sandhills Railway Station as this has the benefit of a bus service to the ground, which runs for a

couple of hours before the game and around 50 minutes after the final whistle. The bus drops you off within easy walking distance of Anfield. It costs £2.

Kenilworth Road

1 Maple Road, Luton, LU4 8AW

What is the ground like?

On one side is the Main Stand, which is an old two tiered covered stand. This stand is mostly wooden and is really beginning to show its age, which is not surprising at the central part of the stand dates back to 1922. This Main Stand only runs around two thirds of the length of the pitch with another more recent structure 'bolted' onto one end. This area is known as the 'David Preece Stand' (after a former player) was opened in 1991 and is used a family area. Opposite is a rather smaller affair. It is predominantly just a row of executive boxes, beyond which can clearly see residential houses. Apparently restrictions placed on the Club by the Local Authority mean that they are unable to have anything taller on this side of the ground than the houses behind. Netting has been suspended between the floodlight pylons on its roof to reduce the number of footballs being kicked out of the stadium.

At one end is the Oak Stand, which is a small covered stand that has a simple electric scoreboard mounted on its roof. Whilst opposite is the larger Kenilworth Road End, which is also covered and is the traditional home end of the ground.

What is it like for visiting supporters?

Away fans are housed on one side of the Oak Road Stand (on the Executive Stand side) at one end of the ground. The entrance to the Oak Stand must be one of the most unusual in the country. After going down a rather small alleyway at the side of the stadium (or down the cordoned off Oak Road), the impression is of queuing to go into someone's house and then through their back garden and into the stand! Just over 1,500 supporters can be accommodated in this stand, however as this stand is now shared with home fans, visiting supporters are allocated around half this number of tickets.

Still the acoustics of this stand are very good and with Luton fans in close proximity this makes for a good atmosphere. On the downside, there always seems to be a large Police presence, which seems unnecessary for the majority of games, although the Club stewards themselves seemed pretty relaxed. Also there are a number of supporting pillars in this stand, which may hinder your view. The leg room is tight (although I noted that away fans stood throughout on my last visit) and the toilets are small and have seen better days.

The refreshments are not bad, although rather limited in selection to: Burgers (£4), Rollover Hot Dogs (£3), Cheese and Onion Pasties (£3) and Sausage Rolls (£2).

Club nickname: The Hatters	Ground name: Kenilworth Road	Capacity: 10,226 (all seated)	Opened: 1905
Pitch size: 110 x 72 yards	Undersoil heating: No	Record attendance: 30,069 v Blackpool FA Cup 6th Round March 4th, 1959	Home kit: Orange and White
Telephone: 01582 411622	Ticket Office: 01582 416976	Website: lutontown.co.uk	Programme: £3

Pubs for away fans

Just inside the away turnstiles, is located a small bar, which serves both draught and bottled beers. Although fairly simple looking inside and with no seating, it serves its purpose. You can also purchase hot pies inside the bar (£3.50) and there is one small television showing the early kick off.

Mick O'Sullivan adds; 'A good place to drink is the Beech Hill Conservative Club on Leagrave Road, which welcomes both home and away supporters. You will be charged a small entrance fee (£1), but you make it up on the cheaper than pub beer.'

Whilst in the town centre on the Bedford Road, only a few minutes' walk away from the train station is the English Rose. This CAMRA Good Beer Guide listed pub has received good reports from visiting fans who have drank there.

Alex Winter a visiting Cheltenham Town fan adds; 'Near the train station on High Town Road is the Bricklayers Arms. It is a charming old pub which offers an excellent selection of real ale, shows live sport and is only 15-20 minute walk from Kenilworth Road.'

Directions & Car Parking

Leave the M1 at Junction 11 and take the A505 towards Luton. Go through one set of traffic lights and at the first roundabout, turn right into Chaul End Lane. At the next roundabout turn left into Hatters Way, whilst continuing down Hatters Way the ground will be seen on your left, although it is not accessible from this road.

At the end of Hatters Way turn left and start looking for street parking from here on (the ground will now be on your left). Or you can park at Beech Hill Conservative Club (£4).

By train

Luton Station is a 15 minute walk away from the ground. Turn right out of the station. Go straight across at the traffic lights into Mill St. Turn left at the junction into New Bedford Rd, then right into Collingdon St. On reaching the dual carriageway, turn left along the carriageway and then bear right to go along the footbridge over the busy road and bear right again where it divides. This leads to Dunstable Rd. Then fifth left for the ground.

One Call Stadium
Quarry Lane, Mansfield, NG18 5DA

What is the ground like?

During the late 1990's and into the early part of this decade, Field Mill was largely transformed into a modern stadium, with the building of three new stands. Both ends, the North Stand & Quarry Lane End plus the Ian Greaves Stand on one side of the pitch were re-developed. The ends are almost identical single tiered stands, each accommodating just under 2,000 supporters.

The last addition to the ground was the West Stand, which was opened in February 2001. This is a cantilevered two tiered stand, with a capacity of 5,500. In 2010 this stand was renamed the Ian Greaves Stand, after a former manager of the club. On the other side of the ground is the rather small Bishop Street Stand, a covered seated stand that only runs half the length of the pitch. This now looks rather dowdy alongside its new shiny neighbours and due to safety concerns it has been closed for some time. It has boards placed in front of it to prevent access to the stand, which gives the impression that it is a building site, which does little to enhance the overall feel of the ground. The team dugouts are located in front of this stand.

What is it like for visiting supporters?

Away fans are housed in the North Stand, which is unpopular with a number of home supporters, as the North End of the ground had been the traditional home end for many years.

As you would expect from a relatively new stand that is free of any supporting pillars, then the views of the playing action are pretty good, as are the facilities. Around 1,800 supporters can be accommodated. The stand has a low roof meaning that visiting supporters can really make some noise from this end.

I had a fairly uneventful trip to Mansfield and did not encounter any problems, although there did seem to be quite a lot of Police in attendance. Stewarding was fine and amicable. Food on offer inside includes a range of Pies including the Chicken Balti Pie (£3.20).

Rob Ferguson adds; 'For those away fans arriving by coach, please note that buses should drop off at Portland Street and pick up at Portland Street at the end of the match.'

Club nickname: The Stags	Ground name: One Call Stadium	Capacity: 9,295 (all seated)	Opened: 1861
Pitch size: 115 x 70 yards	Undersoil heating: No	Record attendance: 24,467 v Notts Forest FA Cup 3rd Round January 10th, 1953	Home kit: Amber and Blue
Telephone: 0623 482 482	Ticket Office: 0623 482 482 (Option 1)	Website: mansfieldtown.net	Programme: £3

Pubs for away fans

There is a bar at the ground called the Sandy Pate (underneath the Ian Greaves Stand), which welcomes away fans and is free to enter. However, as you would expect it gets quite busy on matchdays.

Near to Mansfield Railway Station is the Midland Hotel as Nick Meadows a visiting Luton Town fan adds; 'The Midland Hotel is on Station Road and is only a ten minute walk away from the stadium. Although rather basic inside, the beer was reasonably priced and visiting fans were welcomed.'

Chris Patrick informs me; 'There is the Sir John Cockle pub, which is located on the A38 going into Mansfield from the M1 and again serves good food'. Whilst Gordon Cleugh adds; 'About a quarter of a mile past the John Cockle on the A38 there is The Bold Forester which has about 10 real ales and also serves good value food' and is listed in the CAMRA Good Beer Guide.

Please note that alcohol is not made available for away fans to purchase inside the ground.

Directions & Car Parking

Leave the M1 at Junction 28, take A38 to Mansfield. After passing the Kings Mill Hospital on your left and then the Nell Gwyn pub on your right, turn right at the traffic lights after the pub into Sheepbridge Lane. After passing under a railway bridge you will reach a set of traffic lights where you turn left into Quarry Lane. You will reach the stadium along on the left. There is some parking at the ground which costs £5. There is also the station car park which costs £3 for 4 hours. It is located behind the adjacent Retail Park.

By train

Mansfield Railway Station is around ten minutes walk away. The station is on a local line and is served with trains from Nottingham. To get to the ground from the station; Leave the station and turn left along the dual carriageway, (away from the town centre), you should see a retail park on the right. Go straight ahead at the first set of traffic lights, along Portland Street and then right at the next lights and into Quarry Lane.

Etihad Stadium
Rowsley Street, Manchester M11 3FF

What is the ground like?

The Etihad Stadium has a bowl design and is totally enclosed. Now expanded to a capacity of over 55,000 it has become one of the best stadiums in the country, not only in terms of size but also in its fantastic facilities.

Both stands on either side of the pitch are virtually identical, being semi-circular in shape, three tiered, with a row of executive boxes running across the stands, located in-between the second and third tiers. Both ends were originally smaller in size, being two tiers high, but during the 2014/15 season a large third tier was added to the South Stand,

adding another 6,250 seats.

The roof runs continuously around the stadium stretching up over the stands and down to the North end, creating a spectacular effect. There is a perspex strip just below the roof and the spectator areas, allowing light to reach the pitch. The upper tiers are steeper than the lower, ensuring that spectators are kept close to the playing action. The stadium also has two large video screens in opposite corners. Near the main club entrance is a memorial garden, which includes a tribute to Marc-Vivien Foe.

What is it like for visiting supporters?

Away fans are located in one side of the South Stand at one end of the ground, spread across the upper, middle, and lower tiers, where up to 3,000 fans can be accommodated (4,500 for cup games). The view of the action is pretty impressive although the atmosphere within the stadium is a bit 'hit and miss' at times. I did hear though on my last visit one very good rendition of the Man City fans anthem 'Blue Moon'.

My only real complaint was the lack of distance between the home and away supporters. Only a few seats and a row of stewards stood in-between the two sets of fans, which led to a lot of unpleasant baiting

between the two. And of course it was always the away fans who were adjudged to be causing the problems by the stewards (although I'm sure that if I visited on another occasion I probably would have seen the same Man City fans baiting in the same manner) and this led a number of away fans on my visit being escorted out of the stadium.

The facilities are also pretty good with spacious concourses and large plasma flat television screens showing the game. There is also the usual selection of food on offer; including Hot Dogs (£4.50) and a range of pies; Peppered Steak, Chicken Balti, Potato and Meat, plus Cheese & Onion (all £4 each).

Club nickname:	Ground name:	Capacity:	Opened:
The Blues or Citizens	Etihad Stadium	55,097 (all seated)	2002

Pitch size:	Undersoil heating:	Record attendance:	Home kit:
116 x 77 yards	Yes	54,693 v Leicester Premier League February 6th 2016	Sky Blue and White

Telephone:	Ticket Office:	Website:	Programme:
0161 444 1894	0161 444 1894 (Option 1)	www.mcfc.co.uk	£3

Pubs for away fans

There are not a great deal of pubs around the stadium, and the few available, including the FanZone at the ground, are predominantly for home support. However, 'The Stanley' (aka Sports Bar) pub does let in away fans in small numbers. It is about a ten minute walk away from the stadium, just set back from the main A6010 (Pottery Lane), going towards Ashburys train station.

Alan Finneran informs me; "I would recommend the Townley on Albert Street, which is only a five minute walk away from the stadium. The pub has a good atmosphere and as long as away fans arrive early and are discrete (i.e. no colours) then they should be okay.'

Dave Clinton adds; 'If you want a pint beforehand then it is probably best to drink in the city centre. My tip, would be to head to the Printworks in Manchester, near Victoria station. There is a connecting tram service from Piccadilly. There are loads of pubs at the Printworks, with plenty of choice of food.' Otherwise alcohol is available inside the stadium; Fosters Lager, Strongbow Cider, John Smith's Bitter (all £4 a pint).

Directions & Car Parking

Leave the M62 at J18 and then join the M60 Ashton Under Lyne. Leave the M60 at Junction 23 and take the A635 towards Manchester. Branch off onto the A662 (Ashton New Road) towards Droylsden/Manchester. Stay on the A662 for around 3 miles and you will reach the Stadium on your right. There is some parking available at the stadium itself which costs £10. The East Car Park is near the away entrance. Some unofficial car parks are located around Pottery Lane mostly charging £5 per car.

By train and Metrolink

The Etihad Stadium has its own Metrolink stop on the East Manchester line, called Etihad Campus; this is only a five minute walk from the away end. Trams can be caught from either Victoria or Piccadilly railway stations. The closest railway station is Ashburys which is a short five minute train ride away from Manchester Piccadilly Station. The stadium is about a 15 minute walk away from Ashburys station.

Old Trafford

Sir Matt Busby Way, Manchester M16 0RA

What is the ground like?

Old Trafford's sheer size makes it a bewildering sight. It has been steadily expanded over the last couple of decades raising its capacity to a staggering 73,310, making it the largest Club ground in Britain. Both ends, which look almost identical, are large two tiered stands, which were originally built in the early 1990's and had an additional tier added at the turn of the millennium. Each are quite steep, with a large lower tier and smaller upper tier. The three tiered Sir Alex Ferguson Stand, opened in 1996, at one side of the ground, is the largest capacity stand of any League Ground in England. It has 25,500

seats. The corners to each side of this stand are also filled with seating and extend around to meet both ends.

These re-developed stands dwarf the older Main (South) Stand opposite. This stand (part of which dates back to 1910) is single tiered, with a television gantry suspended below its roof. All the stands have a row of executive boxes at the back of the lower tier. In April 2016 the Main (South) Stand was renamed the Sir Bobby Charlton Stand.

What is it like for visiting supporters?

Away supporters are normally located in one corner of the ground, taking up part of the East and Sir Bobby Charlton Stands. The views from the away sections are excellent and up to 3,000 away supporters can be accommodated. Entrance into the stadium is gained by first being searched by a steward and then placing your ticket into an electronic bar code reader. It is then up a few flights of rather steep stairs to the concourse.

Although the concourse looks a little cramped, it is adequate and there seems to be enough food and drinks outlets that the queues never seem to get too long. These sell a range of pies; Meat & Potato, Steak, Chicken & Mushroom (all £3.80) The Club also offer

a "United" Pie (£3.80), which I believe is a Chicken Curry Pie. Other refreshments on offer include; Cheese & Onion Pasties (£3.50), Foot long Sausage Rolls (£4) and Rollover Hot Dogs (£4.40). At the far end of the concourse is a large flat screen television showing Sky Sports.

The away fans section is set back from the pitch as there is a disabled area to its front. The leg room between rows is a little tight, as well as the space between the seats themselves. This results in most away fans standing throughout the game. The good thing though, is that the away fans can really make some noise from this part of the stadium.

Club nickname:	Ground name:	Capacity:	Opened:
The Red Devils	Old Trafford	73,310 (all seated)	1910
Pitch size:	**Undersoil heating:**	**Record attendance:**	**Home kit:**
116 x 76 yards	Yes	76,098 v Blackburn, Premier League, March 31st, 2007	Red, White and Black
Telephone:	**Ticket Office:**	**Website:**	**Programme:**
0161 868 8000	0161 868 8000 (Option 1)	www.manutd.com	£3.50

Pubs for away fans

The three pubs nearest the ground (The Trafford, Sam Platts and The Bishops Blaize) generally won't let you in if you wear away colours. The best bet is probably the city centre or along one of the stops on the Metrolink.

Luke Burns a visiting Birmingham City fan adds; 'There is also the Lime Bar in nearby Salford Quays. Good beer, quick service and good mix of home and away supporters.' Also in Salford Quays (which is about a mile away from Old Trafford) is the Matchstick Man pub, which is part of the Hungry Horse chain and serves visiting supporters.

On my last couple of visits I have drank at the Quadrant pub which had a mixture of home and away fans and a couple of handy Chinese/Chippies nearby. The pub is about a 10-15 minute walk away from Old Trafford, in the direction of the Cricket Ground.

Alternatively alcohol is normally served within the ground, although for some high profile games the Club opt not to sell any.

Directions & Car Parking

Leave the M6 at Junction 19 and follow the A556 towards Altrincham. At the junction with the M56 take the A56 towards Altrincham. Keep on the A56 for six miles and then you will come to see Sir Matt Busby Way on your left. The ground is half a mile down

this road on your left, although on matchdays this road may well be closed to traffic. There are lots of small private car parks near to the ground, otherwise it is street parking. Or you can park at Old Trafford Cricket Ground, which costs £10.

By train or Metrolink

Probably the best way to get to the stadium is by Metrolink or train from Manchester Piccadilly mainline station, as Old Trafford has both its own railway station next to the ground and a Metrolink station which is

located next to Lancashire County Cricket Club on Warwick Road, which leads up to Sir Matt Busby Way. Normally the railway station, which is called Manchester United Football Ground, is less busy than the Metrolink.

Riverside Stadium
Middlesbrough, Cleveland, TS3 6RS

What is the ground like?

The Club moved to the Riverside Stadium in 1995 after leaving its former home of Ayresome Park where it had played since 1903. The stadium is totally enclosed, after the previous open corners to either side of the West Stand were 'filled in' with seating in 1998. All the stands are two-tiered, although the West Stand is slightly larger than the other three sides, which makes the overall appearance of the stadium look somewhat imbalanced. This stand also has a row of executive boxes running across its middle and has the players tunnel and team dugouts in front. The roof around the stadium is raised up above the seating areas to allow more light to get to the pitch, through perspex panels located between the roof and the back of the seating areas. There is also a large video screen situated in the South East corner.

Although the stadium looks a little bland on the inside, externally it looks great. This is especially so at night, when the stadium is illuminated and is visible from some miles around. Outside the main entrance you will find the old entrance gates to Ayresome Park, which is a nice link with the Club's history.

What is it like for visiting supporters?

Away supporters have now been moved to one side of the East Stand (towards the South East corner) at one side of the stadium. Just under 3,000 fans can be accommodated in this area. The turnstiles are electronic which means that you have to insert your ticket in a reader, to gain entry. Once inside then the leg room is okay and the view from the away section is excellent. There is a betting outlet available and there are a number of flat screen televisions, showing Sky Sports (and the match itself once it has kicked off).

The catering has a fair choice of grub on offer, including the intriguingly named "Parmo in a bun". Apparently this is inspired by the local Middlesbrough dish that consists mostly of chicken in breadcrumbs, creamy sauce and cheese, it costs £4.20. For the less adventurous then there is the regular fayre of; Cheeseburgers (£3.80), Burgers (£3.50), Hot Dogs (£3.50), Pizza (£3), Chicken Balti Pies (£3), Cheese & Onion Pasties (£3) and Minced Beef Pies (£3).

In an effort to boost atmosphere inside the ground the Club have encouraged a singing section in the South Stand which is called the 'Red Faction'. Including a drummer and looking colourful with flags and banners, they try and sing for the whole match. They certainly are noisy!

Club nickname:	Ground name:	Capacity:	Opened:
Boro	Riverside Stadium	35,100 (all seated)	1995

Pitch size:	Undersoil heating:	Record attendance:	Home kit:
115 x 75 yards	Yes	34,836 v Norwich Premier League 28th December 2004	Red and White

Telephone:	Ticket Office:	Website:	Programme:
0844 499 6789	0844 499 1234	www.mfc.co.uk	£3

Pubs for away fans

The main pub that away fans frequent is Doctor Browns, which is a ten minute walk away from the ground at the bottom of Corporation Road, in the town centre. This pub serves real ale, has SKY TV and on my last visit had a good mix of home and away fans, both inside and outside of the pub. On the corner opposite the pub, is also a sandwich bar, which was doing a brisk trade in amongst other things, trays of roast potatoes and gravy.

Dave Ellis a visiting Leicester City fan informs me; 'We found a pub called "The Lord Byron" on Dock Street, which is only around a five minute walk away from the ground. It was reasonably priced, had a very friendly atmosphere and kids were welcome too!'

Otherwise, there is a bar at the back of the away stand within the ground which serves pints of John Smiths Bitter (£3.50), Fosters Lager (£3.70), Bulmers Cider (Bottle £3.70) and Wine (Small bottle £3.60).

Directions & Car Parking

From the A1 follow the A66 (signposted Teesside) to Middlesbrough. Carry along the A66 through the centre of Middlesbrough and you will pick up signs for the Riverside Stadium. There is a small amount of parking available at the stadium itself (in Car Park E), which costs £6 per car and spaces can be pre-booked through the ticket office. Otherwise there are a number of private parks located nearby costing around £4.

By train

The Riverside Stadium is around a 15-20 minute walk from Middlesbrough Railway Station which is located on Albert Road.

Although there is a direct train service from Manchester, fans travelling from other parts of the country, will most likely find themselves changing at Darlington, for Middlesbrough.

The Den
Zampa Road, London SE16 3LN

What is the ground like?

The Club moved the relatively short distance to their new stadium, which was nicknamed the New Den after leaving their original Den ground which had been their home for 83 years. This was first new major football ground to be constructed in London since before the Second World War.

The stadium is made up of four separate two-tiered stands that are of the same height and look fairly similar. On one side is the Barry Kitchener Stand (named after a former player) which has the players tunnel and team dugouts at its front. This simple looking stand has the same characteristics as both ends with windshields to either side in the upper tier and with the upper tier slightly overhanging the lower tier.

The Dockers Stand on the other side is slightly different having a row of executive boxes running across its middle. Between the East & North Stands in one corner is a large video screen.

What is it like for visiting supporters?

Away fans are located at one end of the ground in the North Stand (usually in the upper tier only). Around 4,000 away fans can be accommodated in this end. Like the general improvement in football, a trip to Millwall is not as threatening as it once was. However, it is hardly a relaxing day out and I found the Den to be quite intimidating. I would advise that you exercise caution around the ground and not to wear club colours.

Food on offer inside includes; a range of pies from the 'Pie Factory' including Steak & Ale and Chicken Balti (£3.40). There are also Cheese & Onion Pasties (£3.40), Sausage Rolls (£3.10), Burgers (£4) and Chips (£2.10).

Luke Fern a visiting Bolton Wanderers fan informs me; "Inside the ground the concourse is mostly concreted and looks very dull. It is also very cramped with little space available for fans to get around those queuing for food and drinks. However the view from our seats was excellent and the stewards were very tolerant and friendly. We had traveled by official Club coach and had to wait 45 minutes after the game had ended before we were allowed to exit the stadium car park".

Most away fans travel to the Den by official club coach or by train from London Bridge. The Police are well drilled in dealing with the coaches and supporters arriving by train.

Club nickname:	Ground name:	Capacity:	Opened:
The Lions	The Den	20,146 (all seated)	1993

Pitch size:	Undersoil heating:	Record attendance:	Home kit:
105 x 68 yards	Yes	20,093 v Arsenal FA Cup 3rd Round January 10th, 1994	Blue With White Trim

Telephone:	Ticket Office:	Website:	Programme:
020 7232 1222	0844 826 2004	millwallfc.co.uk	£3

Pubs for away fans

There are not many pubs located near to the stadium and those should be avoided by away supporters. If travelling by train then it is probably best to grab a beer around London Bridge before moving onto the ground. I would advise keeping any colours covered, even when drinking in the London Bridge area. Inside the ground alcohol is available in the form of; cans of Tetley's Smooth (£4.10), plus plastic bottles of Carlsberg (£4.10) or Somersby Cider (£4.60).

Chris Lynskey a visiting Scunthorpe United fan recommends; 'The Shipwright Arms on Tooley Street, near London Bridge. Come out of London Bridge tube station, turn right and its only 200 yards down the road on your right hand side. A lovely little pub which also serves food. We left the pub at 2.15pm to go and catch the train to the stadium and made it comfortably for kick off.' On the Borough High Street by London Bridge is the Barrow Boy & Banker, which is a Fullers pub and has the benefit of a large screen showing Sky Sports. Further down the High Street is the Borough Market, which on nearby Stoney Street is situated the legendary Market Porter pub, which has nine real ales on tap.

Directions & Car Parking

Follow the A2 into London from Junction 2 of the M25. The A2 actually passes the ground. Once you go past New Cross Gate tube station on your right the ground is about a mile further on. The only awkward bit is about half way in-between New Cross Gate and the ground where the road splits into two. Keep to the right following the signs A2 City/Westminster. You will come to the Den on your right. There is no car parking for away fans cars at the ground itself, so street parking.

By train

South Bermondsey Railway Station is only a few minutes walk from the ground. There is a direct walkway specifically built for away fans which takes you directly to the away end and back to the station afterwards. This has made the Police's job of keeping rival supporters apart so much more manageable. If your team brings a sizeable following, then an 'away fan' football special may be laid on from London Bridge.

Stadium MK
Denbigh, Milton Keynes, MK1 1ST

What is the ground like?

The Club moved to the new Stadium MK in 2007. The stadium it is a 'cut above' some other new comparable venues, in terms of quality and standards of spectator facilities. From the outside it has a modern look, with good use of silver coloured cladding and a large amount of glass on view. The most striking feature of the stadium is its roof, which sits high up above the football ground with a large gap between in and the back roof of seating. This allows more natural light to reach the pitch. The stadium is totally enclosed and has a bowl like design.

The overall look of the stadium has benefited from the installation of seating into the previously unused upper tier. It certainly looks a large and imposing stadium, one that is worthy of football at a higher level. It is two tiered, with on three sides having a large lower tier being over hung by a smaller upper tier. The West side of the stadium is slightly different, with the seating areas in the upper tier being replaced by the Director's Box and executive and corporate hospitality areas. Unusually the spacious concourse areas at the back of the lower tier see directly into the stadium.

What is it like for visiting supporters?

Away supporters are normally located in the upper tier of the stadium in the North East Corner, where around 3,000 fans can be accommodated. If demand requires it then the North Stand upper tier behind the goal can also be allocated as well as the lower tier. This generous allocation has led to some huge away followings at Stadium MK in recent years, which has led to some memorable away days. For example in 2014 Wolverhampton Wanderers had almost 9,000 fans in attendance. On the further plus side the stadium is a quality one i.e. it has not been built on the cheap. So the facilities are first class. The stadium also has such creature comforts as big "Emirates Style" comfy seats and the ability to continue to watch the game in progress, whilst eating a burger

on the concourse. The view of the playing action and leg room are both good and the atmosphere not bad. The concourses are spacious and offer a good range of food. The stadium also has electronic turnstiles, so no paying at the gate here. Instead you gain entrance by putting your tickets into a bar code reader to gain entrance. Alan Burgess a visiting Sheffield Wednesday fan adds; "The seating is marvellous both for comfort and leg room, the concourses very impressive and the sight lines fantastic. The serving areas were plentiful and well organised; there wasn't a bad atmosphere either, although the PA was deafening. Even the toilets had soap and hot running water - a luxury!"

Club nickname:	Ground name:	Capacity:	Opened:
The Dons	Stadium MK	30,500 (all seated)	2007
Pitch size:	**Undersoil heating:**	**Record attendance:**	**Home kit:**
115 x 74 yards	Yes	28,127 v Chelsea FA Cup 4th Round January 31st 2016	All White
Telephone:	**Ticket Office:**	**Website:**	**Programme:**
01908 622 922	0333 200 5343	www.mkdons.com	£3

Pubs for away fans

There is little choice of drinking establishments for away fans near to the ground. However if you are looking for something to eat as well as a drink, then on the Retail Park surrounding the stadium there is a choice of Nando's, Frankie & Benny's, TGI Friday's and Pizza Express.

If arriving into Bletchley Railway Station then nearby, is the Park Inn and Bletchley Working Mens Club. Just turn left out if the station entrance, then left along the main road. After passing under a railway bridge, you will see both these venues on the right hand side.

Please note though it is then a good 35-40 minute walk to the stadium.

Guy Plumb adds; 'There is also Fenny Stratford which is located a mile south of the stadium along Watling Street. Fenny has seven pubs within a five minute walk of each other plus a fish and chip shop.'

Inside the stadium, alcohol is made available to away fans, including bottles of ale from the local Concrete Cow Brewery.

Directions & Car Parking

Leave the M1 at J14 and take the A509 towards Milton Keynes. Cross over the first roundabout and at the next, turn left onto the V11 Tongwell Street. Proceed across one roundabout and at the next turn right onto the H8 Standing Way (A421). Continue alone

the Standing Way going across a number of roundabouts. On reaching the Bleak Hall Roundabout turn left into the V6 Grafton Street. At the next roundabout, turn right and the stadium entrance, is further down on the left. Parking at the stadium costs £7.

By train

The nearest railway station is Fenny Stratford which is just over a mile away from Stadium, however this is on the local Bletchley to Bedford line. As you exit the station turn right and at the top of the road turn right onto the

main Watling Street. Just go straight along this road and you will see the stadium over on your right. There is also Bletchley Railway Station which is around about two miles away from the stadium.

Globe Arena
Christie Way, Morecambe LA4 4TB

What is the ground like?

The Globe Arena which was opened in 2010, is dominated by the Peter McGuigan Stand one side. This stand which is named after the current Club Chairman, has a capacity of just under 2,200 seats. This all seated, covered stand, has a box like feel, with a corporate glassed area to the rear. It is though free of supporting pillars and has windshields to either side, essential for a football ground located near the coast.

Opposite is the North Terrace, which is a very small open terrace that is only a few steps high. The terrace is split into two separate parts, with a large gap between them located around the half way line. Above this gap is an area for a television gantry.

Both ends are covered terraces. The West Terrace is for home supporters and houses 2,234 fans, whilst the East Terrace is substantially smaller and is for the away support. In the North East corner of the stadium, adjacent to the away terrace is a Police Control Box. Also located in this area, attached to a wall beside the Control Box is a small electronic scoreboard.

What is it like for visiting supporters?

Away fans are mostly housed in the Bay Radio Terrace at one end of the ground, where just under 1,400 supporters can be accommodated. In addition the Club also make around 300 seats available in the Peter McGuigan Stand, which is shared with home fans. As you would expect with a new stadium the view of the playing action is good. However the facilities are not that great, more to do with lack of space at the back of the terraced stand, more than anything. They also have separate queues at the refreshment hatch for food and alcohol, which is not great when you want something to eat with your drink and vice versa. However, if you get chance try one of the Club's pies (£3.10), which are highly acclaimed. They also serve hot dogs which cost £2.60.

Rob Parker adds; 'I sat with the Rotherham fans in the Peter McGuigan Stand. To gain entrance I had to edge through the tightest turnstile block I've ever known, and then proceed down a narrow four-foot wide open alleyway into the stand, passing the entrance to the toilets and the refreshments kiosk, where there was a small scrum of fans around the serving window, which is built into the back of the stand.'

Club nickname:	Ground name:	Capacity:	Opened:
Shrimps	Globe Arena	6,476	2010

Pitch size:	Undersoil heating:	Record attendance:	Home kit:
110 x 76 yards	No	5,003 v Burnley League Cup Rd 2 24th August 2010	Red and Black

Telephone:	Ticket Office:	Website:	Programme:
01524 411 797	01524 411 797 (Option 1)	morecambefc.com	£3

Pubs for away fans

Just outside the stadium entrance is a relatively new Marston's pub called the Hurley Flyer. Family friendly and offering food too, it has its own car park which costs £10 before the game, but this can be refunded against a food purchase. Otherwise the closest bar that admits away supporters is on the nearby Regent Leisure Holiday Park. David Foster a visiting Chesterfield fan adds; 'I had a drink across at the Regent Caravan Park. This was fully accessible, offered a decent pint and food, plus had Sky television on a big screen and generally had a good atmosphere.'

Otherwise if you turn left out of the stadium entrance then around a ten minute walk away (located opposite a Lidl supermarket on Westgate) is the William Mitchell pub, which also shows Sky Sports. If driving to the stadium from the direction of Lancaster you will pass a Toby carvery which offers reasonably priced food.

Otherwise alcohol is served inside the stadium in the form of Carling, Guinness, Caffreys and Strongbow.

Directions & Car Parking

Exit the M6 at junction 34 and follow the signs for Morecambe. After around five miles you will reach a crossroads (with a McDonalds over on the right) where you turn right onto the Morecambe Road. You will then reach a roundabout, (where there is a Toby Carvery) where you take the first exit into Westgate Road (signposted Sandylands).

Continue along this road for about one mile and you will reach the stadium on your right. No parking is available at the ground. So street parking or Regent Holiday Park (£3)

By train

Morecambe Railway Station is around a 25-30 minute walk away. As you exit the station turn left down Central Drive past Frankie & Benny's, and a Morrisons superstore and you will reach the sea front. Turn left along the

promenade passing the Ranch House pub on your left and then take the 5th left into Regent Road. Proceed straight up Regent Road and continue along into Westgate. You will reach the stadium on your left hand side.

St James' Park
Newcastle, NE1 4ST

What is the ground like?

The ground was largely rebuilt in the 1990's and is now unrecognisable from the St James' Park of old. On approaching the stadium, it looks absolutely huge, as it appears to have been built on raised ground. In 2000 an additional tier was added to the Milburn and Leazes (Sir John Hall) Stands increasing the capacity to over 52,000. These stands have a huge lower tier, with a row of executive boxes and a smaller tier above. It has a spectacular looking roof, which at the time was the largest cantilever structure in Europe. The transparent roof allows natural light to penetrate through it (and hence is good for the pitch). However the ground now looks somewhat unbalanced with one half of the ground being significantly larger than the other two sides. These remaining two sides the Gallowgate End and East Stand are both of the same height and are two-tiered. The stadium is also totally enclosed with all four corners being filled with seating.

In October 2014 a large video screen was installed on the upper side of the Sir John Hall Stand, which looks rather odd, in terms of its position. Outside the stadium is a statue of former manager Sir Bobby Robson.

What is it like for visiting supporters?

Away fans are housed on the very far side of the Sir John Hall Stand, in the top tier. Up to 3,000 supporters can be accommodated in this section for league games and a larger allocation is available for cup games. Be warned though that it is a climb of 14 flights of stairs up to the away section and that you are situated quite far away from the pitch. So if you are scared of heights or have poor eye sight then this may not be for you. On the plus side you do get a wonderful view of the whole stadium, plus the Newcastle skyline and countryside in the distance. Also the leg room and height between rows are some the best that I have come across and the facilities on offer are pretty good. Away fans also get the best view of the new video screen that has been installed as it is located on that side of the stand.

The concourse is spacious and there is a fair selection of pies on offer including the Chicken Balti Pie (£3.50). There are also televisions on the concourse, showing live the game being played, with separate refreshment areas which serve alcohol.

The atmosphere in St James' Park can be electric and it is certainly one of the best footballing stadiums in the country. I personally found the Geordies friendly and helpful and a trip to Newcastle can be one of the better away trips in the League.

Club nickname:	Ground name:	Capacity:	Opened:
The Magpies or The Toon	St James' Park	52,401 (all seated)	1892 (the land had been used for football since 1880)
Pitch size:	Undersoil heating:	Record attendance:	Home kit:
115 x 75 yards	Yes	68,386 v Chelsea Division One September 3rd, 1930	Black and White Stripes
Telephone:	Ticket Office:	Website:	Programme:
0844 372 1892	0844 372 1892 (Option 1)	www.nufc.co.uk	£3

Pubs for away fans

St James' Park is one of the few remaining football grounds in the country that is located in the centre of the city. You are only a few minutes walk from the main shopping areas of Newcastle. There are plenty of bars to choose from in the city centre, but most away fans tend to favour some of the pubs opposite and around Newcastle Railway Station. The 'A Head Of Steam,' 'The Lounge' and 'O'Neills' are all popular with visiting supporters, but some of these bars will only admit fans if colours are covered and none of them admit children. Nearby is a former Wetherspoons pub called the Union Rooms, which is now is now under new ownership. This pub is happy to admit away fans and is family friendly.

On my last visit I went to the Bodega on Westgate Road and had no problems. This pub is listed in the CAMRA Good Beer Guide and had a friendly atmosphere. Closer to the ground (and just around the corner from China Town) is the Newcastle Arms on St Andrews Street. This pub is also known for its real ale, but you need to arrive early and not wear colours to gain entrance. Alcohol is also served within the ground.

Directions & Car Parking

At the end of the A1(M) continue onto the A1 North and then the A184 towards Newcastle. Continue along this road, bearing left onto the A189. Continue over the River Tyne on the Redheugh Bridge, from which the ground can be clearly seen. Carry on straight up the dual carriageway (St James Boulevard). This leads directly to the Gallowgate End of the ground. As the ground is so central there are a number of pay and display and multistorey car parks in the vicinity.

By train

Newcastle Central Railway Station is located half a mile from St James' Park and takes around 10-15 minutes to walk.

As you exit the main station entrance, turn left and proceed along Neville Street. Continue past the blue NHS building and Central Bar and at the next traffic lights turn right into St James' Boulevard (A189). You will soon spot the ground further up this street.

Rodney Parade
Newport, Gwent, NP19 0UU

What is the ground like?

On one side is the Bisley Stand that was opened in 2011. This covered all seated stand has a capacity of just over 2,500 seats. It is single tiered and incorporates a row of executive boxes. The roof is situated quite high up above the spectators area and pleasingly there are no supporting pillars to obstruct your view of the playing action.

Opposite is the much older but classic looking Hazell Stand. This covered stand has seating to the rear (with windshields to either side) and terracing to the front. There are a row of thin supporting pillars running across the middle of this stand. It does not run the full length of the pitch and has a portion of open terracing on one side towards the North End. The team dugouts are situated at the front of this stand.

The North or Town End as it is also known was rebuilt in 2010. It is a small open terrace which is quite set-back from the playing area. At the South is a small open temporary stand of seating. There is also an electric scoreboard in one corner of the stadium. The ground is shared with Newport and Newport Gwent Dragons Rugby Clubs.

What is it like for visiting supporters?

Away fans are mostly housed on one side of the Bisley Stand, where around 580 fans can be accommodated. This stand is all seated and covered and being a relatively new stand the facilities inside are good. The stand is shared with home supporters who are separated by a portion of green netting, draped over the seats. In addition a small temporary block of open seating is also made available at the South End. This has a capacity of just over 400. As to be expected the seating in the Bisley Stand gives the better and more comfortable view of the game, but both areas share the same facilities. There is a food outlet just inside the ground by the turnstiles serving amongst other things; Burgers (£3), Hot Dogs (£3), a selection of Pies & Pasties (£2.60), Sausage Rolls (£1) and Chips (£2).Away Supporters Entrance

The entrance to the away supporters section is at the opposite end of the stadium to the home areas and is accessed along Corporation Road (so no need to go through the main stadium entrance). It is poorly signposted and is literally a small pathway situated in-between some residential houses. Outside the turnstiles there is a small portakabin that serves as the away ticket office. I found my visit to be an enjoyable one, with the stewards certainly taking a relaxed and friendly approach. The atmosphere was good emanating from all sides of the ground.

Club nickname:	Ground name:	Capacity:	Opened:
The Exiles or Ironsides	Rodney Parade	7,850	1877

Pitch size:	Undersoil heating:	Record attendance:	Home kit:
112 x 72 yards	No	7,326 v Notts County League Two 6th May 2017	Amber and Black

Telephone:	Ticket Office:	Website:	Programme:
01633 670690	01633 670690 (Option 1)	newport-county. co.uk	£3

Pubs for away fans

Inside the stadium away fans are treated to their own bar that is situated at the top of the Bisley Stand and is accessed from steps at the front. With plush seating, Sky Sports television and great views across the stadium, you would have easily thought that you had walked into a corporate area by mistake. The only downside is that the bar is closed whilst the game is in progress (including 10 minutes before the first half kick off) and fans are not allowed to be in the bar whilst the match is being played. This is enforced (in a nice way) by a doorman.

Along Corporation Road is the Excelsior Club which allows in away fans, shows televised sports and is family friendly. There is also a Wetherspoon pub on Chepstow Road called the Godfrey Morgan. This spacious pub is only a 10 minute walk from the away turnstiles

Neil Le Milliere a visiting Exeter City fan informs me; 'On our visits to Newport we've used the Lamb pub on Bridge Street in the town centre. It is both welcoming and serves great real ale.' This pub is listed in the CAMRA Good Beer Guide.

Directions & Car Parking

Leave the M4 at J26 and take the A4051 towards Newport. After going under a flyover you will reach a large roundabout where you take the 2nd exit keeping in the filter lane towards the City Centre/Railway Station. At the next roundabout take the 1st exit going across the river onto the B4591 towards Maindee. At the traffic lights bear right onto Chepstow Road and then take the first right into Corporation Rd. Take the next right into Grafton Rd and the entrance is down on the left. Street parking although note restrictions.

By train

Newport Station is situated around a 1/4 of a mile away from the stadium. Exit the main station entrance and turn left along the main (Queensway) road. Follow this road until you reach a large roundabout. Take the pedestrian underpass down underneath, and at the centre turn left towards River Usk. After you have come back up to street level cross the river bridge and then take the first right hand turn into Rodney Parade.

Sixfields Stadium
Northampton, NN5 5QA

What is the ground like?

The Club moved from their old County Ground to the Sixfields Stadium in October 1994. This neat all seater ground is located on the outskirts of Northampton.

On one side is the new East Stand, which is still a work in progress. It has a lower tier of 1,900 seats, which are currently available to supporters, however the rest of the stand is still very much of a shell, with large areas above the lower seating tier still to be put in place.

On the other side of the ground is the large

West (Main) Stand. This two tiered affair, is all seated and covered and is free of any supporting pillars. The team dug outs are located at the front of it.

Both ends are smaller stands and are of similar size to one another. Again both are all seated and covered. The South end of the stadium is allocated to away supporters. A large hill overlooks the ground, where small numbers congregate to watch the game free, even though they can only see half the pitch!

What is it like for visiting supporters?

Away fans are located in the Moulton College at one end of the pitch, where 800 supporters can be accommodated. If demand requires it then an additional 423 seats can be allocated in the East Stand. One slight pain about Sixfields is that you can't pay at the turnstiles. You have to buy your ticket first from a Portakabin and then you have to queue again. Some away fans have got caught out by this when arriving late. However, I have received a number of reports complementing the standard of stewarding, other club officials and the Northampton fans themselves. Please note that if you club has a large away following to make sure that you have a ticket before travelling as it has not be unknown for away fans turning up on the day, to find that

the away section has sold out. Food on sale inside the ground includes: Cheesburgers £4.20, Burgers £4, Hot Dogs £3.70, Various Pies £3.30 and Sausage Rolls £3.30.

Having lived in Northampton for a year and watched Northampton Town win the old fourth division (giving away my age now...), I have a soft spot for them. The fans themselves are quite passionate and this makes for a great atmosphere especially at cup games.

Robert Dunkley informs me; 'Outside the West Stand there is a used programme stall stocking a wide range of programmes from different clubs and seasons.'

Club nickname:	Ground name:	Capacity:	Opened:
The Cobblers	Sixfields Stadium	7,750 (all seated)	1994

Pitch size:	Undersoil heating:	Record attendance:	Home kit:
116 x 72 yards	No	7,798 v Man United League Cup 3rd Rd 21st September 2016	Claret and White

Telephone:	Ticket Office:	Website:	Programme:
01604 683 700	01604 683 777	www.ntfc.co.uk	£3

Pubs for away fans

At Sixfields Stadium itself is Carrs Bar (the entrance to which is at the back of the Main Stand) which allows in away supporters. It also shows televised football.

As Sixfields Stadium is built on a leisure complex on the outskirts of Northampton, then visiting fans on arrival are pretty much confined to the complex. Just going past McDonalds towards the top end there is a Flaming Grill pub, which offers real ale, serves food and shows televised sport. Behind the Flaming Grill is a Tenpin Bowling Alley which also has a bar and also shows televised sports. Nearer to the stadium there is a Frankie & Benny's restaurant, which also serves alcohol. There are also a variety of other eating places nearby including a KFC, McDonalds and a Pizza Hut.

Kevin Roberts informs me; 'For those supporters travelling from the North and leaving the M1 at Junction 16 and taking the A4500 towards Northampton, then you will pass on your left the recently refurbished Turnpike pub, which as far as I am aware is still welcoming away supporters.'

Directions & Car Parking

Leave the M1 at Junction 15A or 16, following the A43 or A45 respectively towards Northampton. The Sixfields stadium, which you will reach on your right, is well signposted around the area. There is a fair sized car park located at the ground, which costs £4. Make sure though that you arrive early as it has been known for it to get full for the more popular games. Near to the stadium, off the roundabout by TGI Fridays is a hard standing area, known as Duston Mill. On matchdays it is used as a car park (£4).

By train

Northampton Station is 2 miles from the stadium. You can take the 25-30 minute walk as Dave Brown directs; "Go across the station car park and then turn right onto Black Lion Hill. Go over the bridge and continue straight on. At HSS Hire (& the handily placed Thomas A. Beckett pub opposite) turn left onto St James' Mill Rd. Then turn right at the Fabric Warehouse onto Harvey Reeves Rd. After one mile this road brings you out at Sixfields".

Carrow Road
Norwich, NR1 1JE

What is the ground like?

Carrow Road has been steadily redeveloped since the late 1970's, with all four sides of the ground having new stands. The newest of these is the Jarrold South Stand at one side of the pitch which was opened in 2004. It is an impressive looking cantilever, single tier, all seated stand, that can house up to 8,000 supporters. It is has a large television gantry suspended beneath its' largely perspex roof. This stand was further extended in 2005 and now surrounds the corner of the ground where it joins the Norwich & Peterborough Stand. The rest of the ground is also all seated and all stands are covered.

Both ends look particularly smart, being large two tiered affairs, complete with a row of executive boxes and distinctive pairs of large floodlight pylons protruding from their roofs. The first of these to be built was the River End in 1979 (it was later renamed the Norwich & Peterborough Stand), with the Barclay End opposite opening in 1992. On the remaining side is the Geoffrey Watling City Stand. Named after a former club president and opened in 1986, this single tiered stand is smaller than both ends. In one corner the Club have installed the World's first (for a football ground) revolving LED big screen.

What is it like for visiting supporters?

Away fans are housed on one side of the South Stand, on one side of the ground. As you would expect from a modern stand the facilities and view of the playing action are good. The normal allocation in this area is 2,500 fans although this can be increased further for cup games. If you are located at the very back of this stand then you can enjoy some fine views across the city, including Norwich Cathedral.

The Club I found to be particularly friendly and relaxed. I certainly would rate it as one of the better away days, even though it seems an eternity to get there. Alas the days of the Club producing its own range of pies have long since gone instead you can enjoy the

standard range of Pukka Pies (£3), Sausage Rolls (£2) and Rollover Hot Dogs (£3.50).

Tom Jameson a visiting Sheffield United fan informs me; 'I recently visited Carrow Road and found it to be a pleasant, relaxing atmosphere which made for a very enjoyable day out. The stand is very modern, and offers a decent view of the action with plenty of leg room. One problem I did encounter was the tendency of the stewards to order away supporters to keep seated throughout the game, which I did find rather all annoying.'

Club nickname:	Ground name:	Capacity:	Opened:
The Canaries	Carrow Road	27,220 (all seated)	1935

Pitch size:	Undersoil heating:	Record attendance:	Home kit:
114 x 74 yards	Yes	43,984 v Leicester FA Cup 6th Round 30th March 1963	Yellow and Green

Telephone:	Ticket Office:	Website:	Programme:
01603 760 760	0844 826 1902	www.canaries.co.uk	£3.50

Pubs for away fans

The Compleat Angler pub which for many years was the main pub for visiting fans, is now under new management and has changed its policy to now only admit home supporters. Further along the same road as the Compleat Angler, is the Prince of Wales pub which admits away fans. This pub has televised sport and also serves food. The Prince of Wales pub is located around a five minute walk from Norwich Railway Station and a 15-20 minute walk away from Carrow Road. Rob Emery informs me; 'Not far away from the ground and towards the City Centre a new leisure complex called the Riverside has opened. This has a number of drinking and eating establishments, including a Wetherspoons Lloyds No.1 outlet.'

Whilst Nicholas Mead suggests; 'The Coach and Horses on Thorpe Road brews its own beer and is around a 10 minute walk away from the ground.' Also on Thorpe Road is the Fat Cat and Canary. This pub which like the Coach and Horses is listed in the CAMRA Good Beer Guide, has a number of real ales available as well as Sky Television. Inside Carrow Road alcohol is on sale to away fans.

Directions & Car Parking

The ground is well signposted from the A11 and A47. From the southern bypass (A47) take the A146 into the city. At the traffic lights turn right towards the city centre on the A1054. At the next roundabout stay in the left hand lane and continue towards the city centre along the A147. At the next set of traffic lights, turn right into King Street. This street as it bends around to the right and crosses the river becomes Carrow Road, the ground is further down on the right. You can park at nearby Norfolk County Hall at a cost of £7.

By train

Carrow Road ground is walkable from Norwich Railway Station. If you ignore all those wonderful pubs it should take you no more than ten minutes to walk to the ground. From the station turn left and head for the Morrisons supermarket and you should see the ground behind that.

City Ground
Nottingham, NG2 5FJ

What is the ground like?

The City Ground from a distance looks quite picturesque sitting on the banks of the River Trent. Both ends were re-developed during the 1990's, much improving the overall appearance. At one end, the Bridgford Stand houses away fans in the lower tier; it is odd because one third of this stand was built lower than the rest, due to a local Council planning requirement to allow sunlight through to the houses in nearby Colwick Road. Opposite, the Trent End, is the most recent addition to the ground. It is a large two tiered stand that looks quite smart. One unusual feature of the stand is that running across the middle are a number of rows of seating enclosed within a covered shaded glass area.

On one side there is a similarly impressive two tiered stand, with executive boxes in between, which was built in 1980. Once called the Executive Stand, it was recently renamed the Brian Clough Stand in honour of their greatest manager. Facing this is a smaller and much older Main Stand (built in the mid 1960's) that now looks quite tired in the company of its shiny new neighbours.

What is it like for visiting supporters?

Visiting supporters are housed on one side of the lower tier of the Bridgford Stand (towards the Brian Clough Stand), where around 2,000 fans can be accommodated. The facilities and view of the action in this stand are good. If demand requires it then an additional 1,000 away supporters can be seated in a lower block of the Brian Clough Stand. Food inside the ground includes a range of Pukka Pies; Chicken Balti, Meat and Potato, Cheese and Onion (all £3.20), plus Cornish Pasties (£3.20) and Sausage Rolls (£2.50). Also available are Cheeseburgers (£3.80), Burgers (£3.60) and Hot Dogs (£3.60).

The concourse behind the stand is a little tight for space but it does have good acoustics if your fans burst into song prior to the game starting. Also inside the ground the upper tier of the stand overhangs the lower tier somewhat, again helping to further reverberate some noise. Following complaints that objects were being thrown down onto away fans from the so called Forest fans above, then some netting has been put in place to try and catch anything 'accidentally falling' below. Also I have received reports of stewards insisting on fans sitting in seats, but on my last visit away supporters stood throughout the match unchallenged. I have always enjoyed my visits to the City Ground and coupled with the number of great pubs located in Nottingham, it is one that I normally look forward to.

Club nickname:	Ground name:	Capacity:	Opened:
The Reds	City Ground	30,576 (all seated)	1898
Pitch size:	Undersoil heating:	Record attendance:	Home kit:
115 x 78 yards	Yes	49,946 v Man United Division One 28th October 1967	Red and White
Telephone:	Ticket Office:	Website:	Programme:
0115 982 4444	0115 982 4388	nottinghamforest. co.uk	£3

Pubs for away fans

Nearly all pubs near to the ground are for home fans only. Police normally direct away fans to the Notts County Supporters Club bar at the nearby Meadow Lane ground. Carl Fitzpatrick a visiting Coventry City fan adds; 'Very near to the ground on the banks of the River Trent, we came across the Nottingham Rowing Club, which displayed a banner outside saying that away fans were welcome. They charged £1 entry and the beer was good and very reasonable, plus the Forest fans that we met inside were chatty and friendly.' Simon Phillips recommends the Stratford Haven, just down the road from the Larwood and Voce; 'It has great beer and food, it bustles and is used by both home and away fans.'

Tim Cooke a travelling Millwall fan has a different angle (so to speak); 'Definitely one for the lads! Hooters on the outskirts of the city centre has very nice waitresses wearing just enough to cover things up, serves lovely beer, and great food. Take my advice, make a weekend of it, Nottingham is a top city!' Otherwise, beer is available inside the ground.

Directions & Car Parking

Leave the M1 at Junction 24 and take the A453 towards Nottingham. Then take the A52 East towards Grantham and then onto the A6011 into Nottingham. The ground is situated by the A6011. There is little parking available at the stadium itself for visiting supporters. There is though some street parking to be had, especially in the roads near to the Meadow Lane ground across the River Trent. The council also provide parking at their Eastcroft depot (NG2 3AH) at £4 a car.

By train

Nottingham Railway Station is located one mile from the City Ground and takes around 20 minutes to walk. As you come out of the main station entrance, turn left and then left again. Follow the road down to the dual carriageway and then turn right. The ground is about 3/4's of a mile down the dual carriageway on the left, just over Trent Bridge.

Meadow Lane
Nottingham, NG2 3HJ

What is the ground like?

During the early 1990's the ground was completely rebuilt, creating an attractive all seater stadium. Although the ground comprises four separate stands, it is quite smart looking. Both sides are single tiered stands, the larger of which is the Derek Pavis Stand. This is the Main Stand containing the Directors Area and having the players tunnels and team dugouts at its front. Opposite is the Jimmy Sirrel Stand which has a gable on its roof reminiscent of those old grounds, where they were once a common sight.

At one end is the large Kop Stand, which can

house up to 5,400 supporters. Again this is a newish stand with excellent facilities. The other end is the smaller, covered Family Stand. This stand has one sizeable solitary supporting pillar, which may affect your view as it is situated right at the front of the stand in the middle. This stand also has a small electric scoreboard on its roof. The stadium is completed with a set of four modern floodlight pylons.

Outside the stadium there is a statue of Notts County legends Jimmy Sirrel and Jack Wheeler.

What is it like for visiting supporters?

Away fans are housed on one side of the Jimmy Sirrel Stand, located on one side of the ground. The normal allocation for this area will be around 1,300, although this can be increased for cup games.

On my last visit I was very impressed with the standard of the ground. The views were generally good and the concourse spacious. I was quite impressed also to see a proper queueing system in place for refreshments. I wish more clubs would do this as I personally hate the scrum around kiosks that is common place at most other Clubs.

The only disappointments were that the substantial supporters club didn't allow

in away supporters and that the ground generally lacked atmosphere, however this may improve with home fans now once again back in their traditional home end of the Kop. A visit to Meadow Lane is usually a hassle free and enjoyable day out.

Andy McLaren a visiting Hartlepool United fan adds; 'The stewards at the back of the away section let us stand and even joined in with some friendly banter. There was a reasonable number but they kept a low profile and let the fans enjoy themselves. Overall they were a credit to the club and made the day enjoyable!'

Club nickname:	Ground name:	Capacity:	Opened:
The Magpies	Meadow Lane	20,300 (all seated)	1910

Pitch size:	Undersoil heating:	Record attendance:	Home kit:
114 x 76 yards	No	47,310 v York City FA Cup 6th Round 12th March 12th 1955	Black and White Stripes

Telephone:	Ticket Office:	Website:	Programme:
0115 952 9000	0115 955 7210	nottscountyfc.co.uk	£3

Pubs for away fans

The Supporters Club at the ground and the nearby Trent Navigation Inn on Meadow Lane, tend to be for home fans only. So it is either a case of going for a drink on the other side of the River Trent (by the Forest ground) or near the train station/in the city centre. Both areas are around a 10-15 minute walk away.

Probably the nearest pub would be the Southbank Bar as Steve from the Pie Fanzine website informs me; 'Just on the other side of Trent Bridge is the Southbank Bar. It serves excellent food and has sport on the numerous televisions and normally three real ales are offered here'. A little further on up from this pub near to the cricket ground is the 'Trent Bridge Inn' which is a Wetherspoons pub.'

If arriving by train then just across from the front of the station down Queensbridge Road is the "Vat and Fiddle" which is located next to the Castle Rock Brewery. It offers ten real ales, food and is family friendly. It is also listed in the CAMRA Good Beer Guide. Alcohol is also available within the ground.

Directions & Car Parking

Leave the M1 at Junction 26 and take the A610 towards Nottingham and then follow the signs for Melton Mowbray. Turn left before the River Trent in to Meadow Lane.

Parking is available at the Cattle Market (opposite the away end) which costs £3.50 a car or at Nottingham City Council's Eastcroft depot (NG2 3AH) a five minute walk from Meadow Lane, It costs £4. Roads near to the ground are mostly Pay and Display bays. Some street parking can be had further away.

By train

The Meadow Lane ground is a 10-15 minute walk away from Nottingham Railway Station.

As you come out of the main station entrance, Turn left from the station across the car park and then turn right at the traffic lights. The stadium is about a quarter of a mile down the dual carriageway on the left.

SportsDirect.com Park
Boundary Park, Oldham, OL1 2PA

What is the ground like?

The look of Boundary Park has been greatly enhanced with the opening of the new North Stand on one side of the ground. This new stand is pretty smart looking both inside and out, and is of a good size, being the tallest at the stadium. It has a single tier of seating that comprises 2,340 seats. Above this area is a large panelled back wall that encompasses corporate hospitality areas and club offices. This is all located below a slightly curved roof that has two large windshields to either side.

At one end is the comparatively new Jimmy Frizzell Stand, which is named after a former Oldham player and manager.

This is a good sized all seater covered stand which enjoys excellent views of the pitch and has an electric scoreboard on its roof. The other end, the 'Chaddy End', is a medium sized all seater covered stand, which has a number of supporting pillars running across the front of it. On one side there is the old two-tiered George Hill Main Stand. This used to have terracing in front, but has since been filled with seating. The ground also benefits from four large traditional floodlight pylons, leaving the visitor in no doubt that this is a football ground.

What is it like for visiting supporters?

Away fans are housed in the ZenOffice Stand (the Chaddy Road End) at one end of the ground. This stand has a capacity of around 3,750 fans. This is the opposite end to where the away fans have been housed for many years and has caused some upset with some Oldham supporters, as this was always seen as the traditional "Home" end.

Although the ZenOffice Stand is covered it does have a number of supporting pillars running across the front of it, which could impede your view of the action. The facilities are adequate albeit a little dated and generally the stewards are fine. Away fans can really make some noise from the visitors stand and the atmosphere is "helped" further by the

presence of a drummer in the home end.

If you get chance, make sure to try one of the pies on offer; Cottage, Steak & Pepper, plus Cheese & Potato (all £3). Some fans reckon that this is the best part of a visit to Boundary Park!

Make sure you wrap up well though as the location of Boundary Park on the edge of the Pennines, means that it always seems to be cold, with a biting wind that goes right through you.

Club nickname:	Ground name:	Capacity:	Opened:
The Latics	SportsDirect.com Park	13,500 (all seated)	1906

Pitch size:	Undersoil heating:	Record attendance:	Home kit:
106 x 72 yards	No	47,671 v Sheff Wed FA Cup 5th Round 25th January 1930	Blue With White Trim

Telephone:	Ticket Office:	Website:	Programme:
0161 624 4972	0161 785 5150	oldhamathletic. co.uk	£3

Pubs for away fans

The closest pub is the Clayton Green, which is a Brewers Fayre outlet and can be found two hundred yards from the corner of the Main Stand and the Chaddy End, on Sheepfoot Lane. This pub allows in visiting supporters and there is normally a good and friendly mix of home and away fans inside.

There is also the Greyhound pub, which is across Broadway down Holden Fold Lane.

Chippy Lees, an exiled Latics fans in Cornwall, recommends the following; 'The Old Grey Mare on Rochdale Road is worth a visit. If you walk to the top of Sheepfoot Lane and turn left at the newspaper shop, the pub is about 100 yards down the road on the right. There's a varied selection of beers available, and again a warm welcome is assured. Further down on the right is The White Hart.'

Alcohol is also sold to away fans inside the ground, albeit from a separate kiosk to food.

Directions & Car Parking

Leave the M62 at J20 and take the A627(M) towards Oldham. Leave the A627(M) following the signs for Royton (A663). At the top of the slip road you will find a large roundabout that on the left has a McDonalds. Take the second exit onto the A627 towards Oldham. After passing a Vauxhall Garage, turn left at the traffic lights. Follow the road around to the right and then bear left onto Westhulme Way. You will then reach the ground at the end of this road. Oldham Royal Hospital offers matchday parking at £3.

By train/Metrolink

The closest Metrolink station is Westwood which is around a 15-20 minute walk away. The nearest railway station is Mills Hill, which just over a two miles away Park and a 40-45 minute walk. Both these services depart from Manchester Victoria. Whilst the Metrolink also has a number of other pick up points in Manchester City Centre and takes around 21 minutes, the train to Mills Hill takes around 8-10 minutes.

Kassam Stadium
Grenoble Road, Oxford, OX4 4XP

What is the ground like?

The club moved to the Kassam Stadium in 2001, after leaving the Manor Ground, which had been its home for 76 years. The stadium is named after the former Club Chairman Firoz Kassam. It was built at a cost of around £15m and is located on the outskirts of Oxford. It has only three sides, with one end remaining unused. Each of the stands are of a good size, are all seated, covered and are roughly of the same height. The South Stand on one side of the pitch, is a two-tiered stand with a row of executive boxes. This is a particularly impressive looking stand with police control and press boxes situated at the back. Opposite is the single tiered North Stand, primarily given to away supporters. This has a number of strange looking floodlights protruding from its roof. At the one end is the Oxford Mail Stand, which is also single-tiered. There is a special type of pitch, one of the first to have artificial grass woven into the live turf. One disappointment are the large gaps in the corners, which sets the stands back from the playing surface and means cold winds whistling through in winter. Outside the stadium at the West End, there is a statue of an Ox.

What is it like for visiting supporters?

Away fans are normally housed on one side of the North Stand, towards the open end of the ground. This stand may be shared with home supporters, or if demand requires it, then the whole of this stand can be allocated providing just over 5,000 seats in total. The facilities within and the views of the playing action are excellent, and there is also good leg room. The atmosphere within the ground is not bad, with the home fans in the Oxford Mail Stand doing their best to raise it. There is not much around the ground in terms of pubs and eating establishments, although refreshments inside the stadium are okay, although if there is a large away support, then it can take quite a while to get served. Refreshments on offer include:

Cheeseburgers (£3.80), Burgers (£3.40), Hot Dogs (£3) and a selection of Wrights Pies (£3). With one end of the ground being open, there is always the remark 'of watch my car' as another wayward shot flies into the car park behind. On the whole I found the Kassam Stadium to be an enjoyable and a largely friendly day out.

Derek Fennel a visiting Blackburn supporter adds; 'The stewards at the Kassam seemed very helpful and accommodating which led to a feeling of watching the game in relaxed frame of mind. There was great vocal support from the home supporters who really got behind their team.'

Club nickname: The U's	Ground name: Kassam Stadium	Capacity: 12,500 (all seated)	Opened: 2001
Pitch size: 112 x 78 yards	Undersoil heating: No	Record attendance: 12,243 v Orient League Two 6th May 2006	Home kit: Yellow and Blue
Telephone: 01865 337 500	Ticket Office: 01865 337 533	Website: www.oufc.co.uk	Programme: £3

Pubs for away fans

There are no pubs in close vicinity to the stadium Kim Rockall informs me; 'There is a cinema and bowling alley complex located adjacent to the stadium, called Ozone. Inside the bowling alley there is a bar, which also has Sky television and a fast food outlet.' There is also on the complex a Chinese buffet restaurant called Oxy Oriental, as well as a fish and chip shop called the Ozone Plaice.

Dave Langford a visiting Northampton Town fan tells me; 'I found a small local pub called the George Inn, situated in Littlemore just off the ring road (not far from Sainsburys). It had a number of television screens showing the early kick off and we were served fairly quickly. The Oxford fans at the pub made us very welcome. The stadium was then only a ten minute walk away.' Also in Littlemore is the British Legion Club (OX4 4LZ) which also welcomes away fans. Please note though that for certain high profile games (on Police advice) that both the pub and Club do not admit visiting supporters.

Otherwise alcohol is also served within the ground.

Directions & Car Parking

The Kassam Stadium is quite well signposted from the main routes into Oxford, with brown football signs pointing the way. The stadium can be found in between the Oxford Science Park & Blackbird Leys Estate. From the A423 Ring Road, take the A4074 towards Reading. After the roundabout with Sainsbury's on one corner, take the left turning sign posted Cowley/Wallington/Oxford Science Park and you eventually come to the ground on your left. There is a large free car park available at the stadium itself.

By train

Oxford Railway Station is over four miles from the ground and it is really not advisable to try to walk it.

You can get the Oxford Bus Company Service, Number 5 from Oxford Railway Station (use bus stop R2) via the city centre to Knights Road in Blackbird Leys, which is a short walk away from the ground.

ABAX Stadium
London Road, Peterborough, PE2 8AL

What is the ground like?

On one side of the ground is the Norwich & Peterborough South Stand, which was opened in 1996 and replaced a former open terrace. Encased in supporting tubular steelwork, the 5,000 capacity stand is an impressive sight. The two tiered stand, is covered and all seated. There is also a row of executive boxes running across its middle. The other side, the Main Stand, is a much older stand, being first opened in 1957. It is two tiered, covered stand and is all seated. At one end is the London Road Terrace. This covered terrace has a bright white roof and is a classic looking old stand, having its roof put in place in the early 1950's. As to be expected from a terrace of such vintage it does have a number of supporting pillars running across the front of it, which could impede your view of the game. Opposite at the Moy's End, is a new all seater stand that was opened in November 2014. It is a single-tiered all seated stand that has a capacity of 2,500. In one corner of the ground is a Police Control Box, whilst on the other corner is a tall, old fashioned floodlight pylon. The ground had a set of four at one time, but three have been taken down as the London Road ground has been redeveloped.

What is it like for visiting supporters?

Although the new Moy's End stand is now open, the Club have decided to continue housing away fans in part of the Main Stand (towards the Moy's End) where just over 1,800 fans can be seated. The view from this stand is quite good, although the facilities inside (such as the refreshment area and toilets) are on the small side and are quite basic. In the upper part of the stand the seating is wooden, giving an indication of the age of the stand.

Food available inside the ground includes the standard fayre of; Cheeseburgers (£3.60), Burgers (£3.50), Hot Dogs (£3.50), Various Pies including Chicken Balti, Steak and Cheese & Onion (£3.20), Pasties (£3.20) and Jumbo Sausage Rolls (£3.20). On the whole on each of my visits, I have found Peterborough to be a good and fairly relaxed day out, with some good pubs in the locality too.'

Andrew Bartlett a visiting Southampton fan adds; 'Away fans sitting in Block A of the Main Stand, should be made aware that the leg room is quite tight. Otherwise a very pleasant old fashioned ground with welcoming stewards.' Please note that the away fans seating area is situated at the opposite end of the ground to the main London Road.

Club nickname:	Ground name:	Capacity:	Opened:
The Posh	ABAX Stadium	14,319	1934

Pitch size:	Undersoil heating:	Record attendance:	Home kit:
112 x 76 yards	No	30,096 v Swansea C FA Cup 5th Round February 20th 1965	Blue and White

Telephone:	Ticket Office:	Website:	Programme:
01733 563 947	01733 865 674	www.theposh.com	£3

Pubs for away fans

With the recent closing of the Cherry Tree pub on Oundle Road then there is limited choice of pubs close to the ground. One exception is Charters, which is certainly worth a visit and is also listed in the CAMRA Good Beer Guide. This former Dutch barge, is moored on the River Nene, just a few minutes walk away from London Road.

Alun Thomas a visiting Wrexham supporter adds; 'We enjoyed the Palmerston Arms on Oundle Reload. It is away fan friendly and has around 10 real ales on offer. It is around a 15 minute walk away from London Road.'

Alternatively, the ground is in walking distance (10 minutes) of the city centre (which is very pleasant and complete with a cathedral) where there are plenty of good pubs to be found. Most have doormen present on matchdays, but seem happy enough to admit away fans. If you are arriving by train then the Brewery Tap near to the station on Westgate, is worth a visit.

Please note that alcohol is NOT made available to away supporters inside the stadium.

Directions & Car Parking

Leave the A1 at J17 and take the A1139 towards Peterborough. Then take the third exit slip road onto the A1260 (signposted City Centre). Leave the A1260 at the first exit (signposted Orton Malborne) and at the roundabout take the third exit onto Morley

Way. Then at the next roundabout take the first exit onto Shrewsbury Avenue. After half mile you will reach a set of traffic lights where you turn right onto Oundle Rd (A605). You will reach the stadium on your right. Pay & Display Car Park on Oundle Rd (£3).

By train

Peterborough Railway Station is around a mile away from the London Road Ground. Turn right out of station and follow the main road, passing an Asda store on your right. At the traffic lights near to the Rivergate

Shopping Centre, turn right. Go over the bridge and you can see the floodlights of London Road, over on your left. It takes about 20 minutes to walk from the station to the ground.

Home Park
Plymouth, PL2 3DQ

What is the ground like?

During 2001 Home Park was transformed, with three sides of the ground being completely re-built. This included both ends and one side of the ground. They were replaced by single tiered, covered all seated stands, that are of the same design and height. The corners between these stands were also filled with seating so that the ground is totally enclosed on those sides, making an impressive sight. There is a gap between the roof and the back of these stands, which is filled with a perspex strip to allow more light to get to the pitch.

The Grandstand at one side of the pitch is the only remnant of the old Home Park. This classic looking stand dates back to 1952, although its appearance makes it look much older. Although it is much older than the other sides, it is still taller than the other stands and is still the focal point at Home Park. It is a two-tiered stand, with an upper tier of seating and a lower tier of terracing, most of which is uncovered by the stand's roof. There are a couple of modern floodlight pylons situated on either side of the Grandstand.

What is it like for visiting supporters?

Away fans are housed in the Barn Park End, which is all seated and covered. As you would expect from a modern stand the facilities and views of the playing action are both good. The normal allocation for visiting supporters in this area is 1,300 seats, although this can be increased to 2,022, if demand requires it.

The atmosphere is normally good and even though I have received a number of reports of the stewarding being somewhat over zealous in the away end, on my last visit it was fine. No problems were encountered outside the ground and on the whole it was a good day out.

The only down side was that the concourse was a bit cramped and if there is a good away support then it can get uncomfortably crowded.

In keeping with the naval tradition of the area the teams emerge to the Marines tune of Semper Fidelis. You may also be interested to know that Home Park is the most westerly and southerly League Ground in England.

Club nickname:	Ground name:	Capacity:	Opened:
The Pilgrims	Home Park	16,388 (all seated)	1893

Pitch size:	Undersoil heating:	Record attendance:	Home kit:
112 x 73 yards	No	43,596 v Aston Villa, Division Two 10th October 1936	Green and White Stripes

Telephone:	Ticket Office:	Website:	Programme:
01752 562 561	01752 907700	www.pafc.co.uk	£3

Pubs for away fans

Probably the best bet is the Britannia which is a sizeable Wetherspoons outlet and around a 10 minute walk away from the ground (from the car park outside the football ground, turn left and the pub is down the road on the right hand corner). For most matches the pub which is busy normally, has a queue of fans waiting to get in outside, but this is controlled by the security staff, so you don't normally have to wait too long to gain entrance.

Although away fan friendly, the pub doesn't tolerate away supporters singing their clubs

songs and any who do are quickly ejected from the premises, so you have been warned.

Near to the pub is normally a van selling pasties, which looked to be doing a roaring trade on my last visit. Opposite the Britannia is the Embassy Club which is best avoided by away fans.

Otherwise alcohol is available within the ground.

Directions & Car Parking

Take the M5 to the South West and at the end of the motorway continue onto the A38 (The ground is well signposted from the outskirts of Plymouth on the A38). On entering Plymouth, turn left onto the A386 (towards Plymouth). When this road splits into two, keep on the left hand side (again signposted

Plymouth) and after about a mile you will see the ground on your left. The ground is well signposted 'Plymouth Argyle Home Park' on the way into Plymouth. There is a large free car park at the ground itself.

By train

Plymouth Railway Station is about one and a half miles away, so either grab a taxi or embark on the 20 minute walk.

As you come out of the station turn right and down the hill and under the railway bridge. Just keep walking straight along this road (A386) and you will eventually reach the ground on your right.

Vale Park
Hamil Road, Burslem, ST6 1AW

What is the ground like?

The ground has a good mixture of the old and the new. On one side is the Lorne Street Stand, which was opened in 1999. It is a smart two-tiered stand that has a row of executive boxes situated between its large lower tier and much smaller upper tier. It is of a good size with a planned capacity of 5,000. However the stand was never fully completed with a portion of the lower tier still remaining empty and is largely just a concrete base.

On the opposite side is the Railway Stand. Opened in 1954, it is a fair sized stand that is covered to the rear. It has a number of supporting pillars that run across its middle. At one end is the Hamil Road End, which is a good sized single tiered stand. It also has an electric scoreboard situated just below its roof. Opposite is the Bycars Road End, which although old looking was built in 1992. It also is partly covered to the rear and has some supporting pillars to either side.

Situated in one corner, in-between the Bycars & Railway Stands is an odd looking two-tiered structure that is the only portion of the old ground that still remains.

What is it like for visiting supporters?

Up to 4,500 away supporters can be accommodated in the Hamil Road End, where the view and facilities located on the concourse behind the stand are good. Even a relatively small number of away fans can really make some noise from this stand, as the acoustics are excellent. However, the slope is quite shallow, which might affect your view should a tall person be seated in front. Normally though, you could still move to another seat if necessary.

Vince Smith a visiting Northampton Town fan adds; 'I must say it was an enjoyable day out at Vale Park, with very friendly stewards, turnstile operators and very good food served by friendly staff. All in all a very pleasant experience and far more enjoyable than a visit to their near neighbours.'

And for a bit of trivia, Dave Seddon, a visiting Brentford supporter informs me; 'The roof of the Hamil Road End was originally that of the Main Stand at Chester City's old Sealand Road ground.'

The food available on the concourse includes Rollover Hot Dogs (£2.50) and a selection of Wrights Pies; Steak (£2.50), Meat & Potato (£2.50), Cheese & Onion Pasties (£2.10) and Sausage Rolls (£2). The P.A within the ground is quite deafening at times and there is no escape, even in the toilets, as it is piped through!

Club nickname:	Ground name:	Capacity:	Opened:
The Valiants	Vale Park	18,947 (all seated)	1950

Pitch size:	Undersoil heating:	Record attendance:	Home kit:
114 x 77 yards	No	49,768 v Aston Villa FA Cup 5th Round 20th February 1960	Amber with Black Pinstripes

Telephone:	Ticket Office:	Website:	Programme:
01782 655800	01782 655800 (Option 1)	www.port-vale.co.uk	£3

Pubs for away fans

Just outside the away turnstiles is a Club Bar called the Vale Social. Normally it does admit away fans but at a cost of £2 per person, although Over 60's and Under 18's are admitted free. Otherwise the choice of pubs for visiting supporters to drink in near to the ground or in the town centre is very limited as Nick Williams a visiting Plymouth Argyle fan informs me; 'Apart from the Bulls Head, which was very welcoming, every other pub in the town that we found had signs up saying "Home fans only" this also included the closest pub to the ground, the Vine.'

Luckily the Bull's Head which is located in St John's Square, is a cracking pub. It is the local outlet for the nearby Titanic Brewery and is listed in the CAMRA Good Beer Guide. It is friendly for away fans. It has a BBQ on matchdays, has up to nine real ales on offer as well as up to 10 traditional ciders and perries. It is a about a ten minute walk from the ground.

Otherwise inside the stadium alcohol is available, albeit in plastic bottles of Carling (£3.50) and Cider (£3.50).

Directions & Car Parking

The ground is located in the town of Burslem, one of the six towns comprising Stoke On Trent. Leave the M6 at junction 15 or 16 and take the A500 towards Stoke on Trent. Follow A500 until the A527 Tunstall/ Burslem exit, where you take the A527

towards Burslem. Continue into Burslem town centre and just after the main traffic lights turn left into Hamil Road for the ground. There is a large car park located outside a superstore next to the ground which costs £5, otherwise street parking.

By train

Longport Railway Station is the closest to the Vale Park ground, but is a good 30 minute walk away and is not well served by trains, unlike Stoke-on-Trent Station which is.

Therefore most fans end up at Stoke-on-Trent station, which is over four miles away from Vale Park and then take a taxi up to the ground.

Fratton Park
Frogmore Road, Portsmouth, PO4 8RA

What is the ground like?

Fratton Park is a traditional looking ground and one which oozes character. Both side stands are two tiered and originally had terracing at the front, which has now been replaced with seating. The South Stand dates back to 1925 and was originally designed by Archibald Leitch who also designed a number of grounds and stands around this period. Although showing its age in parts, it has plenty of character with an old fashioned looking media gantry perched on its roof and raised team dugouts at its front. Opposite the North Stand opened in 1935, looks somewhat plain and functional. Both the North and South Stands are two tiered and have a number of supporting pillars.

At one end is the Fratton End, which is a more modern single tiered stand that was opened in 1997. It is of a good size and is the tallest stand at the ground. The seating in this stand contains an outline resembling a former player, Jimmy Dickinson, who still holds the record for the most club appearances. Opposite is the covered Milton End, which is all seated. The ground is completed with a superb looking set of tall floodlights that were first used in 1962.

What is it like for visiting supporters?

Away fans are housed on one side of the Milton End (on the North Stand side) where the normal allocation is 2,000. If demand requires it, then the whole of this end can be allocated, raising the allocation to 3,200 seats. Although this end now benefits from having cover, the facilities within are pretty basic and the leg room tight, as this stand was a former terrace that has been converted to all seating. There are also some supporting pillars along the front of the stand that may impede you view. On a positive note, away supporters can really make some noise from this stand, further contributing to what is normally a great atmosphere, which is further aided by a drummer and bell ringer in the Fratton End.

Although the Milton End is shared with home supporters, the Pompey home support get behind their team but generally in a non-intimidatory way towards the away contingent. Fans were literally separated by a netted area only three seats wide, but on my last visit there were no problems whatsoever. Entrance to the stand is gained by inserting your ticket into a bar code reader. If you have not pre-purchased a ticket for the game, then allow yourself plenty of time as the ticket booth is located at the opposite end of the ground to the away end. On the whole though try to sit back and enjoy Fratton Park such older grounds now are becoming few and far between with the advent of new stadia being built.

Club nickname:	Ground name:	Capacity:	Opened:
Pompey	Fratton Park	20,700 (all seated)	1898

Pitch size:	Undersoil heating:	Record attendance:	Home kit:
115 x 73 yards	No	51,385 v Derby FA Cup 6th Round 26th February 1949	Blue, White & Red

Telephone:	Ticket Office:	Website:	Programme:
02392 731204	0345 646 1898	portsmouthfc.co.uk	£3

Pubs for away fans

On my last visit I went to the Good Companion pub, which is on the main A2030 about a five minute walk away from the ground. It is a large pub serving real ales and had a good mix of home and away support. I also noticed that it was doing a brisk business in food.

On Milton Road close to the ground is the Brewers Arms which is popular with away fans. Close by is the Milton Arms, which at one time was for home fans only. However since a new landlord had taken over, it now welcomes visiting supporters. This pub also

has the added advantages of showing the early televised kick off match on a huge screen and serving food (even having outdoor BBQs if the weather is good).

If travelling by train then near to Portsmouth & Southsea Station are a couple of Wetherspoons pubs that have been recommended to me.

Please note that alcohol is NOT on sale to visiting supporters within the ground.

Directions & Car Parking

Go along the M27 (ignoring the M275 turn off for Portsmouth town centre) and continue on to the A27. At the junction with the A2030 turn right towards Southsea/Fratton and just continue straight along the A2030 and eventually you will see the ground in front of you, just slightly to your left.

Mostly street parking along or off the A2030 (Eastern Road). Miltoncross School on Milton Road which is a five minute walk from the ground also offers parking at £6 per car.

By train

The nearest local railway station is Fratton, which is around half a mile, or a ten minute walk away from the Fratton Park ground. It is served by trains from London Waterloo, Cardiff, Brighton and Portsmouth & Southsea.

Portsmouth & Southsea which is the main train station located in Portsmouth is located just over one a half miles away or at least a 25-30 minute walk to the ground.

Deepdale

Sir Tom Finney Way, Preston, PR1 6RU

What is the ground like?

With the addition of the new Invincibles Pavilion Stand in 2008, it now means that Deepdale has now been completely modernised. What was a great looking stadium, is now an even a better one as the new stand completely fills the remaining side of what was the Pavilion side of the ground.

Three sides of the stadium are composed of some excellent looking all seater stands, complete with some spectacular looking floodlights. They are of the same height and style and are all large, covered, single tiered stands. Each has a likeness of a past player outlined on the seats and is named after that player. Tom Finney, Bill Shankly and goalkeeping legend Alan Kelly, are all honoured and this makes a welcome change from the boring letters outlined on most new stands. The first of these stands to be built was the Sir Tom Finney Stand in 1995. This was followed by the Bill Shankly Kop in 1998 and the Alan Kelly Stand in 2001. The fourth new stand, the Invincibles Stand is slightly different in design to the other three. Even though it is of the same height and has a similar roof, it has a smaller tier of seating, with 22 executive boxes sitting above.

What is it like for visiting supporters?

Away fans are housed in the modern Bill Shankly Kop at one end of the pitch. Normally the allocation for away fans is approximately half of this stand (3,000 seats). However for teams with a large away support, then the whole end can be allocated, raising the allocation to 6,000.

The views of the playing action and facilities within this stand are excellent. The stand is particularly steep, meaning that fans are kept relatively close to the pitch. On the concourse there are TV's by the refreshment serving areas showing the game live and with the bars being open during the game, this is too much of a temptation for some. There is a wide range of food available including; Cheeseburgers (£3.70), Burgers (£3.50), Hot Dogs (£3.70), Meat & Potato Pie (£2.80), Chicken Balti Pie (£2.80), Steak & Kidney Pie (£2.80) and the Potato & Butter Pie (£2.80). You can also get a pie, peas and gravy for £3.70, plus the Club offer a 'Pie & a Beer' for £5.70. James Prentice adds; 'I would recommend the Butter Pie, which is a bit of a local delicacy. It is just a normal pie but with a filling of very buttery mashed potato and onion. I was attracted to it by a flag at the top of the new Invincibles Stand that read 'True Prestonians Love a Butter Pie!' I particularly enjoyed my last visit as the fans, stewards and even police all seemed to be fairly friendly and there was a good atmosphere being generated within the ground.

Club nickname: The Lilywhites	**Ground name:** Deepdale	**Capacity:** 23,408 (all seated)	**Opened:** 1875
Pitch size: 110 x 77 yards	**Undersoil heating:** No	**Record attendance:** 42,684 v Arsenal Division One 23rd April 1938	**Home kit:** White and Navy
Telephone: 0344 856 1964	**Ticket Office:** 0344 856 1966	**Website:** www.pnefc.net	**Programme:** £3

Pubs for away fans

There is not a great deal in the way of pubs in close proximity to the ground. Further up Tom Finney Way (which used to be called Deepdale Road) from the stadium, is Sumners. This pub normally has a good mix of home and away supporters, although for certain high profile games and local derbies the pub does not admit away supporters.

There are also a couple of nearby clubs that welcome away fans. First there is St Gregory's Catholic Club, which is around a five minute walk away on Blackpool Road. The Club allows entry for a charge of £1, but offers reasonably priced drinks, hot pies, plus has Sky television. You can also park at the Club at a cost of £3. Secondly, there is the Fulwood Conservative Club, situated around ten minutes walk away from Deepdale, at the junction of Blackpool Road and Garstang Road across from Moor Park. Parking is available at the Club at a cost of £3 per car and non-members are admitted free into the club on matchdays.

Otherwise beer can be purchased inside the Deepdale ground.

Directions & Car Parking

Leave M6 at Junction 31 and take the A59 towards Preston. Go up a steep hill and follow the road down to a mini roundabout (note the speed camera by the BP garage on the left). At the roundabout with the Hesketh Arms turn right into Blackpool Road. Go straight on over three sets of lights and just before a fourth set, the ground appears set slightly back on the left. Parking is mainly in the streets surrounding the ground. There is some parking available at the ground itself, but at a cost of £12.50 per car.

By train

Preston Railway Station is around a mile and a half from the ground and takes around twenty five minutes to walk, although you will pass some good pubs on the way, so it could take you longer!

Preston Station is well connected with regular services to London, Liverpool, Manchester, Leeds and the Midlands.

Loftus Road Stadium
South Africa Road London, W12 7PA

What is the ground like?

Loftus Road has a compact feel, as the ground is totally enclosed, with supporters being close to the pitch. An unusual aspect is that all four stands are roughly the same height, their roofs meet at all four corners with no gaps.

The South Africa Road Stand on one side has a larger upper tier, compared to the lower tier, with a row of executive boxes running across the middle. There are a couple of supporting pillars in this stand. The other side, the Ellerslie Road Stand, is single tiered, with a television gantry suspended below its roof.

Both ends are similar looking two tiered stands. On one of these, the School End (where the away fans are located) there is a large video screen located on the centre of its roof. Below this and situated between the lower and upper tier is a small electric scoreboard.

The ground oozes character and there is nothing similar in the league.

What is it like for visiting supporters?

Away fans are situated in the upper tier of the School End, where around 1,800 fans can be accommodated. If demand requires it then the lower tier can also be allocated, increasing the number of places available to about 2,500. If the away club only takes the upper tier allocation, then the lower tier is allocated to home supporters.

The ground has electronic turnstiles meaning that you need to insert your ticket into a reader to gain entrance and normally fans are searched. Inside the facilities look a little dated and the concourse can get a bit cramped especially if the away end is sold out. Although most get a reasonable view of the game, the leg room between rows is tight.

Although I have never experienced problems at the ground I have always found it a little off putting in terms that there is normally quite a large number of Police and stewards present. Plus I have found the atmosphere a bit hit and miss at times.

Food on offer includes Hot Dogs (£3.70), Pukka Pies (Beef & Onion, Chicken Balti, all £3.50), Cheese & Onion Slice (£3.50) and Sausage Rolls (£3.10).

Club nickname:	Ground name:	Capacity:	Opened:
The Superhoops	Loftus Road Stadium	18,360 (all seated)	1917

Pitch size:	Undersoil heating:	Record attendance:	Home kit:
112 x 72 yards	Yes	35,353 v Leeds Utd Division One 27th April 1974	Blue and White Hoops

Telephone:	Ticket Office:	Website:	Programme:
020 8743 0262	08444 777 007	www.qpr.co.uk	£3

Pubs for away fans

There are no pubs for away fans in the immediate vicinity around the stadium. In nearby Shepherds Bush Green there are a number of bars however most do not welcome visiting fans and employ doormen to enforce this.

One exception is Belushi's Bar, which is located in the Vue Complex. This basic bar also shows Sky and BT Sports. Otherwise alcohol is generally available inside the Loftus Road Stadium, although for some high profile games the Club opt not to sell any to visiting supporters.

On the eating front David Frodsham adds; 'On my travels to many football grounds, I have yet to find a wider selection of food available than on the Uxbridge Road. The cosmopolitan inner city nature means that you can almost eat your way around the world. From the normal range of cafes, burger bars, fried chicken outlets and chippies, there are Indian, Chinese, Thai and Jamaican outlets. There are Lebanese and Indian kebab shops, the latter selling doner kebabs made with Indian spices!'

Directions & Car Parking

At the end of the M40, take the A40 towards Central London. At the point where the A40 becomes the A40(M), turn off onto the A40 towards White City/Shepherds Bush and turn right into Wood Lane, turn right into South Africa Road for the ground.

There is no parking available at the ground itself and restricted on-street parking close by. There is some metered street parking further away of you could park at the nearby Westfield Shopping Centre at a cost of £8 (or £6 if you sign up online beforehand).

By tube

The nearest tube station is White City on the Central Line, which is about a five minute walk away. Also nearby is Wood Lane Station, which is on the Hammersmith & City line. Otherwise there are two other tube stations close by; Shepherds Bush Market on the Hammersmith & City line and Shepherds Bush on the Central Line. The former is about a ten minute walk away from the ground, whilst the other is about 15 minutes.

Madejski Stadium
Bennett Road, Reading, RG2 0FL

What is the ground like?

The Club moved to the stadium in 1998, after spending 102 years at their former home of Elm Park. The stadium is of a fair size and is totally enclosed, with all four corners being occupied. Three sides are single tiered, whilst on one side the West (Main) Stand is two tiered, including a row of executive boxes. This stand has a curve in its roof and the team dug outs are located in front.

Unlike the West Stand, the others stands have a more conventional look to their roofs, although there is a gap between the roofs and the back of the stands, that contains

perspex, to allow more light to reach the pitch.

The ground has been designed with the supporter in mind as the fans are housed very close to the pitch and the acoustics are very good.

The stadium also has a video screen in the South East corner. The stadium, named after Reading's co-chairman John Madejski is shared with London Irish Rugby Club.

What is it like for visiting supporters?

Away fans are located in one end of the stadium, in the South Stand, where up to 4,300 can be accommodated (although the normal allocation is 2,100). The facilities in this stand are good with plenty of leg room and the views of the pitch are superb, as there is good height between rows. Away fans can really make some noise in this stand, so make the most of it. The atmosphere is also boosted by a drummer in the home section. Entrance to the stadium is by ticket only and if tickets are still available for away supporters then they can purchase them on the day at the South Stand ticket office located between gates 9 & 10. You enter the stadium by inserting your ticket into a ticket reader which scans the bar code on the ticket

and illuminates a green light to go in.

I first visited this stadium shortly after it opened and then a few times in recent seasons. When I first went in 1998 I truly believed that it was a fantastic stadium. Subsequently after going back and with a number of other new stadiums being built during that time, the Madejski seems just like another nice functional ground. Considering that as it also lacks character and that essential 'wow' factor and coupled with the fact that there are few facilities around the stadium such as pubs for away fans, then there is not a lot to 'write home about'.

Club nickname: The Royals	Ground name: Madejski Stadium	Capacity: 24,200 (all seated)	Opened: 1998
Pitch size: 102 x 70 metres	Undersoil heating: Yes	Record attendance: 24,184 v Everton Premier League 17th November 2012	Home kit: Royal Blue and White
Telephone: 0118 968 1100	Ticket Office: 0118 968 1313	Website: readingfc.co.uk	Programme: £3

Pubs for away fans

There are a couple of mobile bar units located outside the East Stand which normally both home and away fans can use. Otherwise there no pubs as such close to the stadium. However I did locate a Holiday Inn which was around a 15 minute walk away. The hotel had a small bar inside it, but then attached had a larger Irish themed separate bar area, called Callaghans. This bar had Sky Television, but as you would expect was very crowded with away fans and served drinks at what I can only term as 'hotel prices'. Across the road from the hotel is a very good fish & chip shop.

On my last visit the Holiday Inn was mobbed, so I went in search of another pub. Passing the Holiday Inn on my left I turned left onto Basingstoke Road and walked up over a hill to find a pub on the right called 'The World Turned Upside Down.' This chain pub had a mixture of home and away fans and also was popular for food. From the pub it is around a 15 minute walk to the stadium.

Otherwise alcohol is available to away fans inside the ground.

Directions & Car Parking

If you are travelling along the M4 from the West you can see the stadium on your left. Leave the M4 at Junction 11, bear left on to the A33 relief road which leads you directly to the stadium. The Madejski Stadium is well signposted from Junction 11.

There is some limited parking available at the stadium itself for a cost of £8, but it can be a bit of lengthy process to get out of the car park at the end of the game. There are also a number of unofficial car parks in the area sited at local businesses, charging around £5.

By train

Reading Railway Station is situated just over three miles away from the Madejski Stadium. Probably the easiest way to get to the ground is to catch the F1 'Football Special' bus, which leaves just down from the Railway Station on Station Hill (as you exit the station from the main entrance turn right and head down the steps, the buses line up on the left hand side).. The bus service starts at 1pm for Saturday afternoon games and costs £4.

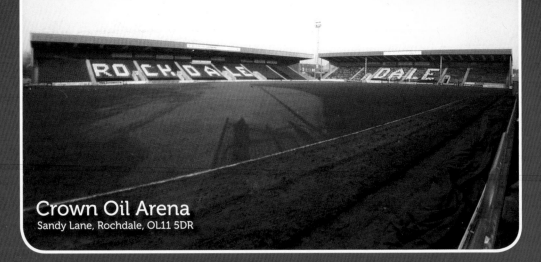

Crown Oil Arena
Sandy Lane, Rochdale, OL11 5DR

What is the ground like?

The Spotland football ground has benefited greatly with the construction of three new stands during the 1990's and year 2000. It is quite picturesque, with a number of trees being visible behind the stands. The last of these new stands to be opened was the smart looking Willbutts Lane Stand at one side of the pitch, which was opened in 2000. This single tiered stand replaced a former terrace and has a capacity of 4,000. On the other side is another single tier, the all seated Main Stand. This has a number of supporting pillars and some executive boxes at the back. At one end the Pearl Street Stand is the third of the new stands. This is also all seated and serves as a Family Stand. It has a couple of supporting pillars that are right at the front of the stand. The Sandy Lane End is the only terraced area remaining. It is one the small size but does at least benefit from having a roof. There is a Police Control Box located in one corner, between the Main & Pearl Street Stands. Spotland is shared with the Rochdale Hornets rugby league team.

In 2016 Spotland was renamed the Crown Oil Arena in a five year corporate sponsorship deal.

What is it like for visiting supporters?

Away supporters are housed on one side of the Willbutts Lane Stand, where around 1,500 fans can be housed. If demand requires it, then the whole of this stand can be given to visiting fans increasing the allocation to 3,650. The stand is normally shared with home supporters with away fans being seated towards the Sandy Lane End. The view of the action and facilities within, are both pretty good. The acoustics are excellent, so away fans can really make some noise from within it. This, coupled with both home ends singing, makes for a good atmosphere.

Teresa Jewell a visiting Sheffield Wednesday fan adds; 'The ground is homely, with the staff being helpful and polite. The pies on sale (£2.80) were worth every penny. The club house to the front of the ground is welcoming to away fans. There is also a chip shop facing the away end for something more substantial to eat, which does a roaring trade on matchdays.'

I would say that Spotland is certainly one of the better footballing days out in the country. Friendly and knowledgeable fans, good stewards, good facilities, a couple of pubs located at the ground, a great range of pies on offer and not a bad atmosphere to boot. In other words all the right elements to make for a great day out. Add a pretty lady on my arm, my team winning six nil and I'll think that I have been transported to heaven!

Club nickname: The Dale	Ground name: Crown Oil Arena	Capacity: 10,249	Opened: 1906
Pitch size: 114 x 76 yards	Undersoil heating: No	Record attendance: 24,231 v Notts Co FA Cup 2nd Round 10th December 1949	Home kit: Blue, White and Black
Telephone: 0844 826 1907	Ticket Office: 0844 826 1907 (Option 8)	Website: rochdaleafc.co.uk	Programme: £3

Pubs for away fans

At the ground itself, there are two bars to choose from, Studds and the Ratcliffe Arms. Studds is located underneath the Pearl Street Stand and is worth a visit, if only to sample the large range of tasty pies & pasties on offer. No real ales here, but the bar has lots of memorabilia/pictures on the walls and some lovely looking barmaids which softens the blow. The Ratcliffe Arms is located at the car park entrance to the ground, on Sandy Lane. This pub has SKY TV, real ale, hot food and is family friendly. On my last visit this pub had a mixture of home and away fans.

If you arrive early, the Cemetery Hotel, located at the bottom of Sandy Lane and on the corner with Bury Road, is also worth a visit. This comfortable historic pub has a range of real ales on offer and again friendly clientele. I am unclear at the moment whether alcohol is on sale inside the ground to away fans.

Please note that alcohol is NOT made available to away fans inside the Spotland Ground.

Directions & Car Parking

Exit the M62 at Junction 20 and take the A627(M) towards Rochdale. At the end of the A627(M) you should be in the left hand lane to turn left at the traffic lights. Now follow the road and with Tesco on your left, go straight through the next set of lights (approach in the middle lane) into Roch Valley Way. At the next crossroads (where the Cemetery pub is on the corner) go straight onto Sandy Lane, where the ground can be found on the right after approximately 3/4 mile. Street parking although be wary of local restrictions.

By train

Rochdale Railway Station is located just under two miles away. It served by direct trains from Manchester Victoria and Leeds. Rochdale station is around a 35-40 minute walk from Spotland, so best jump in a taxi, rather than walking. Alternatively you can shorten the walking journey a bit by catching a Metrolink tram from outside the station into Rochdale town centre, which is around a 20 minute walk away.

AESSEAL New York Stadium
New York Way, Rotherham, S60 1AH

What is the ground like?

The new stadium, which cost in the region of £20m to build, is located close to the old Millmoor ground where Rotherham played for 101 years. Set beside the River Don, the stadium from the outside looks far larger than its 12,000 capacity and is quite striking in its design, especially its eye-catching roof. The stadium is totally enclosed and all seated.

On one side is the Eric Twigg Foods Pukka Pies (West) Stand. This is the largest of the four single tiered stands. It is unusual in so much that the middle seated area of the stand is situated at a lower level than either of the wings. There is an executive area above this with seating outside and yet further above is a television gantry, set into the red panelled wall. The other sides of the stadium are much smaller in size. Both ends are virtually identical, except that the Mears (South) Stand has a small electric scoreboard situated at the back of it. On the remaining side is the Ben Bennett (East) Stand, which is slightly less taller than both the ends. This simple looking stand has two large areas built into the front of the stand for the use of disabled supporters. There is a large video screen situated in the North West corner.

What is it like for visiting supporters?

Away fans are normally housed in the Mears Stand at one end of the stadium, where around 2,500 supporters can be accommodated. If only a small away following is expected then part of the Ben Bennett Stand (towards the Mears South Stand) is allocated instead. The stadium has electronic turnstiles meaning that you have to insert your ticket into a reader to gain admission.

As you would expect from a new stadium the facilities and views of the playing action are generally good. The angle of the Mears Stand is quite steep, meaning that it is a bit of a hike to get to the top. On the concourse the food and drink available includes: a range of Pukka Pies (Chicken Balti, Meat & Potato, Steak & Kidney, Cheese & Onion, all £3.20), Pasties (£3.20), Jumbo Sausage Rolls (£2.70), Hot Dogs (£3.70), Cheeseburgers (£3.90) and Burgers (£3.90). The stewards were generally laid back and friendly and I thought it was a nice touch that fans were allowed to go outside the stadium for a cigarette at half time if they wished. There is also a large television screen on the concourse showing Sky Sports.

Unlike most new stadiums which are situated way out of town in the middle of nowhere, the New York Stadium is close to the town centre. This means good transport links, but also a fair choice of eating & drinking outlets.

Club nickname:	Ground name:	Capacity:	Opened:
The Millers	AESSEAL New York Stadium	12,021 (all seated)	2012

Pitch size:	Undersoil heating:	Record attendance:	Home kit:
110 x 72 yards	No	11,758 v Sheff Utd League One 7th September 2013	Red and White

Telephone:	Ticket Office:	Website:	Programme:
0844 4140733	08444 140754	themillers.co.uk	£3

Pubs for away fans

There are a number of pubs in the nearby town centre, which are only a few minutes walk from the stadium.

The main pub for away fans is the Bridge Inn, which is located quite close to the railway station (turn right out of the station and the pub is across the road on the left). This pub which is listed in the CAMRA Good Beer Guide serves beers from the Old Mill Brewery as well as guest beers and a real cider. This pub was welcoming towards away fans on my visit and it wasn't too bad to get served inside.

Colin Hall a visiting Leicester City fan adds; 'We discovered the Cutlers Arms on Westgate (turn right off the Main Street), which turned out to be a most welcoming and hospitable tavern. It had a mixture of home and away fans and sold beers from the local Chantry's brewery.' Also nearby along Westgate is the New York Tavern, which also serves Chantry's beers.

Alcohol is also available inside the stadium in the form of: Fosters and John Smiths (Both £3.40 a pint) and Bulmers (£3.20 a bottle).

Directions & Car Parking

Leave the M1 at Junction 33 and take the A630 towards Rotherham. After around two miles and crossing over three roundabouts you will reach the stadium on your right. You will pass the floodlights of Millmoor on your left and at the next roundabout (called the Masbrough roundabout with the Liquid night club on one corner) turn right onto Main Street and the entrance to the stadium is down on the right. Plenty of Pay & Display Car Parks in the town centre or some street parking over by the old Millmoor Ground.

By train

Rotherham Central is only a five minute walk from the stadium. Exit the station entrance & turn right along Bridge St. Opposite the Bridge Inn is a footpath that goes along one side of the River Don. Walk along this footpath and then cross the car park towards the entrance. Then turn left going up over the bridge across the river and then take the next right into Market St. Then right into Main Street and the stadium is down on the left.

Glanford Park

Doncaster Road, Scunthorpe, DN15 8TD

What is the ground like?

Glanford Park was opened in 1988. At this time it was the first new league football ground to be built in England since the Second World War. With the Club's intention to build a new stadium nearby, then it may not be around for much longer. From the outside Glanford Park is somewhat uninspiring, mostly a grey drab affair. In fact it if were not for the tops of the floodlights being visible, you would probably not know it was there as it is obscured by the adjacent retail park and trees.

Inside it is a simple affair with all four stands being of equal height and similar in appearance. The ground is totally enclosed, although the corners are not used for spectators. The home end is terracing, whilst the other three sides of the ground are all seated. The main downside is the many supporting pillars running along the front of the stands that may impede your view. There is a small electric scoreboard suspended below the roof of the South Stand. The stadium is completed with a modern looking set of four floodlight pylons

What is it like for visiting supporters?

Away fans are housed in the South Stand at one end. This is all seated and can house 1,678 supporters. If demand requires it, then extra seats can be made available in the south corner of the West Stand.

Normally away fans can really make some noise from end and the stewarding is normally tolerant and relaxed. Although there is a concourse area located near the stand entrance, there is in fact another small food kiosk located on the other side of the stand, which is accessed from within the stand itself. Although there are a couple of supporting pillars in this stand, the view is generally okay.

James Broadbent adds; 'The ground is very

easy to find on the edge of town. Scunthorpe is generally a friendly place to visit, where you can have decent banter and a good day out. To help boost the atmosphere the club allow drums and musical instruments to be brought into the stadium.'

Inside the ground a range of pies are on offer at £2.80 each. For an extra 40p you can even enjoy your pie with mushy peas! Otherwise just outside the nain entrance to Glanford Park there are a number of fast food outlets and eating places such as McDonalds, KFC and a Frankie & Bennys.

Club nickname:	Ground name:	Capacity:	Opened:
The Iron	Glanford Park	9,088	1988
Pitch size:	Undersoil heating:	Record attendance:	Home kit:
111 x 73 yards	No	9,077 v Man Utd League Cup 3rd Rd 22nd Sept 2010	Claret and Blue
Telephone:	Ticket Office:	Website:	Programme:
01724 840 139	01724 747 670	scunthorpe-united.co.uk	£3

Pubs for away fans

At Glanford Park itself is the Iron Bar which admits visiting supporters. Near to the ground there is 'The Old Farmhouse' pub, which also allows in away fans providing though that they are not wearing team colours. A little further way along Doncaster Road (towards Scunthorpe town centre) is the Berkeley Hotel, which is also popular with away supporters and is listed in the CAMRA Good Beer Guide.

Steve Tucker adds; 'We found a great little pub called the Ironstone Wharf which is about a mile and a quarter away from the ground. It's on the A18 going away from Scunthorpe towards Gunness. After going around the left hand bend, the pub is located down on the right.'

If arriving by train, then the Honest Lawyer on Oswald Road is well worth a visit. Although a modern pub inside, it has been listed in the CAMRA Good Beer Guide and has a number of beers on offer. Also on Oswald Road is the Blue Bell which is a Wetherspoons outlet. Otherwise alcohol is available inside the stadium.

Directions & Car Parking

Glanford Park is located is on the very outskirts of Scunthorpe, making it easy to find from the motorway. Leave the M180 at Junction 3 and take the M181 for Scunthorpe. At the end of this motorway, you will see the ground on your right. Turn right at the first roundabout onto the A18 and right again for the ground entrance.

There is a large car park at the ground, which costs £3.

By train

Scunthorpe Railway Station is over two miles away from Glanford Park. Taxi or if you are feeling fit... Turn left out of the station and head towards the crossroads (facing a church) and turn right into Oswald Road, going past a set of traffic lights and the Blue Bell pub. At the next traffic lights turn left into Doncaster Road. Then just go straight down this road and you will eventually reach Glanford Park on your left.

Bramall Lane
Sheffield, S2 4SU

What is the ground like?

Bramall Lane has to me been one of the most underrated grounds in the country. The construction of three large modern looking stands, plus the filling in of the corners (albeit one corner is filled with administrative offices), makes it a great ground and one that has character. Both sides of the ground are large single tiered stands. Whilst the South Stand is a fairly plain looking stand, the North Stand which sits opposite, is probably the smartest looking stand at Bramall Lane. This stand which was opened in 1996, has had the corners to either side of it filled in, by offices on one side and a family seated area on the other. At the back of the stand are a row of executive boxes and on its roof is a small gable, reminiscent of when many older grounds featured them.

At one end is the Kop Stand, which is slightly disappointing as it has two large supporting pillars. Opposite is the Bramall Lane Stand, which is a two tiered and also has an electric scoreboard, perched between the two. The stadium is balanced, with all four stands being of the same height.

What is it like for visiting supporters?

Away fans are housed in the lower tier of the Redbrik Estate Agency (aka the Bramall Lane) Stand at one end of the ground, where around 3,000 supporters can be accommodated. For cup games if the demand requires it, then the upper tier can be made available too.

Fans are normally searched on entry into the ground by the stewards. The Club have automatic turnstiles, meaning that you have to insert your ticket into a bar code reader to gain admittance.

Bramall Lane is a great place to watch football as the stands are located close to the pitch, the views are generally good, as well as the atmosphere too. On the concourses there are television screens showing the game going on inside as well as a betting outlet. Food is available in the form of Pukka Pies (Meat & Potato, Chicken Curry, or Cheese & Onion (all £3.50), Sausage Rolls (£2.90), Cheeseburgers (£3.50) and Hot Dogs (£3.50).

Sheffield as a city has a young vibrant feel. Coupled with the fact that it has a number of good pubs and that Bramall Lane is located not too far from the town centre, then most fans look forward to their day out in the 'Steel City.'

Club nickname:	Ground name:	Capacity:	Opened:
The Blades	Bramall Lane	32,702 (all seated)	1862
Pitch size:	Undersoil heating:	Record attendance:	Home kit:
112 x 72 yards	Yes	68,287 v Leeds Utd FA Cup 5th Round 15th February 1936	Red and White Stripes
Telephone:	Ticket Office:	Website:	Programme:
0114 253 7200	0871 995 1889	www.sufc.co.uk	£3

Pubs for away fans

About a ten minute walk away at the bottom of Eccleshall Road is a Wetherspoons Outlet called the 'Sheaf Island'. This good sized pub tends to have a mix of home and away fans. Whilst a little further away on Wellington Street is the Devonshire Cat. This pub has around 12 hand pulled beers on offer, serves food, has a large screen tv, welcomes families (until 7pm) and is listed in the CAMRA Good Beer Guide.

Near to the railway station is the Globe, which Simon a visiting Chelsea informs me: 'I found that the Globe pub around a five

minute walk from the station and a 15 minute walk from the ground welcomed home and away fans as long as there was no singing. The majority of fans there where Chelsea and the doors where policed two hours before the game but it was a nice friendly pub serving good ale'.

Dave Barraclough informs me; 'In the station itself is the Sheffield Tap which serves real ales and is run by the Thornbridge Brewery' (please note though that no football colours are allowed to be worn at the Sheffield tap). Beer is also on sale inside Bramall Lane.

Directions & Car Parking

Leave the M1 at Junction 36 and follow the A61 into Sheffield. Follow the A61 into Sheffield passing Hillsborough Stadium on your right. Continue along the A61, which becomes the ring road around the western side of the city centre. You will eventually

reach a roundabout at the junction with the A621. At the roundabout turn right onto the A621 Bramall Lane. The ground is a short way down on the left. There is no parking at the ground for visiting fans, so street parking or a town centre 'pay and display' car park.

By train

Sheffield Railway Station is located just under a mile away from Bramall Lane. It is around a 15 minute walk. As you come out of the station, walk left along the main road. Where the road splits at the traffic lights, take the

right fork which is Shoreham Street. Continue straight down this road going through two more sets of traffic lights. At the mini roundabout turn right for the ground.

Hillsborough
Sheffield, S6 1SW

What is the ground like?

Hillsborough may be to some to be old and out dated but to me it is a beautiful ground that oozes character. On one side is the North Stand. This large single tiered stand was opened in 1961. It was hailed as an architectural marvel, as at the time it was the largest cantilever stand ever built in Britain.

Opposite is the South Stand which is the largest of the stands and is superb looking. It was originally opened in 1914 and was designed by the famous football ground architect Archibald Leitch. A second tier and new roof were added in 1996. The stand

has a large lower tier with a small upper tier above.

At one end is the Spion Kop. This was previously a huge open bank of terrace that was at one time the largest in Britain. It gained a roof in 1986 and was made all seated in 1993. Opposite is the West Stand or Leppings Lane End. This two tiered stand was opened in 1966. Like the Kop, it has a number of large supporting pillars. One corner of the ground is also filled with seating and another corner has a large video screen.

What is it like for visiting supporters?

Away fans are normally placed in the upper tier of the West Stand (the Leppings Lane) end of the ground, where up to 3,700 away supporters can be accommodated. If there is a particularly large following (or for an FA Cup Tie) then the lower tier can also be allocated, plus the open corner of seating next to the West Stand. This can take the allocation up to 8,000.

Fans are normally searched on entry to the stadium. Once inside you proceed up a concrete gangway up to the upper tier. The concourse although not spacious is normally adequate and some of the kiosks accept card payments. Food on sale includes; A range of Pies (£3.20), Sausage Rolls (£2.60), Burgers

(£3.80) and Hot Dogs (£3.80).

The low hanging roof over the away end helps with amplifying the sound of the away support, further boosting what is normally a good atmosphere. There are a couple of supporting pillars in the West Stand, which could impede your view. The stewarding is usually polite and friendly.

I had an enjoyable day out at Hillsborough, where I found the atmosphere outside the ground to be relaxed. I thought the ground was certainly one of the best in the League, if not the country, in terms of setting and attractiveness.

Club nickname:	Ground name:	Capacity:	Opened:
The Owls	Hillsborough	39,812 (all seated)	1899

Pitch size:	Undersoil heating:	Record attendance:	Home kit:
115 x 75 yards	Yes	72,841 v Man City FA Cup 5th Round 17th February 1934	Blue and White Stripes

Telephone:	Ticket Office:	Website:	Programme:
03700 20 1867	03700 20 1867 (Option 1)	www.swfc.co.uk	£3

Pubs for away fans

A pub that admits away supporters is the Railway Hotel on Penniston Road, which is the main A61 that runs by the stadium. Walk up the A61 in the opposite direction to Sheffield City Centre (Meadowhall & M1), passing a Burger King and Garage on your left, and you will reach the pub on the right. Also I did pass a couple of pubs (the Norfolk Arms & The Red Lion) on the way into Sheffield on the A61 from the M1, where away fans were drinking.

Bill Harris a visiting Millwall fan adds; 'I found an excellent Pub called The New Barrack Tavern on the A61 just before McDonalds on the way to the ground, from the city centre. Although on my own I was made to feel very welcome and spent a good couple of hours talking football to the locals.'

For those with a little bit more time on their hands or planning to travel to the ground by Supertram, then the Hillsborough Hotel near the Langsett/Primrose View tram stop (two stops from Hillsborough going towards Meadowhall/Halfway) is worth a visit. Otherwise alcohol is on sale to away fans within the ground itself.

Directions & Car Parking

Leave the M1 at Junction 36 and follow the A61 into Sheffield. Continue along the A61 for approximately eight miles. You will see Hillsborough Stadium on your right. This is not the shortest route to the ground, but this is definitely the easiest and avoids Sheffield City Centre. There is some street parking to be had if you arrive early, although some roads near to Hillsborough are permit only, so make sure to check for warning signs before you park. Otherwise there are some unofficial car parks along the A61.

By train

Sheffield Railway Station is located over three miles away from the ground. Either get a taxi up to the ground (which cost around £10), or take the Supertram. Jeremy Dawson adds; 'The trams run every 10 minutes and take 20 minutes up to Hillsborough. Take a blue tram, going towards Malin Bridge. At the Hillsborough stop (10 minutes walk from the ground) take a yellow line tram to Leppings Lane which is right by the stadium.

Greenhous Meadow
Oteley Road, Shrewsbury, SY2 6ST

What is the ground like?

The Greenhous Meadow is comprised of four separate stands and at first glance looks similar in design to some other new stadiums that have been recently built. Yes it is smart looking, functional and tidy, but lacks that certain something to make it stand out from the others.

Each of the stands are simple single tiered stands, that are covered. Below the roof at the back of the stands is a sizeable strip of perspex that runs along the length of the stands. This is to allow more light into the stadium to facilitate pitch growth. Each of the stands are 18 rows high, with the Roland Wycherley Stand (named after the Club Chairman) on one side, being the 'Main Stand'. This stand has a slightly different layout to the others with a press area and eight corporate boxes at its rear, the type of which that you can sit outside of.

The North Stand at one end of the stadium where the away fans are located also houses a prominent looking Police Control Box. Four small floodlights pylons are present on the roofs of the side stands.

What is it like for visiting supporters?

Away fans are located in the North Stand at one end of the ground. Leg room is good and the stands are quite steep keeping the fans close to the action and there is good height between rows. The concourses are quite well laid out, although the swing doors at the entrances to the toilets were met with a bit of trepidation. Although they were clearly marked one for entrance and one for exit, the inevitable occurs with fans piling out of each.

The catering has a selection of pies made by Wright's, including; Steak and Ale, Chicken Balti and a 'Pie of the Day' (all £3). There are also Cornish Pasties (£2.50), Cheese and Onion Pasties (£2.50) and Sausage Rolls (£2). Plus Hot Dogs (£3) and Burgers (£3). The club provide plastic forks to tackle those hot pies, which come in handy. I have to say that my steak and ale pie was very tasty, one of the better that I have had on my recent travels. There are also large plasma screens on the concourses showing Sky Sports throughout the afternoon.

I had a pleasant visit to the Greenhous Stadium and was surprised by the reasonable atmosphere inside. This is boosted by a drummer in the home end, whilst most of the Shrewsbury singers tend to congregate close to the right of the away supporters in the West Stand. Even though I was at a local derby, the atmosphere was not hostile and I encountered no problems.

Club nickname:	Ground name:	Capacity:	Opened:
Shrews, Salop, Town or Blues	Greenhous Meadow	9,875 (all seated)	2007

Pitch size:	Undersoil heating:	Record attendance:	Home kit:
115 x 77 yards	No	10,210 v Chelsea League Cup 4th Rd 28th October 2014	Blue, Amber and White

Telephone:	Ticket Office:	Website:	Programme:
01743 289177	01743 273943	shrewsburytown. com	£3

Pubs for away fans

The Brooklands Hotel is around a five minute walk away from the stadium, located just off Meole Brace Island. Normally it admits away fans but for certain high profile games it reverts to a home fans only pub..

There is also the Charles Darwin pub; which is around a ten minute walk away and in the opposite direction to the Brooklands Hotel (with the stadium entrance behind you turn left for the Brooklands or turn right and then left into Sutton Road) for the Charles Darwin. The Charles Darwin is family friendly, shows Sky Sports, as well as offering cask ales and food. Opposite the pub is the Tasty Plaice fish & chip shop.

Neil Le Milliere a visiting Exeter City fan recommends; 'The Prince of Wales Hotel on Bynner Street. Although near the town centre (albeit on the new stadium side), in the Belle Vue area, this CAMRA Good Beer Guide listed pub was an excellent find. Good ale, food and a friendly welcome. The pub also runs a coach to the stadium for each home game, which away supporters can use for £2.50 (if there is space).' Alcohol can also be bought inside the away end at the stadium.

Directions & Car Parking

At the end of the M54 continue onto the A5. After about seven miles, there is a traffic roundabout which is at the junction with the A49. Bear left at this roundabout still following the A5. At the next roundabout take the third exit onto the B4380 (Thieves Lane).

Continue along Thieves Lane going straight over two roundabouts and this will lead you into Oteley Road. You will reach the stadium down further down Oteley Road on the left. There is limited parking at the stadium costing £7 or Brooklands Hotel (£5).

By train

Shrewsbury Railway Station is just over two miles away. If you do decide to walk it is going to take around 40 minutes. Otherwise you can grab a taxi up to the ground or you can catch the Meole Brace Park & Ride service on Saturdays only from the railway station which takes you to the Meole Brace Retail Park, which is close to the stadium and costs £1.60. Also a Football Special Bus Service runs from the Bus Station (£2.50).

St Mary's Stadium
Britannia Road, Southampton, SO14 5FP

What is the ground like?

The Club moved from The Dell to the new St Mary's Stadium in 2001. In some ways this saw the Club returning to its roots as it was originally founded as 'Southampton St Marys', hence the club nickname 'The Saints'. Although a fairly standard design, the stadium does look quite superb.

The stadium is completely enclosed, with all corners being filled with seating. There are also two great looking screens sitting on the roofs at each end. Running around three sides of the stadium, just below the roof, is a transparent perspex strip allows more light and facilitates pitch growth. On the remaining side there is a row of executive boxes. The crowd are set well back from the playing action, as firstly there is a cinder track surrounding the playing surface and secondly the pitch itself must be one of the largest in the League (although the playing area does not use all of it).

Outside the stadium behind the Itchen Stand is a statue of former Southampton legend Ted Bates.

What is it like for visiting supporters?

Away fans are located in the Northam Stand at one end of the stadium, where normally up to 3,300 fans can sit. For cup games this allocation can be increased to 4,750. The view of the playing action and the facilities within this stand are excellent. Leg room is good, although the width of the seating seemed to be a bit narrower than other grounds (either that or I am putting on weight!). The sizeable concourse behind the stand features a betting outlet, has TV's which show the game as it is played and a number of eating and drinking kiosks. There are plenty of staff and the queues never seemed to get particularly long, which was a pleasant surprise. There is also a 'Pie & Pint' outlet, that as the name suggests, only serves beer and pies. Perhaps they should rename it as 'Heaven'!

I thoroughly enjoyed my visit to St Mary's and would happily return. The stadium has (contrary to other reports) a great atmosphere and the facilities are first class. I particularly commend the Club for the friendliness of their staff, from the stewards to the catering staff. Even as I left the stadium, a steward wished me an enjoyable journey home! Considering that away supporters are almost treated with contempt at some other clubs, this was a refreshing change. Coupled with the relaxed attitude of the home supporters and the excellent facilities, then this to to me makes a visit to St Mary's one of the better days out in the League.

Club nickname:	Ground name:	Capacity:	Opened:
The Saints	St Mary's Stadium	32,689 (all seated)	2001
Pitch size:	Undersoil heating:	Record attendance:	Home kit:
112 x 74 yards	Yes	32,363 v Coventry Championship Lge 28th April 2012	Red & White Stripes
Telephone:	Ticket Office:	Website:	Programme:
0845 688 9448	02381 780 780	southamptonfc.com	£4

Pubs for away fans

There are not many pubs located close to the stadium, so the choice for away fans is limited. There is the Waterfront Bar in William Street, which is an area called Shamrock Quay. Nic Hallam a visiting Wolverhampton Wanderers fan adds; 'In the Ocean Village we found a pub called the Admiral Sir Lucius Curtis. This large establishment had an excellent choice of beers, friendly bar staff and a convivial mix of both home and away fans.'

Most fans seem to end up in the city centre before the game, where there are plenty of pubs to choose from. Paul Hunt a visiting Bristol City fan adds; 'On our last visit the Standing Order Wetherspoons outlet was for home fans only, with bouncers on the door. We ended up in Yates Wine Lodge in the central shopping area. There were also a lot of away fans in the Slug & Lettuce next door.'

Please remember though that if you do drink in the centre, that the stadium is a good twenty minute walk away. Otherwise alcohol is served within the ground.

Directions & Car Parking

From the M3 take the A33 into Southampton. Continue on the A33 until you reach the junction with the A3024 Northam Road and turn left onto this road towards Northam. Then turn right onto the B3038, Britannia Road for the stadium. There is no parking at the stadium for away fans, nor street parking nearby. You can park at Ocean Village (£1 per hour or free after 6pm) or a 15-20 minute walk away there is free street parking on the other side of the Itchen Toll Bridge (which costs 60p) in Woolston.

By train

The stadium is located around one and a half miles away from Southampton Central Railway Station (where there is also quite a large car park), which should take about 30 minutes to walk. There is also a 'Stadium Shuttle bus in operation taking fans from the station to the ground. This operates from the Blechynden Terrace bus stop outside the station. It starts two hours before kick off and costs £2 return.

Roots Hall
Victoria Avenue, Southend, SS2 6NQ

What is the ground like?

At one end of the ground is the relatively modern South Stand. This stand which was opened in 1994, is a small 'double decker' type of stand, the upper tier hanging over the lower. It is all seated and covered, but unfortunately has a few supporting pillars. On its roof is a small clock, dedicated to former player, Director and Chairman, Frank Walton. Opposite is the North Stand, which like the West Stand at one side of the pitch, is single tiered and has an old looking 'barrel' shaped roof (that dates back to the 1950's), with the West Stand having a unique double barrel roof. The West Stand extends around

to the North Stand so that one corner is filled with seating. It has a number of supporting pillars right at the front, which may hinder your view of the action. It also has the most precarious looking TV gantry that stands on stilts and is accessed by a long ladder.

On the other side is the East (Main) Stand which is another single tiered, covered stand, that has a row of executive boxes running across the back of it. At the front are some strange looking dugouts. The ground has four tall traditional looking floodlight pylons. In other words a proper football ground!

What is it like for visiting supporters?

Away fans are normally housed on one side of the North Stand (on the Main Stand side of the ground), where up to 1,200 away supporters can be accommodated. If demand requires it then the whole stand can be allocated bringing the allocation up to 2,000 seats. The stand is covered, but there are a number of supporting pillars running across the front of the stand that could impede your view. The stand is a former terrace and like most former terraces that have had seats bolted onto them, the leg room and height distance between each row is less than desirable. One good thing for away fans in the North Stand is that comparatively few numbers of fans can really make some noise from it, making for a good atmosphere.

Refreshments within the away area are served from a 'Transport Cafe' type establishment, complete with tables and chairs. Bear in mind though, that getting your drinks in one piece back to your seat can be quite a challenge. The front of the stand is below pitch level, with stairs leading up to each pitch access point where the stewards stand. Going up and down these flights of stairs, with a cup of coffee in each hand, can present a problem.

Even though Roots Hall is an older ground it has some rather modern electronic turnstiles. Each match ticket has a bar code printed onto it and fans insert their ticket into a bar code reader at the turnstile to gain entrance to the stadium.

Club nickname:	Ground name:	Capacity:	Opened:
The Shrimpers	Roots Hall	12,392 (all seated)	1955

Pitch size:	Undersoil heating:	Record attendance:	Home kit:
110 x 74 yards	No	31,090 v Liverpool FA Cup 3rd Round 10th January 1979	Blue With Sky Blue Trim

Telephone:	Ticket Office:	Website:	Programme:
01702 304050	08444 770077	southendunited. co.uk	£3

Pubs for away fans

At the ground is the Shrimpers Bar. Although primarily for home fans, it does admit away supporters, apart from 'high profile' matches. It serves real ale and has a number of television screens showing the early kick off. Otherwise there is the Blue Boar pub which is located on the main Victoria Road, just up from the ground (going towards Southend town centre) on one corner of the crossroads.

A bit further away is the 'The Bell', a large Toby Carvery, which you pass on your way into Southend on the A127. The town centre is around a 20 minute walk away, where there are plenty of pubs including a Wetherspoons outlet (the Last Post on Weston Road).

Please note that alcohol is NOT served to away fans within the stadium. There is also a good fish and chip shop located across the road from the Blue Boar by the traffic lights, called the 'Fish House', which I found to be excellent. Judging by the amount of fans standing outside eating fish and chips (there is some seating inside as well), then I'm not the only one that thinks it is good.

Directions & Car Parking

From M25 take Junction 29 and follow the A127 to Southend. Continue towards the town centre, through the lights near to the Bell Pub. At the next roundabout turn right (3rd turning), continuing on the A127. The ground is on the right just past the next traffic lights. If you turn right as you reach the ground, this will put you behind the away end where there is plenty of street parking to be found. Otherwise there is a car park at the ground which costs £5 or there is Southend High School For Boys on Prittlewell Road (£5)

By train

Prittlewell Railway Station is the closest to Roots Hall, being located about a five minute walk away. It is served by trains from London Liverpool Street. As you exit the station turn right, you will then come to a crossroads with traffic lights. On your right is the 'Fish House', fish and chip shop. Pass this and turn right. Walk about 100 yards and the ground is tucked away on your left. Southend Central Station is about a 25 minute walk away.

Lamex Stadium
Broadhall Way, Stevenage, SG2 8RH

What is the ground like?

To be honest, the Lamex Stadium doesn't look much from the roads running past it, as most of the stadium is obscured behind trees. Inside though, you will find a nice tidy stadium that although generally modern, still has a bit of character about it.

On one side is the all seated covered Main Stand that looks quite impressive and is single-tiered. Opposite is the fair sized East Terrace, which is covered and quite steep. Even though like the rest ground, the stand is relatively new, it does have a gable with a clock sitting on its roof above the half way

line, which gives it a touch of character. Oddly though it has a sizeable service tunnel located towards the centre of the stand with the terracing extending around it.

At one end is the South Stand, which is another single tiered, all seated, covered stand. This stand which was opened in 2001 is given to away supporters. There is an electric scoreboard on the roof of this stand. Opposite at the North End of the ground, is a small covered terrace. This terrace is mostly covered (around three quarters) with a portion of open terrace to one side.

What is it like for visiting supporters?

Away fans are located at one end of the ground in the South Stand, where up to 1,400 supporters can be housed. As you would expect from a relatively new stand the facilities and views of the playing action are good. If demand requires it then part of the Main Stand can also be given to visiting supporters, bringing the total allocation up to 2,000.

Once inside the Lamex Stadium, the away end has good views of the action with no obstructing pillars and being elevated above the action. The only slight negative was that the catering consisted of just one small hut (Pies and Cornish Pasties cost £2.50).

The atmosphere within the stadium is aided by a drummer on the home East Terrace, who keeps the Stevenage fans going throughout most of the game. However, I found the public address system though within the away end to be particularly loud, which interrupted a few conversations. If you are into plane spotting then from the away stand you can watch a steady stream of airplanes descending into Luton airport.

A visit to the Lamex Stadium is normally an enjoyable day out and one that fans of most other clubs look forward to.

Club nickname:	Ground name:	Capacity:	Opened:
Boro	Lamex Stadium	6,920	1980

Pitch size:	Undersoil heating:	Record attendance:	Home kit:
110 x 70 yards	No	8,040 v Newcastle FA Cup 4th Round 25th January 1998	Red And White

Telephone:	Ticket Office:	Website:	Programme:
01438 223 223	01438 223 223 (Option 1)	stevenagefc.com	£3

Pubs for away fans

There is a large Club House bar at the ground, behind the South Stand, which is popular with both home and away fans alike. However, for some high profile games, the bar will be open to home fans only, but this is only for a small minority of games.

Otherwise there is not much in the way of pubs near to the ground. Still if you like your real ale then it is worth taking the 15 minute walk to the 'Our Mutual Friend' pub in Broadwater Crescent. This pub which is listed in the CAMRA Good Beer Guide offers seven beers on hand pump.

Tim Rigby a visiting Wolves fan adds; 'The Roebuck Inn on London Road, about a ten minute walk away from the away end is certainly worth a visit. It's an old tudor looking pub with a Best Western Hotel attached. It serves real ale and on my visit it was quite easy to get served.'

Across the roundabout from the ground there is the 'Roaring Meg' Retail Park that has a Harvester restaurant and bar, plus other various eating outlets such as Pizza Hut, McDonalds and Burger King.

Directions & Car Parking

Leave the A1(M) at Junction 7 and take the A602 towards Stevenage. Go straight across the first roundabout and as you approach the next roundabout you can see the floodlights of the ground over on the right. However, if you go straight across the roundabout then you will see the entrance to a large car park on your left, which is free to park in. The car park though has only one entrance/exit, so this can lead to bit of a bottleneck after the game has finished. Otherwise there is street parking to be found in the local area.

By train

Stevenage Railway Station is about one mile away from the Lamex Stadium and is around a 20 minute walk. Alan Chapman informs me; 'There is a shuttle bus service operated by Arriva Buses on matchdays that runs on a loop covering Stevenage Bus Station, Railway Station (Stop N) and the Lamex Stadium. It costs £1 return. The first shuttle bus starts two hours before kick-off.'

bet365 Stadium
Stanley Matthews Way, Stoke-on-Trent, ST4 4EG

What is the ground like?

The bet365 stadium looks imposing from afar, as it is perched upon a hill with hardly any buildings around it. It especially looks good at night when it is lit up. The ground is of a fair size. On one side is the Q-railing (Main) Stand, which is the tallest at the bet365 Stadium. This imposing stand has a large lower tier of seating with a smaller tier above. Situated between the tiers is a row of Executive Boxes. There are open areas to each side of this stand. On one side towards the Boothen End a large video screen has been installed, whilst on the other towards the Sharp (South) Stand there is the players tunnel. As unusually the teams come onto the pitch from this corner of the ground. The team dug outs are located in front of this stand. The rest of the stadium is comprised of three single tiered stands that extend around two corners of the stadium. The corner in-between the DPD and Sharp Stands was filled with 1,800 covered seats, at the end of the 2016/17 season, much improving the overall look of the stadium.

Outside the stadium there are statues of former player Sir Stanley Matthews and on the main road by the stadium there is one of England World Cup winner Gordon Banks.

What is it like for visiting supporters?

Away fans are housed on one side (towards the Players Tunnel) of the Sharp Stand at one end of the ground, where around 2,800 supporters can be accommodated. This stand is shared with home fans on the other side. At first I was quite perturbed by a large sign advising fans that persistent standing would result in ejection from the ground, however the facilities and view of the action from this stand are good. The concourse is adequate and there is a large choice of refreshments available such as Wrights Pies, Pasties (£3.20 & £3.10) and Sausage Rolls (£2.60).

The stadium is quite high up in an exposed position and the open corners can mean that a cold wind can whip through the stadium, so bear this in mind, especially in the winter months. I thought the inside of the stadium was quite disappointing being rather bland and lacking character, although I'm sure that this can be developed in time. Listen out though for the Stoke anthem 'Delilah' being sung by the home fans, they can still give a great rendition of that Tom Jones classic song.

If you want to try something a little different then on the canal located behind the Main Stand (look for the semi-circular looking bridge beyond the car park) are two moored barges, one which sells the traditional locally produced Oatcake, whilst the other sells beer. Both are proving very popular on matchdays!

Club nickname:	Ground name:	Capacity:	Opened:
The Potters	bet365 Stadium	30,183 (all seated)	1997

Pitch size:	Undersoil heating:	Record attendance:	Home kit:
115 x 75 yards	Yes	28,218 v Everton FA Cup 3rd Round 5th January 2002	Red and White Stripes

Telephone:	Ticket Office:	Website:	Programme:
01782 367 598	01782 367 599	stokecityfc.com	£3.50

Pubs for away fans

Next to the stadium is a Harvester Pub and Restaurant that does allow in away fans. A bit further away on Dennis Viollett Road (off Sir Stanley Matthews Way) is a Power League complex that also has a bar, which also allows in away supporters and shows SKY television.

Further down Sir Stanley Matthews Way (and turning left along Eastern Rise) is the Longton Rugby Club, which has two bars also showing SKY Sports. Parking is also available at £5 a car. It is around a 20 minute walk to the away turnstiles from the Club.

If arriving by train then the Terrace Bar on Leek Road has been designated as an official away fans pub. The pub which is only five minutes walk from the railway station (turn right out of the station entrance, left at the crossroads and the pub is down on the left) also shows Sky Sports and offers food too. The shuttle bus to the ground (return cost £3 adults) that runs from near the station, also stops at the pub and returns after the game.

Otherwise alcohol is available on the concourses at the back of the away end.

Directions & Car Parking

Leave the M6 at Junction 15 and take A500 towards Stoke, then passing the junction with the A34. Leave the A500 at the slip road following signs for the A50 towards Derby. At the top of the slip road turn right at the roundabout (still A50) and then move into the second from left lane. Turn right at the top of the slip road and then right at the next roundabout for the stadium. The Bet 365 Stadium is quite well signposted, although a few may still say the Britannia Stadium! Car parking at the stadium costs £5.

By train

Stoke Station is just over two miles away, so either a taxi or catch one of the stadium shuttle buses that run from Glebe Street. Colin Bell adds; 'It took us less 30 minutes to walk from the station: Exit the station and turn right. At the lights, turn right along Leek Road (A52), under the railway line and then left down on to the tow path of the Canal. Follow the tow path all the way until you are level with the stadium.'

Stadium Of Light
Sunderland, SR5 1SU

What is the ground like?

The stadium is of a good size, is totally enclosed and on the whole is quite impressive. It is composed of two three tiered stands (at the North end and the West side of the pitch), whilst the others are two tiered. The West (Main) Stand on one side also has a row of executive boxes (which you can sit outside if you wish), that are situated just below the top tier. Currently, with half the stadium being larger than the other, it looks a little imbalanced, when looking from the South Stand. However, if at some point the Club were to add an additional tier to the two remaining sides, then an even more remarkable stadium would emerge. There is also a large video screens perched upon the roof at either end.

Outside the stadium there is a statue of former FA Cup winning manager Bob Stokoe. Also outside one corner is a large miners lamp, a reminder of the former Wearmouth Colliery that the stadium was built upon. If you feel a little mischievous, then ask the nearest Sunderland fan whether it is a Geordie Lamp. Don't worry you won't get any physical abuse, just a long lecture that the lamp is in fact a Davy lamp!

What is it like for visiting supporters?

Away fans are housed in the Upper Tier of the North Stand at one end of the stadium, where around 3,000 fans can be housed for league games. For cup games then up to 9,000 visiting supporters can be accommodated in this tier. Although the facilities are fine in this area, you do have to climb a large number of flights of stairs to reach this top tier. It almost feels if this area has been 'tucked in' under the stadium roof, as it comes down over this section. It means that if you are sitting towards the back of the tier, then although you can see the pitch, you get a limited view of the majority of the rest of the stadium, giving the feeling of being a bit cut off from it all. On the food front, then the club offer; Fish & Chips (£5.50), Various Pies (£3.50) including the Chicken Balti Pie, Cornish Pasties (£3) and Jumbo Sausage Rolls (£3).

When people ask me which grounds are 'the best' to visit, then Sunderland inevitably comes out as one of my top five recommendations. On its day the place can be rocking, the PA system deafening, especially when the classical piece 'Dance Of The Knights' from Prokofiev's 'Romeo & Juliet' is played before the players come on to the pitch at the start of the game and the Sunderland supporters exceptionally friendly (I was even given a Sunderland shirt by one supporter!). But bear in mind you are not allowed to swear inside the stadium, so if you persist you may find yourself being ejected!

Club nickname:	Ground name:	Capacity:	Opened:
The Black Cats	Stadium Of Light	48,707 (all seated)	1997

Pitch size:	Undersoil heating:	Record attendance:	Home kit:
105 x 68 metres	Yes	48,353 v Liverpool Premier League 13th April 2002	Red and White

Telephone:	Ticket Office:	Website:	Programme:
0371 911 1200	0371 911 1973	www.safc.com	£3

Pubs for away fans

The Club have a Fan Zone which is located outside the South East part of the stadium. The area has entertainment in the form of live bands, large screens etc.. Plus food and drink outlets. It is available to both home and away supporters. It is open three hours before kick off and for one hour after the game has ended. Entry is free.

Marcus Bowen a visiting Swansea City fan informs me; 'Just across the road from the stadium (near to the entrance where the Davy Lamp is situated) is the Colliery Tavern. Although predominantly a home fans pub,

it does allow in away fans and we had an enjoyable time on our visit. It shows live football on a number of tv's and to cope with the large number of fans it has a marquee outside, also serving beer as well as a burger van.' Stephen Lundell adds; 'There are two social clubs; the Sunderland Companions club, and the New Democratic Club, both on North Bridge Street (the road approaching the Wearmouth Bridge), which are about a five minute walk away from the ground.'

You can also buy a beer inside the Stadium of Light.

Directions & Car Parking

Exit the A1 at Junction 62 and take the A690 towards Sunderland. After about eight miles, you will reach a roundabout, at which turn left onto the A19, signposted Tyne Tunnel. Stay in the left hand lane and take the second slip road towards Sunderland (signposted

A1231 Sunderland). Continue along the A1231 into Sunderland and you will eventually reach the stadium on your right. Park at the Metro Station (£4), or use the Park & Ride (signposted off A1231). Some street parking towards the sea front (check restrictions).

By train and Metro

Sunderland Railway Station is located just under one mile away in the city centre and takes around 15-20 minutes to walk to the stadium.

The ground also has its own Metro Station nearby. Whilst St Peter's Metro Station is only a few minutes walk away from the away turnstiles.

Liberty Stadium
Morfa, Swansea, SA1 2FA

What is the ground like?

The Club moved to the Liberty Stadium in 2005, after spending 93 years at their former Vetch Field home. The stadium was christened White Rock by the Swansea residents, but was renamed the Liberty Stadium under a 10 year corporate sponsorship deal.

Although fairly conservative in its design, the stadium is still impressive. It is completely enclosed with all four corners filled with seating. Each of the four stands is two tiered and three are of the same height. The West Stand at one side of the pitch is slightly taller,

having a row of 28 corporate hospitality boxes, situated above the upper tier. The Club's offices are also located behind this stand. An unusual feature is the great use of transparent roofing towards the South End of the stadium. This allows more natural light into this area, making for an interesting effect. Both ends have an electric scoreboard situated on the front of their roofs.

Outside the stadium by the club shop and ticket office, is a statue of former Swansea legend Ivor Allchurch. The stadium is shared with Ospreys Rugby Union Club.

What is it like for visiting supporters?

Away fans are housed in the North Stand at one end of the stadium. Up to 2,000 fans can be accommodated in this area, although this allocation can be reduced to 1,000 for teams with a smaller following. The views of the playing action from this area are excellent as there is a good height between rows and the leg room is probably one of the most generous of any stadium that I have visited. The concourses are spacious, with food and beverage outlets, plus a number of television sets, for pre-match and half time entertainment.

Away fans are separated from home fans by two metal barriers, with a line of stewards and Police in-between. Interestingly, the

main singing contingent of home fans, have, in the traditions of the Vetch Field, situated themselves along one side of the pitch in the East Stand, rather than at the South end of the stadium.

David McNeil a West Brom fan informs me; 'The stadium is very impressive and the facilities inside the stadium are excellent. Large concourse and great views from the stands. The atmosphere generated by the Swansea fans was excellent throughout the 90 minutes. Pre-match entertainment was enjoyed by my kids especially the antics of Cyril the Swan. Great day out, would love to visit the ground again.'

Club nickname:	Ground name:	Capacity:	Opened:
The Swans or The Jacks	Liberty Stadium	20,972 (all seated)	2005
Pitch size:	Undersoil heating:	Record attendance:	Home kit:
114 x 74 yards	Yes	20,972 v Liverpool Premier League 1st May 2016	All White
Telephone:	Ticket Office:	Website:	Programme:
01792 616 600	0844 815 6665	swanseacity.net	£3

Pubs for away fans

Phil Weston a visiting Stoke City fan informs me; 'The Liberty Stadium is a lot more friendly than the old Vetch Field. Stoke fans were drinking in The Harvester and Frankie & Benny's just outside the ground.'

John Ellis a visiting Leicester City fan adds; 'Just a few minutes walk away from the stadium on Llangyfeleach Road, is the Plough and Harrow, which admits visiting fans, There was a good mixture of both home and away supporters on our visit.'

Otherwise it is a choice of a drink on the way to Swansea, go into the city centre or drink inside the stadium. Merv Williams informs me; 'There are a number of pubs on Wind (pronounced as winding a watch) Street in the centre of town, such as Yates, the Bank Statement and the No Sign Bar (the latter being listed in the CAMRA Good Beer Guide. Ask for Castle Gardens, and you'll see Wind Street.'

Alcohol in the form of Carling lager and Worthington bitter are served within the stadium.

Directions & Car Parking

Leave the M4 at Junction 45 and take the A4067 towards the City Centre (sign posted A4067 South). Stay on the A4067 for around two and half miles and you will reach the stadium on your left. Car parking at the stadium is for permit holders only and most of the immediate residential areas around the stadium now have 'residents only' parking schemes in place. There is a matchday 'Park and Ride' service to the stadium which is signposted from Junction 46 of the M4. It costs £6 per car.

By train

Swansea Station is about two miles from the Liberty Stadium. Regular local bus services (every ten minutes: routes 4, 4a, 120, 122, 125, 132) and taxis (around £7) are available from the train station to the stadium. Otherwise it is a 25-30 minute walk. Exit the station and turn right up the High Street. At the traffic lights turn right into Neath Road. Proceed straight along Neath Road and you will reach the stadium on your right.

County Ground
County Road, Swindon, SN1 2ED

What is the ground like?

A traditional looking ground that has an interesting mix of stands. Both sides are large two-tiered covered affairs that tower above the two smaller ends. The Main Stand is the Arkells Stand on one side. Built in 1971 the stand is a fairly simple affair and has the players tunnel and team dugouts in front. It has windshields to either side and a few supporting pillars. Opposite is the smarter looking Don Rogers Stand. Opened in 1994, this stand has a cantilevered roof, allowing spectators to have an uninterrupted view of the playing action. It has a large upper tier, with a much smaller lower tier.

The Town End is a small covered stand that is the traditional home end. Unfortunately it has a row of supporting pillars that run across the front of it. Oddly on one side, the base of one of the floodlight pylons is situated within the stand, with the pylon itself rising up through the roof of the stand. At the other end is the Stratton Bank Stand. This area is uncovered and open to the elements. It has a small electric scoreboard situated above it, next to which is a Rolex Clock. Apparently this is the only Rolex clock that can found within a football ground anywhere in the World. The ground also has a striking set of 4 floodlights.

What is it like for visiting supporters?

Away fans are located in the Arkells Stand at one side of the pitch, where up to 1,200 fans can be housed. This is an older stand with facilities to match, but at least you are under cover. If you are at the back of this stand there is one supporting pillar which may impair your view of the goal otherwise it is fine. You even get a view of some of the rolling Marlborough Hills beyond one corner of the ground! There is a small kiosk at the back of stand serving amongst other things a range of pies, but be careful when taking them back to your seat. The entrances to the seating areas are through large solid doors, and to compound matters they open out towards you!

Teams with a larger away following can also be allocated the Stratton Bank End if required. A further 2,100 fans can be accommodated in this area, but the end has no cover and is open to the elements. Fine on a nice sunny day, but on a cold wet, winters day, it can be grim. This area was a former terrace that has had seating bolted onto it, which meant that the height between rows is not great. I found Swindon to be a relaxed and fairly friendly day out, although the size of Police presence on my last visit seemed excessive.

Food on offer inside includes; Chicken Balti Pie (£3.40), Steak & Ale Pie (£3.40), Cheeseburgers (£3.50), Burgers (£3.50), Hot Dogs (£3.80), Cheese & Onion Pasties (£2.50).

Club nickname: The Robins	Ground name: County Ground	Capacity: 15,728 (all seated)	Opened: 1896
Pitch size: 110 x 70 yards	Undersoil heating: No	Record attendance: 32,000 v Arsenal FA Cup 3rd Round 15th January 1972	Home kit: Red and White
Telephone: 0871 876 1879	Ticket Office: 0871 876 1993	Website: swindontownfc.co.uk	Programme: £3

Pubs for away fans

Away fans are treated to their own bar, called Bar 71, which is located by the away turnstiles. However it is quite small and tends to fill up quickly, with door men preventing anyone else going in, so that it does not become over crowded.

There is also the Merlin Pub on Drove Road (near to the Magic Roundabout) that allows in visiting supporters as Derek Shaw a visiting Wolves fan tells me; 'The Merlin pub is friendly and welcoming to away supporters. It's a decent size pub which serves meals and has a number of TV screens installed. I enjoyed the atmosphere in the Merlin which is less than ten minutes away from the County Ground and would recommend it.'

Alcohol is available within the ground to away fans in the Arkells Stand, but not in the open Stratton Bank End.

Otherwise Swindon town centre is a 15 minute walk away, where there are plenty of pubs to be found.

Directions & Car Parking

Leave the M4 at Junction 15 and follow the A4259 (Queens Drive) towards Swindon. Go across one roundabout and at the next take the first exit onto the A4312 (signposted Swindon/Football Traffic). You will see the floodlights of the County Ground over on the right, as you approach the large Magic Roundabout.

There is some parking at the ground (£10), Swindon Cricket Club (£5) or at St Joseph Catholic college in Ocotal Way (£5).

By train

The County Ground is walkable from Swindon Railway Station and will take you around 10-15 minutes. Leave the station, cross the road and proceed up the road between the two pubs (Great Western and Queen's Tap), continue to end of road. Turn left, proceed along Manchester Road, through traffic lights as far as you can go. At the junction turn right. The County Ground is about 300 yards up this road on the left.

Wembley Stadium
Empire Way, London, HA9 0WS

What is the ground like?

With the Club building a new 61,559 all seater stadium, on the existing White Hart Lane site, then the Club will play all their competitive home matches at Wembley Stadium for one season. It is expected that the new White Hart Lane Stadium (or whatever it ends up being called in a likely corporate sponsorship deal) is scheduled to open for the start of the 2018/19 season.

With the Club successfully playing a number of Champions League and Europa League fixtures at Wembley Stadium last season and attracting crowds in excess of 80,000.,

then it seemed logical for the Club to take up residence was their new stadium is being built. Not have the club chosen to play in the largest stadium in the country, in terms of capacity, but in my mind the best also in terms of design and facilities.

The most striking external feature of the stadium is 'The Arch', towering some 133 metres above it. It comprises of white tubular steel that can be seen for many miles across around. It looks particularly spectacular at night when it is lit up. Outside the stadium is a statue of Bobby Moore.

What is it like for visiting supporters?

Away fans are housed in the South East corner of the stadium in the lower tier. Although the stadium has a capacity of 90,000 only 3,000 tickets will be made available for Premier League games to visiting supporters, which is complies with League rules. For Cup games then further blocks in the lower tier of the South Stand extending around towards the half line may also be allocated.

Most English football fans look forward to a trip to Wembley and this should be no exception. For some this will also be quite a novelty this season to see their team play a league or cup game on the hallowed turf.

The facilities within the stadium are excellent and the concourses spacious. On the concourses they also have betting facilities, programme kiosks as well as a number of flat screened televisions. There are plenty of food and drink outlets available, meaning that queues never seem to get too long. Although don't expect to see much change from a tenner if you are buying a pie and a bottle of beer.

The views inside of the game going on are generally good and the leg room adequate. Add in an excellent PA system and some of the largest digital screens in the country, then the stadium may well be rocking!

Club nickname:	Ground name:	Capacity:	Opened:
Spurs	Wembley Stadium	90,000 (all seated)	2007
Pitch size:	Undersoil heating:	Record attendance:	Home kit:
105m x 68m	Yes	85,512 v Leverkusen Champions League 2nd November 2016	White and Navy
Telephone:	Ticket Office:	Website:	Programme:
0344 499 5000	0344 844 0102	tottenhamhotspur. com	£3.50

Pubs for away fans

As this book has been written before the season starts, then it is unclear as to whether any pubs or bars in the local area will be designated for the use of away fans. Or it may be with such a large home support whether indeed any pubs are made available at all.

So it may be an idea to plan to drink in Central London before the game or at a pub located near to one of the tube stations such as Harrow-on-the-Hill, that are on the same tube line to Wembley.

Near to the stadium is the London Designer Outlet which has a number of eating places such as TGI Fridays, Frankie & Benny's and Nando's, which also serve alcohol.

I would also expect that alcohol will be made available to away supporters inside Wembley Stadium itself.

Directions & Car Parking

The stadium is well signposted from the M25 plus M1 and M40. The stadium is just off the A406 North Circular Road. The stadium has been labelled as a 'public transport' destination, meaning that there is very limited parking available at the stadium itself

and there is also a residents only parking scheme in operation in the local area. I would recommend parking at one of the tube stations at the end of the Metropolitan or Jubilee lines such as Uxbridge or Stanmore and then take the tube to Wembley Park.

By train or tube

The nearest tube station is Wembley Park which is about a ten minute walk away. This tube station is on both the Jubilee and Metropolitan lines. Wembley Central is slightly further away from the stadium and

has both rail (from London Euston) and tube connections (Bakerloo line). There is also close by Wembley Stadium Railway Station, which is served by trains from London Marylebone.

Banks's Stadium
Bescot Crescent, Walsall, WS1 4SA

What is the ground like?

The stadium is dominated by the Tile Choice Stand at one end This is a large two tiered affair that houses almost 5,000 spectators. It is smart looking, with a glassed area running across its middle. Unusually, it has a slightly larger upper than lower tier. Originally this end was single-tiered but had the larger upper tier added in 2003.

The rest of the stadium is totally enclosed with three of the stands being roughly the same height, giving it a 'box-like' feel. These stands are not particularly big, around 15 rows high. The corners are filled, but mostly with advertising hoardings. The Main Stand on one side has a small television camera gantry perched on its roof, as well as the players tunnel and team dug outs at its front. Opposite is the Community Stand which is a simple seated stand that has dedicated areas for wheelchair users at its front.

Excluding the Tile Choice Stand then the main disappointment is the large number of supporting pillars in each of the other three stands including the away end. In one corner of the stadium is a large video screen that was installed in 2014.

What is it like for visiting supporters?

Away supporters are housed in the University of Wolverhampton Stand at one end of the ground, where around 2,000 away supporters can be accommodated.

There are a few supporting pillars at the front of this stand which could impede your view, especially if your team has a large following. However normally fans are allowed to sit where they want, so get into the ground early to pick a good spot. As the away end has a rather low look, then this means that even a small amount of away fans can really make some noise and generate a good atmosphere.

Food on offer inside includes a range of Pies; including Chicken Balti (allegedly Walsall were the first Club in the country to stock Balti pies) and Steak & Kidney Pies (£3), Cheeseburgers (£3.40), Burgers (£3.20), Hot Dogs (£3.20), Sausage Rolls (£2.10) and Pasties; Cornish (£2.40), Minced Beef and Onion (£2.40) and Cheese & Onion (£2.40).

A visit to the Bank's Stadium is normally a relaxed one, although sometimes the journey there and back can be a bit of a pain. Just outside the away end is a programme shop that stocks an interesting range of old programmes. Outside the stadium you may notice a huge video screen, designed to catch the attention of the M6 traffic going by. When installed it was the largest in Europe.

Club nickname:	Ground name:	Capacity:	Opened:
The Saddlers	Banks's Stadium	11,300 (all seated)	1990

Pitch size:	Undersoil heating:	Record attendance:	Home kit:
110 x 73 yards	No	11,049 v Rotherham Division One 9th May 2004	Red and Black

Telephone:	Ticket Office:	Website:	Programme:
01922 622 791	01922 651 414/416	www.saddlers.co.uk	£3

Pubs for away fans

This is the Saddlers Club situated just outside the stadium that is happy to admit away supporters on matchdays on payment of a £2 entrance fee, although under 16's are admitted free. The Club has two rooms, a smaller one at the front which is for home supporters and a larger function room at the back, which is for away fans. This area has seating for 300, has a large screen showing Sky Sports news, has food on offer such as pies & burgers plus they have real ale. Overall, I was very impressed with the facilities, but as you would expect if there is a large away following it can get full pretty quickly.

Otherwise, the nearest pub to the ground is the King George V on Wallowes Lane. It is okay, but again understandably busy which can make it a bit difficult to get served quickly. It is about a 15 minute walk away, opposite the Morrisons Supermarket. If you are walking from the stadium, go out of the official car parks and down towards McDonalds. Go past McDonalds on your right and take a left hand turn into Wallowes Lane. At the end of the lane turn left onto the main road and the pub is just setback on the left. Beer is also on sale to away supporters inside the Banks's Stadium.

Directions & Car Parking

Leave the M6 at Junction 9 and take the A461 towards Walsall. Bear right on to the A4148 (Wallowes Lane) and turn right at the second set of traffic lights. You will see the Banks's Stadium on your left.

There is a good sized car park located at the ground behind the away stand (called the Blue Zone), which costs £4. Bescot Railway Station also offers car parking for £2. Alternatively there is some street parking to be had off Wallowes Lane.

By train

The Banks's Stadium has its own Railway Station, called Bescot Stadium which is situated behind the away end and is only a few minutes walk from the turnstiles. Trains run there on a local line from Birmingham

New Street and the journey time is around 20 minutes. There is a regular service on Saturdays along this line and you should not have too many problems getting away after the game.

Vicarage Road
Watford, WD18 0ER

What is the ground like?

Vicarage Road has seen some new investment recently, with the construction of the new Sir Elton John Stand on the East side of the stadium. Opened in December 2014, this covered all seated stand is quite simple looking. It has a capacity of 3,800 seats and its construction has greatly improved the overall look of the stadium.

Opposite to the new Sir Elton John Stand, is the Rous Stand, which was recently renamed the Graham Taylor Stand, after their former manager. This stand which was opened in 1986 is a two-tiered stand that has an interesting roof design, with a number of semi-circular arches. Light is also able to penetrate through the roof aiding pitch growth. It also has a row of executive boxes running across the back. The ground has had both ends re-developed during the 1990's along with the front of the Graham Taylor Stand. Both ends are similar looking large single tiered stands, with some strange looking floodlights perched on the roofs. Away fans are housed in one of these ends in the Vicarage Road Stand. Whilst opposite the Rookery Stand is larger, housing some 6,950 supporters.

What is it like for visiting supporters?

Away fans are housed in the Vicarage Road Stand at one end of the ground. This stand is normally shared with home supporters (with the obligatory 'no-mans land' comprised of empty seats covered in netting in-between). Around 2,200 visiting fans can be accommodated in this area. The stand has electronic turnstiles, meaning that you have to place your ticket into a bar code reader to gain entrance. You should also then expect to be searched by the stewards on the way in.

I've always found this club friendly and the stewarding relaxed on my four visits and have never had any hassle, although at times there can be a heavy Police presence around the ground and in the town centre. My only real gripe is that the size of the concourse at the back of the stand is one of the tightest that I have come across and is wholly inadequate when there is a large away following. If you manage to get to the serving hatch, then you will find on offer the usual fayre available including; Pies (Chicken Balti, Steak and Ale, Bombay Vegetable) £3.40, Pasties £2.90, Jumbo Sausage Rolls £3 and Hot Dogs £3.90.

Adam Hodson a visiting Stockport fan adds; 'I was very impressed with the ground and the modern facilities. There was plenty of leg room in the way end and a good atmosphere. However, the concourses are very small meaning that they easily get crowded.' There is also a betting outlet available.

Club nickname:	Ground name:	Capacity:	Opened:
The Hornets	Vicarage Road	21,977 (all seated)	1922

Pitch size:	Undersoil heating:	Record attendance:	Home kit:
115 x 75 yards	Yes	34,099 v Man United FA Cup 4th Round 3rd February, 1969	Yellow & Black With Red Trim

Telephone:	Ticket Office:	Website:	Programme:
01923 496 000	01923 223023	www.watfordfc.com	£3.50

Pubs for away fans

The main pub for away fans is the 'Odd Fellows' in Fearnley Street, which is only around a five minute walk from the visitors turnstiles. It has a large beer garden, with its own barbecue selling Burgers and Hot Dogs (£2.50). Even though it was very busy on my last visit, I was impressed with the service from behind the bar, getting served in reasonable time (even though it looked like you had no chance of getting near to the bar let alone being served!).

Otherwise the ground is in walking distance of the town centre, where along the High Street you will find a few pubs including a large Wetherspoons outlet called the Moon Under Water, an O'Neils and a Walkabout.

If you are feeling peckish then if you are walking to the ground from the town centre then there are a number of eating establishments en route.

Please note that alcohol is NOT sold inside the ground in the away section.

Directions & Car Parking

Leave the M1 at Junction 5 and take the A4008 into Watford. If on nearing the town centre you can't see the ground over on your left, just go left around the inner ring road (follow signs for Watford General Hospital as this is behind the ground) and you will soon spot it.

No parking available at the stadium itself. There is the Vicarage Road Girls School (WD18 0AD), which is close to the stadium and charges £8 per car. On the inner ring road there is the Church multi-storey costing £1 per hour.

By train or tube

The nearest railway station is Watford High Street, a ten minute walk away from the Vicarage Road ground. However you are likely to come into Watford Junction Railway Station, which is about a 20 minute walk.

Watford also has its own London tube station, which is on the Metropolitan Line and is situated just under one mile from Vicarage Road. However overland trains from London normally have a shorter journey time.

The Hawthorns
Halfords Lane, West Bromwich, West Midlands, B71 4LF

What is the ground like?

With the completion of the East Stand in 2001, the Club achieved its objective in completely re-building the Hawthorns and making it a modern stadium. Not only has the ground received a much needed face lift, but it is now totally enclosed and all seated. The East Stand is an impressive, large single tiered stand, which has been well integrated with the rest of the ground. It has a row of executive boxes running along the back, and to each side of the stand the previous open corners have been filled with corrugated sheeting. There is a thin supporting pillar on each side of the stand to support the corner structures.

On the other side is the smaller Halfords Lane Stand. This stand which was opened in 1982 stretches around two corners of the ground. The home end, the Birmingham Road Stand is large, covered, and quite steep. At the other end away fans are housed in the Smethwick End. Both these ends were built in 1994/95.

Two video screens have been installed in opposite corners of the ground, one at the Smethwick End side of the East Stand and the other in the opposite corner of the Halfords Lane Stand.

What is it like for visiting supporters?

Away fans are housed on one side of the Smethwick End, where the normal allocation is 3,000 seats. This means that this stand is shared with home supporters. For cup games, the whole of this stand can be allocated to away supporters, raising this figure to 5,200. The facilities and the view of the pitch in the Smethwick End are okay, although the leg room is a little cramped.

I have been to the Hawthorns on a number of occasions and have always found it to be a fairly friendly place and normally has a good atmosphere. The only thing against it, in terms of a day out is the lack of nearby pub for away fans, meaning that most elect to drink inside the ground instead. Considering

that the concourse at the back of the Smethwick End is pretty small in comparison to its overall capacity, then it can have uncomfortable feel, especially when there is a capacity away support. Strangely I noticed that fans were not allowed to bring in take away food from the nearby McDonalds.

Food available on the concourse includes; Cheeseburgers (£3.70), Burgers (£3.50), a range of Pukka Pies; Chicken Balti, Chicken & Mushroom, Cheese & Onion, Steak & Kidney (All £3.30), Sausage Rolls (£3.30) and Pasties (£3.30).

Club nickname:	Ground name:	Capacity:	Opened:
The Baggies	The Hawthorns	26,500 (all seated)	1900

Pitch size:	Undersoil heating:	Record attendance:	Home kit:
115 x 74 yards	Yes	64,815 v Arsenal FA Cup 6th Round 6th March 6th 1937	White and Navy

Telephone:	Ticket Office:	Website:	Programme:
0871 271 1100	0871 271 9861	www.wba.co.uk	£3.50

Pubs for away fans

There is a Club 'Fan Zone' located just across the road from the Stadium. This area has live music, a large screen showing the early kick off, plus food and alcoholic drinks are available. This is free to enter and away fans are welcome (although there may be an exception to this when it comes to Wolves and Villa fans!).

The main pub for away fans is 'The Vine' (pictured right) which is about a 15-20 minute walk from the ground. From Junction 1 of the M5 turn left towards West Bromwich town centre (opposite direction to the ground). Take the first left into Roebuck Street. The Vine is down on the left. You can also street park in this area and then walk to the ground. This pub also offers Indian food and has an indoor tandoori barbeque (from 1pm on Saturdays), plus has a beer garden with children's play area.

Both the Park Hotel which is just off junction one of the M5 and the Royal Oak which is down Birmingham Road going past the ground on your right, both admit away fans. You can also get a beer inside the stadium.

Directions & Car Parking

Leave the M5 at Junction 1 and take the A41 towards Birmingham. After half a mile you will reach the Hawthorns on your right. Beware wary though of some speed cameras on this stretch of the A41 which is 30mph.

Street parking or alternatively there is parking at Hawthorns station (£4), Beeches Road Methodist Church (B70 6QE) at a cost of £5 or just around the corner from the Vine pub on Roebuck Lane is a St John's Ambulance Depot that offers matchday parking for £3.

By train or Metro

The Hawthorns has its own Railway and Metro Station which is about a five minute walk away. They can be reached from Birmingham New Street, either by first taking a train to Smethwick Galton Bridge and changing there for the Hawthorns, or by taking a Metro Tram from directly outside New Street Station. Total journey time by train is around 20-25 minutes, whilst the Metro is around 13 minutes.

London Stadium

Queen Elizabeth Olympic Park, E20 2ST

What is the ground like?

Built for the 2012 Olympics, the London Stadium originally it had a capacity of 80,000, but this has since been reduced to 66,000, although licencing regulations currently restrict the Club to a maximum attendance of 57,000. Since 2012 a further £200m has been spent on further upgrading the facilities, including the construction of the largest cantilevered roof in the World. The build quality of the stadium is excellent and it is certainly up there as being one of the best in the country. The stadium is essentially a bowl design, but when you consider that the stadium was primarily built for athletics and it still retains its ability to host large athletic events, then this is understandable. From the outside the stadium looks somewhat unremarkable. Inside though the stadium is bright and 'airy'. Certainly the 14 large triangular towers fitted into the front of the mostly translucent roof, certainly create this feeling and are a unique feature in themselves. The stadium is totally enclosed with all sides being essentially two tiered, although the West Side gives the illusion of having three tiers, as a large corporate area has been installed at the front of the upper tier. There are big digital screens at each end.

What is it like for visiting supporters?

Away fans are housed in the both the upper and lower tiers in the South West part of the stadium, where just under 3,000 can be accommodated for League games (or up to 8,000 for domestic cup ties). Supporters enjoy fine unobstructed views, however fans are housed quite far away from the playing area, especially at the back of the upper tier, so make sure you bring some binoculars, or more practically if you can, get yourself a seat in the lower tier or at the front of the upper tier. Due to the nature of the retractable seating in the lower tier (the seating can be moved backwards for athletics and forwards for football) there is a fair gap between the lower and upper tiers of the visiting fans sections, which hinders the atmosphere.

On the plus side the facilities inside the stadium are excellent, with ample food and drink outlets located on spacious concourses. And of course a visit to a game of football wouldn't be complete without a pie, although it will set you back £4.20 for a choice of Steak and Ale, Chicken and Vegetable or Vegetarian Pie. Even the toilets, which when I compare to other grounds that I have visited, can only be described as more of akin to a hotel standard rather than a stadium one. Most of the food and drink outlets take card payments, which also is handy. Entrance to the stadium is through electronic turnstiles, meaning that you insert your ticket into a bar code reader to gain entrance.

Club nickname:	Ground name:	Capacity:	Opened:
The Hammers or Irons	London Stadium	66,000 (Restricted to 57,000)	2012
Pitch size:	Undersoil heating:	Record attendance:	Home kit:
105m x 68m	Yes	56,996 v Burnley Premier League 2nd December 2016	Claret and Blue
Telephone:	Ticket Office:	Website:	Programme:
020 8548 2748	0333 030 1966	www.whufc.com	£3.50

Pubs for away fans

There is not much in the way of drinking outlets close to the stadium, so it is mainly the case for visiting fans to drink in Central London or en route. Alcohol though is served inside the stadium, although not cheap at around £4.80 for a pint of Amstel, or there are bottles of Fosters, Strongbow or Bulmers (all £4.60), Smirnoff Ice (£4.80) or small bottles of wine (£5.10). There are a number of pubs in the centre of Stratford itself, but nearly all of these are for home fans only. John Ellis a visiting Leicester City fan informs me; 'Having been turned away from the Wetherspoons pub called the Goldengrove, the doormen pointed us in the direction of the Goose pub at 78 Broadway, where we were made welcome. There was a mixture of home and away fans inside and families were also allowed in.' Adam adds; 'Before the game we went to the Hamilton Hall Wetherspoons pub at Liverpool Street Station before journeying onto Stratford and the Stadium. This pub has been popular with fans visiting London for a game over a number of years'. There are a number of eating places, restaurants and even a casino within the nearby Westfield Shopping Centre that also serve alcohol.

Directions & Car Parking

From end of the M11 motorway follow the signs for the North Circular A406 (S). Then at at the roundabout take the fourth exit onto the A12 towards Stratford. Keep on the A12 for around 4 miles. Then exit onto the A106, signposted Stratford. At the bottom of the slip road at the traffic lights, take the left hand filter lane, towards Stratford and Westfield. Continue along this road and you will reach the stadium on the right and the Westfield Centre on the left. Westfield Shopping Centre offers car parking at £9.50 for a day.

By train or tube

The main tube station is Stratford which is located both on the Jubilee and Central tube lines, as well as the DLR. Also nearby is Stratford International railway Station which is served by trains from London St Pancras, the journey time of which is just seven minutes. Both these stations are around a 15 minute walk away from the stadium, although it may take longer after the match due to crowd control measures.

DW Stadium
Loire Drive, Wigan, WN5 0UZ

What is the ground like?

The DW Stadium was opened in 1999 after the Club moved from its former home of Springfield Park, where it had been in residence since the Club's formation in 1932.

The DW is a functional stadium but overall it has somewhat of a bland look. In fact I would say that it looks more interesting from the outside from a distance than it does within. The four separate stands are of roughly the same height and are all single tiered. They are also quite steep meaning that fans are sat quite close to the playing action, although this is mitigated a little by the fact that the stands themselves are set back a fair distance from the pitch perimeter.

Both the side stands have large supporting steel frameworks visible above their roofs, whilst oddly both ends are different, having the steel framework located below the roof line. Unusually for a modern stadium, it does seem to be lacking in the number of corporate areas and executive boxes. There is an electric scoreboard above the Boston (East) Stand, on one side of the ground. The stadium is also shared with Wigan Warriors Rugby League club.

What is it like for visiting supporters?

Away fans are located in the North Stand at one end of the stadium, where up to 4,800 visiting supporters can be accommodated. Although this stand has a capacity of 5,500 seats, the allocation is restricted to 4,800 to prevent over-crowding on the concourse.

The stadium is functional and the facilities adequate, but it just seems to lack something, to give it that memorable feeling. The view of the playing action and leg room are both good. The stewards are generally helpful and relaxed.

To the left of the away section is where the singing Wigan fans tend to congregate, who are aided by a drummer, which provides some atmosphere. The public address within the stadium is particularly loud, none so when 'I'm a Believer' by the Monkees is blasted out just as the teams get ready to kick off.

The concourses are of a good size. There are screens showing the early kick off game and a betting outlet. Food on offer includes a range of Hollands Pies, including Chunky Steak, Meat & Potato and a Cheese Pie (all £2.60). There were also Herta Hot Dogs (£2.90).

Club nickname:	Ground name:	Capacity:	Opened:
Latics	DW Stadium	25,023 (all seated)	1999

Pitch size:	Undersoil heating:	Record attendance:	Home kit:
110 x 60 metres	Yes	25,133 v Man United Premier League 11th May 2008	Blue and White

Telephone:	Ticket Office:	Website:	Programme:
01942 774 000	0871 663 3552	wiganlatics.co.uk	£3

Pubs for away fans

Simon Wright a visiting West Bromwich Albion fan informs me; 'Beside the away turnstiles is an entrance to the large indoor Marquee Bar, specifically for the use of away fans. It has the usual bar, big screen television and sells pies, as well as teas and coffees. It's a great comfortable facility and welcomes families.' I was particularly impressed with this facility and with a stage on one side and low lighting, I was almost waiting for the dancers to emerge! However on my last visit the queues to get served were quite long even though there wasn't a particularly large away following in attendance.

Otherwise the traditional pub for away fans visiting the DW stadium is the Red Robin, which is only a few minutes walk away from the ground opposite the Cinema Complex.

On the concourse alcohol is on sale. There are two counters serving beer. The largest one has a queuing system which is overseen by the stewards, which is good. Plus there is a limit of buying two pints per person, so can you can get served relatively quickly compared to most grounds. However no food is served from these outlets, so you may need to queue up again for a pie.

Directions & Car Parking

Leave the M6 to Junction 25 then take the A49 to Wigan. After around two and a half miles you should approach a large roundabout, that has a McDonalds on the right hand side. Continue straight on but keep in the left lane and then at the lights

take the left hand filter lane by the large Asda superstore. Continue straight on passing the Red Robin pub on your right. At the next roundabout go straight across and at the next traffic lights turn right into Stadium Way for the ground, where you can also park (£5).

By train

Wigan's central railway stations (Wigan North Western & Wallgate stations) are a good 20 minute walk away. So either take a taxi, or you can get Bus No 621 from near Wigan Wallgate or to walk; on exiting North Western

turn left and go down the road heading under a railway bridge. Bear right at the road fork. It is then a fairly straight walk along Wallgate Road to the stadium which will appear on your right.

Molineux Stadium

Waterloo Road, Wolverhampton WV1 4QR

What is the ground like?

The Molineux ground is dominated by the modern Stan Cullis Stand at one end of the stadium, which was opened in 2012. This impressive looking structure towers over the rest of Molineux and the roof steelwork can be seen from miles around on the Wolverhampton sky line. The stand is two tiered, with a larger lower tier, with the upper tier having a large windshield on one side.

Both sides of the stadium are two tiered covered stands, that have a row of executive boxes situated along the middle. They are unusual in being oval in shape, meaning that those sitting on the half way line are furthest away from the playing action. The oldest of these is the Steve Bull Stand, which was opened in 1979, whilst opposite is the Billy Wright Stand which was opened in 1993. This stand is the Main Stand at Molineux, which contains the Directors area and team dugouts in front. At one end is the Sir Jack Hayward Stand, which was also opened in 1993. This is a large single tiered stand. There are a couple of video screens in two of the corners, but unfortunately these are no longer in operation.

What is it like for visiting supporters?

Away fans are normally housed in the lower tier of the Steve Bull Stand along the side of the pitch. Up to 2,750 away supporters can be housed in this area. Fans in this stand are sat quite far back from the playing area, which gives the illusion that the pitch is larger than at most other grounds. Also there are Wolves fans located above in the upper tier, which can sometimes lead to a few exchanges between supporters.

For teams with larger away followings then also part of the Stan Cullis Stand can also be allocated. Around 1,600 fans can be accommodated in this area. Fans are housed in both the upper and lower tiers, of the Stan Cullis Stand, although tickets for the upper sections are sold first. You need to do up quite a few flights of stairs to reach the upper tier (although a lift is normally available to those who need it) and view of the playing action quite distant.

The facilities inside the stadium are fine, including the catering, which offers amongst others a range of pies including; Steak, Rogan Josh, Potato & Meat, Vegetable, Cheese & Onion (all £3.10).

It is probably best to keep away colours covered around the ground and especially in the city centre. I did not experience any problems, but I have received a number of reports of others that have not been so lucky.

Club nickname: Wolves	Ground name: Molineux Stadium	Capacity: 31,700 (all seated)	Opened: 1889
Pitch size: 116 x 74 yards	Undersoil heating: Yes	Record attendance: 61,305 v Liverpool FA Cup 5th Round February 11th, 1939	Home kit: Old Gold & Black
Telephone: 0871 222 2220	Ticket Office: 0871 222 1877	Website: wolves.co.uk	Programme: £3

Pubs for away fans

Well it may be a great stadium, with good atmosphere, but the main drawback with a visit to Molineux is the lack of away friendly pubs for visiting supporters to drink in. Although Molineux is only a ten minute walk away from the city centre, then still most city centre pubs are for home fans only on matchdays, with most having doormen checking match tickets, to prove you are not an away fan.

Tom Rice a visiting Aston Villa supporter informs me; 'The Stonehouse bar on Queen Street, in the city centre seems to be the designated pub for away fans to drink in. The bouncers on the door, checked to make sure that we were Villa fans before entering". The bar which is family friendly normally opens at 1pm on Saturday afternoons.

I have also been advised that there is a small bar called the Bluebrick inside the Premier Inn hotel, located near to the railway station, which is being used frequently by away fans. It does though charge a £2 entrance fee.

Alcohol is also made available to visiting supporters inside the stadium.

Directions & Car Parking

From the South leave the M6 at Junction 10 and take the A454 towards Wolverhampton, or from the North leave the M6 at Junction 12 and take the A5 towards Telford and then turn onto the A449 towards Wolverhampton. On reaching the roundabout that intersects with the ring road, turn right. As you approach the second set of traffic lights you will see Molineux over on the right.

Limited parking available at Molineux itself (£8) or use one of the City Centre car parks.

By train

Wolverhampton Railway Station is around a 15 minute walk away from Molineux.

From the main station entrance proceed straight on towards the city centre and as you reach the inner ring road turn right. Just follow the ring road as it continues in a circular pattern around to the left. Eventually you will see the Molineux Stadium on the right.

Adams Park
Hillbottom Road, High Wycombe, HP12 4HJ

What is the ground like?

On one side of the ground is the impressive looking Frank Adams Stand, opened in 1996. This was named in memory of the man who originally donated to the club their previous ground at Loakes Park. It is a large two tiered stand, complete with a row of executive boxes and it dwarfs the rest of the stadium.

The other three stands are smaller affairs, but are at least all covered. Only the Bucks New Uni Stand at the home end remains as terracing.

Opposite is the Panache Stand, housing away supporters, a medium sized single tiered stand, with windshields to either side.

Along the other side of the ground is the Beechdean Stand. This single tiered stand has a raised seating area, meaning that fans access it by climbing a small set of stairs in front of it. It is set back from the pitch and has the team dugouts situated in front of it.

There is a large video screen situated in one corner of the stadium, between the Panache and Main Stands. The ground has a set of four floodlights.

What is it like for visiting supporters?

Away fans are mostly located at one end of the ground in the Panache Stand, where just over 2,000 supporters can be accommodated. For teams with a larger following then 350 seats are also made available in the Beechdean Stand, increasing the total allocation to 2,350.

I personally had an enjoyable day at Wycombe. The club has a relaxed friendly feel about it. The ground is situated in a nice setting with a wooded hill over-looking the ground (this normally has a small contingent of fans trying to watch the game for nothing) and with green fields surrounding the other sides.

The standard football ground fayre of Cheeseburgers (£3), Hot Dogs (£3), Double Cheeseburgers (£4.50), Chicken Balti Pie (£3.30) and Pasties (Cheese or Cornish £3.30), Sausage Rolls (£2.70) and Chips (£2), are available from the refreshment kiosk.

David Abbott a visiting Northampton Town supporter informs me; 'I have to say what an excellent ground Adams Park is. Good signposting around the ground, good organisation, good atmosphere, excellent view from the away end and friendly fans. It was a very pleasant visit and if all grounds and supporters were as welcoming and well-behaved as Wycombe the game would be all the better for it.'

Club nickname:	Ground name:	Capacity:	Opened:
The Chairboys	Adams Park	10,300	1990

Pitch size:	Undersoil heating:	Record attendance:	Home kit:
115 x 75 yards	No	10,000 v Chelsea Friendly Match 13th July 2005	Navy and Light Blue

Telephone:	Ticket Office:	Website:	Programme:
01494 472 100	01494 441 118	wycombewanderers. co.uk	£3

Pubs for away fans

For larger games the club erect a heated marquee, located just outside the away turnstiles, which is for visiting supporters only. Inside there is a bar selling alcoholic drinks, whilst nearby is a mobile catering unit which sells hot food, including pies.

Also at the ground is the Scores Bar and Vere Suite which normally welcome away fans. There is no entry charge for supporters to enter. As Adams Park is located on the edge of an industrial estate, there aren't many other drinking places around.

Neil Young informs me 'The nearest pub to Adams Park is the Hourglass on Chapel Lane in Sands (about a 15 minute walk, from the end of the road up to the ground). Away fans are normally okay in small groups except for big games or local derbies.' James Goddard adds; 'The Hourglass is a great pub, where home and away fans mix with no problems. The landlady on our visit was on her own and couldn't do food but sent us to the chippie and let us eat them in her bar - even gave us forks; as she said, it kept us drinking ale in her pub!'

Directions & Car Parking

Adams Park is located on the outskirts of Wycombe on the Sands Industrial Estate. Leave the M40 at Junction 4 and take the A4010 towards Aylesbury. Turn left at the fourth roundabout into Lane End Road and then continue straight along this road. Cross another roundabout and into Hillbottom Road. The ground is down at the very bottom of this road. There is a fair sized car park located at the ground which costs £5 per car, or some of the nearby industrial units provide match day parking (at around £3-£4).

By train

Wycombe Station is located around two and half miles away from the stadium and is really too far to walk. It is served by trains from London Marylebone and Birmingham Moor Street. You can either take a Taxi (costs about £8) or get the football special bus that runs from the station to the ground on match days. The Football Special (No.32) departs the Railway Station for the stadium at 13.55 on Saturday matchdays and 18.40 midweek.

Huish Park

Lufton Way, Yeovil, Somerset, BA22 8YF

What is the ground like?

Generally the ground is a tidy looking one, located in a pleasant setting, with lots of trees visible behind the stands. Both sides of the ground are similar looking stands and are of the same height. They are both cantilevered, covered single tiered stands that are all seated. Each stand has windshields to either side. The only differences between these stands, is that the Main Tamburino Stand has some executive boxes running across the back of it, plus the dug outs and players tunnel, whilst the Screwfix Community Stand has a press box suspended from beneath its roof and a small simple looking electric scoreboard. At the home end is the medium sized home Thatchers Gold Stand. This is a covered terrace, which has windshields to either side. Opposite is the Radio Cabs (Copse Road) Terrace, which is given to away fans. This is smaller and uncovered. Oddly the steel work is in place at the back of this stand to incorporate more terrace space, but the concrete rows have so far not been added. Perched above the rear of this stand is a large electric scoreboard. The ground is completed with a set four modern floodlight pylons, one in each corner of the ground.

What is it like for visiting supporters?

Away fans are mostly situated in the Radio Cabs Stand at one end of the ground. This is an uncovered terrace, so hope for a dry day. Up to 1,500 supporters can be housed in this area. Additionally around 600 seats are allocated to visiting fans in the Screwfix Community Stand, along one side of the pitch, which is covered.

Normally a visit to Huish Park is enjoyable, and the atmosphere good, although the open terrace makes it hard for away fans to really generate some noise. The atmosphere is boosted by a very vocal crowd in the home terrace as well as the presence of a drummer and trumpeter in that end (on my last visit the trumpeter was even imitating an ambulance siren as the trainer ran on to treat an injured player!). If Yeovil score then 'Glad All Over' by the Dave Clark Five blasts out around the stadium.

Food on offer inside include Pasties (meat or vegetable £3.20), a range of pies; Chicken Curry, Chicken & Mushroom, Steak & Kidney (all £3.20), Hot Dogs (£3.20) and Sausage Rolls (£2.20).

It may be just me, but every time I have travelled to a game at Huish Park I have ended up missing the kick off, due to traffic congestion, so allow a bit of extra time for your journey.

Club nickname:	Ground name:	Capacity:	Opened:
Glovers	Huish Park	9,665	1990

Pitch size:	Undersoil heating:	Record attendance:	Home kit:
115 x 72 yards	No	9,527 v Leeds United League One April 25th 2008	Green and White Hoops

Telephone:	Ticket Office:	Website:	Programme:
01935 423 662	01935 847 888	www.ytfc.net	£3

Pubs for away fans

There are a couple of pubs within about 10-15 minutes walk of the ground; 'The Arrow' and 'The Airfield Tavern.' The latter has the benefit of a handy fish and chip shop located next door called Palmers.

Richard Reardon a visiting Carlisle fan adds; "The Arrow is only 10-15 minutes walk away. The weather was excellent so most of our substantial following sat outside at a number of picnic tables. Both sets of supporters mixed well and there was Sky TV inside. There was a Police presence outside the pub but it was all very friendly". Rob Laight a visiting Birmingham City fan informs me; "'As we were early for the game we drove to the Arrow and parked in their large car park and then decided to leave our car there during the match. The Arrow is a great pub to visit, very friendly and the home supporters were easy to talk to. The Arrow also serves excellent food at reasonable prices'. Whilst Dave Thornton informs me; 'On visiting the Arrow I was delighted to see seven real ale handpumps on the bar. These included five beers from the Marstons range and two Guest ales, which were both supplied from the local Yeovil Brewery.'

Directions & Car Parking

Huish Park is located on the outskirts of Yeovil and is signposted from the A303. Leave the A303 at the Cartgate roundabout and take the A3088 towards Yeovil. Follow the road for around four miles until you reach a roundabout with the Westlands Airfield directly in front of you. Turn left at this roundabout and then continue straight on, crossing a number of roundabouts. As you pass the entrance to an Asda superstore, take the next left for the ground. There is a fair sized car park at the stadium (£2).

By train

Yeovil has two railway stations; Yeovil Junction and Pen Mill Junction. Both of these stations are located quite a distance from Huish Park, with Pen Mill Junction just under three miles away and Yeovil Junction almost five miles away. From both stations it is advised to get a taxi to the stadium. It may be an idea to look up the number of a local taxi firm and pre-book one as taxis are not always present outside the stations.

Wembley Stadium
Empire Way, London, HA9 0WS

What is the ground like?

To say that it looks superb is really an understatement. 'Fantastic', 'tremendous', such words probably still don't do it enough justice. But what is really great about the stadium, is that it has its own individual identity and character. From the moment you see the Arch towering over the stadium in the distance, then you know that this is going to be something special, and special it is. Plus unlike a number of other stadiums around the world that host a number of sporting events including football, Wembley is primarily for football and is the home of the England team. No wonder that it is labelled the 'Home of Football'.

The stadium is totally enclosed and comprises three tiers, with both sides of the stadium being slightly larger than the ends and having slightly semi-circular shaped upper tiers. Both these side stands have large upper and lower tiers, with a smaller middle tier sandwiched in-between. This middle tier overhangs the large lower tier and has a row of executive boxes at the back of it. At each end there is a large video screen. The stadium has a partly retractable roof that can cover a third of the pitch.

What is it like for visiting supporters?

Seeing Wembley for the first time, you can't help but be impressed with the sheer quality of the place. From escalators to transport fans up to the top tier, to the landscaped concourse, you can see that no expense has been spared. Although not the most generous of leg room that I have come across, it is still more than adequate and there is good height between rows. Add to this that there literally is not a bad seat in the house (even seats at the very top of the upper tier have excellent views) and with the roofs of the stadium being situated very close to the crowd, then a full house normally generates an excellent atmosphere.

Whereas most concourses in new stadiums are normally rather drab affairs, with a combination of breeze blocks and cladded piping, being predominantly on view, at Wembley it is different. For once someone has had the vision to hide these ugly features, with timber rafting and well positioned lighting, giving a modern stylish look. The concourses themselves are spacious, so much so that entertainers and other attractions are brought in onto the concourses to help entertain the crowd, The stadium has plenty of refreshment tills and these are supplemented with a number of 'pop up' so queues are never too long. Prices have always been historically expensive at Wembley but probably not much more than some Premier League Clubs now charge.

Ground name: Wembley Stadium	Capacity: 90,000 (all seated)	Opened: 1924	Rebuilt: 2007
Pitch size: 105m x 68m	Undersoil heating: Yes	All-time record attendance: **126,047 FA Cup Final 28th April 1923**	Modern record attendance: 89,874 FA Cup Final 17th May 2008
Telephone: 0844 980 8001	Stadium Tours: 0800 169 9933	Address: Empire Way London, HA9 0WS	Website: wembleystadium.com

Pubs for away fans

Although there are a number of bars and pubs located within the general area around Wembley Stadium, they certainly combined do not have the capacity to house all the fans who would like a drink before the game. So bear this in mind when planning your arrival time. The closest bars to the stadium such as J.J. Moons (Wetherspoons), the Green Man (both near Wembley Stadium station) and the Torch (near Wembley Park tube station), are usually heaving many hours before kick off.

In recent years for Cup and Play Off Finals the Police normally allocate pubs in a specific area to one teams supporters. This is based on which side of the stadium the fans are housed, on either the East or West side. In addition the Stadium has erected small fan zones for cup finals, which also serve both food and beer.

There are also a number of outlets selling alcohol in the nearby London Designer Outlet and Arena Square. Otherwise most fans tend to either drink in the centre of London before the game, or have drink near one of the tube stations located north of the stadium such as Harrow on the Hill.

Directions & Car Parking

The stadium is well signposted from the M25 plus M1 and M40. The stadium is just off the A406 North Circular Road. The stadium has been labelled as a 'public transport' destination, meaning that there is very limited parking available at the stadium itself

and there is also a residents only parking scheme in operation in the local area. I would recommend parking at one of the tube stations at the end of the Metropolitan or Jubilee lines such as Uxbridge or Stanmore and then take the tube to Wembley Park.

By train or tube

The nearest tube station is Wembley Park which is about a ten minute walk away. This tube station is on both the Jubilee and Metropolitan lines. Wembley Central is slightly further away from the stadium and

has both rail (from London Euston) and tube connections (Bakerloo line). There is also close by Wembley Stadium Railway Station, which is served by trains from London Marylebone.

THE TOOLS TO TACKLE EVERY JOB.
Game on! Hire from our 1000s of top-brand tools and equipment.
With branches all over the country, we're always close by and we deliver too! To find your nearest branch, call 0870 514 3391 or visit www.brandonhire.co.uk.
makita
50% OFF
YOUR FIRST HIRE*
SIGN-UP TODAY!
WE ARE
BRANDONHire
www.brandonhire.co.uk
WHY BUY? WHEN YOU CAN HIRE.

DRAWING THE 92

PREMIER & FOOTBALL LEAGUE
GROUND ILLUSTRATIONS

by Jamie B Edwards

LUXURY HARDBACK EDITION £30

ON SALE NOVEMBER 2017

www.g2books.co.uk

LOVE SPORT?

Subscribe to the UK's leading Sports Titles

NDULGE YOUR PASSION...

UBSCRIPTION FORM:

ease tick your subscription requirements below and return the form along with your payment to:
e Football Paper Ltd, Tuition House, 27-37 St George's Road, Wimbledon, SW19 4EU.

EWSPAPERS:

	10 Weeks/Issues	20 Weeks/Issues	40 Weeks/Issues
e Cricket Paper	£20 ☐	£40 ☐	£80 ☐
e Rugby Paper	£20 ☐	£40 ☐	£80 ☐
e Football League Paper	£20 ☐	£40 ☐	£80 ☐
e Non-League Paper	£20 ☐	£40 ☐	£80 ☐
e Hockey Paper	£20 ☐	£40 ☐	£80 ☐

AGAZINES:

	Six Months	Annual
te Tackle Football Magazine	£13.75 (5 issues) ☐	£25 (10 issues) ☐
acing Ahead Magazine	£16 (6 issues) ☐	£30 (12 issues) ☐

ase note rates are for UK subscriptions only – other country rates on application.

Name:

Address:

Postcode:

Telephone No:

Email:

I enclose a cheque/postal order made payable to:
THE FOOTBALL PAPER LTD